Money and Possessions

INTERPRETATION

Resources for the Use of Scripture in the Church

INTERPRETATION

RESOURCES FOR THE USE OF SCRIPTURE IN THE CHURCH

OTHER AVAILABLE BOOKS IN THE SERIES

Ronald P. Byars, *The Sacraments in Biblical Perspective*
Jerome F. D. Creach, *Violence in Scripture*
Ellen F. Davis, *Biblical Prophecy: Perspectives for Christian Theology, Discipleship, and Ministry*
Robert W. Jenson, *Canon and Creed*
Richard Lischer, *Reading the Parables*
Patrick D. Miller, *The Ten Commandments*

WALTER BRUEGGEMANN

Money and Possessions

INTERPRETATION *Resources for the Use of Scripture in the Church*

WJK WESTMINSTER JOHN KNOX PRESS
LOUISVILLE • KENTUCKY

2016 paperback edition
Originally published in hardback in the United States
by Westminster John Knox Press in 2016
Louisville, Kentucky

16 17 18 19 20 21 22 23 24 25—10 9 8 7 6 5 4 3 2 1

Book design by Drew Stevens
Cover design by designpointinc.com

Library of Congress Cataloging-in-Publication Data

Names: Brueggemann, Walter, author.
Title: Money and possessions / Walter Brueggemann.
Description: Louisville, KY : Westminster John Knox Press, 2016. | Series: Interpretation: resources for the use of scripture in the church | Includes bibliographical references and index.
Identifiers: LCCN 2016009462 (print) | LCCN 2016015078 (ebook) | ISBN 9780664233648 (alk. paper) | ISBN 9781611646771 (ebook)
Subjects: LCSH: Money—Biblical teaching. | Wealth—Biblical teaching. | Bible—Theology.
Classification: LCC BS680.M57 B78 2016 (print) | LCC BS680.M57 (ebook) | DDC 241/.68—dc23
LC record available at http://lccn.loc.gov/2016009462

ISBN: 9780664262808 (paperback)

♾ The paper used in this publication meets the minimum requirements of the American National Standard for Information Sciences—Permanence of Paper for Printed Library Materials, ANSI Z39.48-1992.

For
Peter Block
and
John McKnight

The Three Cries of History

And the great owners, who must lose their land in an upheaval, the great land owners with access to history, with eyes to read history and to know the great fact: when property accumulates in too few hands it is taken away. And that companion fact: when a majority of the people are hungry and cold they will take by force what they need. And the little screaming fact that sounds through all history: repression works only to strengthen and knit the repressed. The great owners ignored the three cries of history. . . .

. . . The great owners formed associations for protection and they met to discuss ways to intimidate, to kill, to gas. . . . Three hundred thousand hungry and miserable; if they ever know themselves, the land will be theirs and all the gas, all the rifles in the world won't stop them. And the great owners, who had become through their holdings both more and less than men, ran to their destruction, and used every means that in the long run would destroy them.

—John Steinbeck, *The Grapes of Wrath*

CONTENTS

SERIES FOREWORD

This series of volumes supplements Interpretation: A Bible Commentary for Teaching and Preaching. The commentary series offers an exposition of the books of the Bible written for those who teach, preach, and study the Bible in the community of faith. This new series is addressed to the same audience and serves a similar purpose, providing additional resources for the interpretation of Scripture, but now dealing with features, themes, and issues significant for the whole rather than with individual books.

The Bible is composed of separate books. Its composition naturally has led its interpreters to address particular books. But there are other ways to approach the interpretation of the Bible that respond to other characteristics and features of the Scriptures. These other entries to the task of interpretation provide contexts, overviews, and perspectives that complement the book-by-book approach and discern dimensions of the Scriptures that the commentary design may not adequately explore.

The Bible as used in the Christian community is not only a collection of books but also itself a book that has a unity and coherence important to its meaning. Some volumes in this new series will deal with this canonical wholeness and seek to provide a wider context for the interpretation of individual books as well as a comprehensive theological perspective that reading single books does not provide.

Other volumes in the series will examine particular texts, like the Ten Commandments, the Lord's Prayer, and the Sermon on the Mount, texts that have played such an important role in the faith and life of the Christian community that they constitute orienting foci for the understanding and use of Scripture.

A further concern of the series will be to consider important and often difficult topics, addressed at many different places in the books of the canon, that are of recurrent interest and concern to the church in its dependence on Scripture for faith and life. So the series will include volumes dealing with such topics as eschatology, women, wealth, and violence.

The books of the Bible are constituted from a variety of kinds of literature, such as narrative, laws, hymns and prayers, letters, parables, miracle stories, and the like. To recognize and discern the contribution and importance of all these different kinds of material enriches and enlightens the use of Scripture. Volumes in the series will provide help in the interpretation of Scripture's literary forms and genres.

The liturgy and practices of the gathered church are anchored in Scripture, as with the sacraments observed and the creeds recited. So another entry to the task of discerning the meaning and significance of biblical texts explored in this series is the relation between the liturgy of the church and the Scriptures.

Finally, there is certain ancient literature, such as the Apocrypha and the noncanonical gospels, that constitutes an important context to the interpretation of Scripture itself. Consequently, this series will provide volumes that offer guidance in understanding such writings and explore their significance for the interpretation of the Protestant canon.

The volumes in this second series of Interpretation deal with these important entries into the interpretation of the Bible. Together with the commentaries, they compose a library of resources for those who interpret Scripture as members of the community of faith. Each of them can be used independently for its own significant addition to the resources for the study of Scripture. But all of them intersect the commentaries in various ways and provide an important context for their use. The authors of these volumes are biblical scholars and theologians who are committed to the service of interpreting the Scriptures in and for the church. The editors and authors hope that the addition of this series to the commentaries will provide a major contribution to the vitality and richness of biblical interpretation in the church.

The Editors

FOREWORD

A proper introduction to Walter Brueggemann and his inspiring lectures and books would require a whole book. But Brueggemann needs no introduction. He is surely the most widely admired and appreciated biblical scholar of this generation. His books on biblical theology have decisively shaped the thinking of a whole generation of teachers, students, ministers, and laypeople. Countless prophetic insights have found their way through his books into preachers' sermons and teachers' lectures. In a time of proliferating specialization in biblical studies, when most scholars concentrate on one section of one book, Walter commands the whole canon. He regularly brings together critical insights from new lines of analysis into his broader exposition of a wide range of texts that speak to key issues of the life of the church or the urgent concerns of our common life.

Among his most remarkable powers, in addressing a wide audience of clergy and laity as well as students and scholars, Walter has an uncanny ability to draw directly upon a broad range of biblical texts to illuminate cantankerous or troubling contemporary issues. Who other than Walter Brueggemann could undertake a survey of attitudes toward money and possessions in the books of the Bible as a whole? Highly unusual among biblical interpreters, Brueggemann has a grasp both of each biblical book and of the larger literary repertoire of which it is a part (e.g., Torah, prophets, Deuteronomic history). For sections of the overall biblical repertoire, such as the books of the Torah and those of the prophets, moreover, he has an uncanny sense of particular symbols or statements or commandments that open toward the whole and provide the door through which we can enter to explore its treasures.

Brueggemann's treatment of money and possessions in the Bible is a decisive departure in theology and biblical studies. In the dominant culture of the modern Western world, economics, politics, and religion have become separate spheres, with religion reduced to individual faith. Economics, which deals with money matters, has become autonomous, no longer required to take people, society, or its devastation of the environment into account. With the Bible having been defined as religious, biblical interpreters rarely deal with economic matters.[1] But Brueggemann sees that money and possessions are unavoidably relational in biblical texts, in which God is concerned with all of life, not just religion. Possessions, which in ancient society consisted primarily of land and what was produced on land by people's labor, belonged properly to communities of people, indeed provided their living. Throughout biblical texts and throughout Brueggemann's treatment, possessions and money are embedded in social relations, often political power relations.

Brueggemann sees the narratives, songs, and legal collections of Israel's origins as a sustained struggle between the insatiable acquisitiveness of Pharaoh and "neighborliness" in commitment to sharing the common good. In treatment both of the origins of Israel in the exodus and covenant at Sinai and of the restatement of the Mosaic covenant as a centralizing reform of the monarchy (or was it the temple-state?), he begins with the commandment against coveting the possessions of others, the very basis of their livelihood. He begins with coveting, surely, because he is addressing us in our life in the belly of the overstuffed beast of consumer capitalism, where the ubiquitous images of the good life that pervade public space and invade all our senses manipulate our desire for commodities. Coveting, greed, the desire to take possession and control, as channeled by advertising, is what drives the consumption of mostly unneeded commodities that generates profits for capital. Coveting, greed, is what enables the wealthy to "grow" their wealth.

Following this compelling way in, Brueggemann opens up the Sinai covenant as guidelines for how to live faithfully outside Pharaoh's world of expropriation of more and more of people's possessions until they are utterly dependent on centralized wealth, even for the seed to sow their fields (Gen. 40; 47). The covenant commandments are principles of durable relations of trust in communities of neighborliness in which people share the common good. That is, the Ten Commandments are not so much rules of morality as guidelines of social-economic relations among the people, so that possessions, resources such as the land, are used for the support of families and communities. Assuming that people have economic rights to a livelihood, covenantal torah demands collective responsibility to guarantee those rights. The key to living faithfully outside

1. Only recently have a few of us started program units on economics and poverty in the Society of Biblical Literature.

Pharaoh's world of increasing extraction of people's possessions until they are impoverished is surely the second commandment. It is important to hear the whole commandment: not just no images, but you shall *not bow down and serve them* with your produce and possessions, which would presumably today mean your salary or wages spent in consumption of more and more commodities that serve to generate more profits for capital. By desiring the images all around us, we are serving the powers that generate those images, symbolized by the idols that induce service of those powers that are false gods.

Critical analysis with the aid of comparative studies of agrarian societies has suggested that the collections of Mosaic covenantal torah and customs in the books of the Torah have adapted what were popular customs and practices in village communities that kept the component families economically viable.[2] Subsistence farmers were perpetually plagued with the threat of falling into debt, when predatory creditors would swoop in to take advantage of a bad harvest. Correspondingly today, credit card companies and banks are only too eager to maneuver the poor into spiraling debt through high interest rates, penalties, and subprime mortgages. Speaking directly to such situations, Brueggemann presents a compelling treatment of the seemingly puzzling passage on cancellation of debts in Deuteronomy 15. If the people were to really follow the covenantal commandments (not coveting, not stealing, not dealing falsely), customs (lending at no interest), and practices (sabbatical cancellation of debts)—that is, sharing resources in social solidarity—then there would be no one in need among them (15:4). But since in fact they do not obey the commandments, they do indeed have poor among them (15:11), making all the more urgent the exhortation to lend willingly, give liberally, and actually practice the sabbatical release of debts. That this covenantal expectation continued in the village communities of the people for centuries comes vividly to the surface in the Matthean version of the Lord's Prayer: "Forgive us (cancel!) our debts as we also herewith forgive our debtors" (Matt. 6:12; my translation).

2. Douglas A. Knight, *Law, Power, and Justice in Ancient Israel,* Library of Ancient Israel (Louisville, KY: Westminster John Knox Press, 2011); Richard A. Horsley, *Covenant Economics: A Biblical Vision of Justice for All* (Louisville, KY: Westminster John Knox Press, 2009), chaps. 2–3, drawing upon James C. Scott, *The Moral Economy of the Peasant* (New Haven, CT: Yale University Press, 1976).

In the historical books, Brueggemann finds much implicit and even explicit critique of the obscene stockpiling of wealth by Solomon and other kings, from which he draws incisive parallels in the practices of transnational megacorporations of global capitalism today. Remarkably, these historical narratives include the rebellions of the Israelites whose labor and produce were coercively extracted and whose land was seized for debts to provide luxury goods for those who wielded power. And the prophetic books provide scathing prophecies calling down God's judgment against the predatory extortion, exploitation, and expropriation by the wealthy and powerful that leave the people destitute of the land that had provided their livelihood.[3]

When he comes to the books that deal with the rebuilding of the temple and the supposed origins of Judaism, Brueggemann follows recent critical departure from previously standard biblical interpretation that seemed largely oblivious to the fact that Judea and the Judeans were henceforth subject to one empire after another. Indeed, the rebuilding of the temple and perhaps even the collection of cultural traditions, including covenantal torah, were sponsored by the Persian imperial regime. The Persians restored descendants of the previously deported Jerusalem elite as the heads of the newly established temple-state, which functioned in effect as a branch of the imperial administration. The narrative in Nehemiah 5 vividly illustrates the devastating effect on ordinary people. In response to the desperate outcry of impoverished and ravished Judeans, Nehemiah, the high-ranking Judean who had been sent by the Persians as governor, forced the predatory wealthy Judeans to cancel the people's debts and restore their lands. But he offered no relief from the tribute the people owed to the Persian regime that had brought them into debt in the first place. Nehemiah appeals to the covenantal customs by which the land and other possessions supposedly purposed for the livelihood of the people would not be expropriated by the powerful. But Judeans were now subject to an

3. The articles by Marvin L. Chaney, such as "'Coveting Your Neighbor's House' in Social Context," in *The Ten Commandments: The Reciprocity of Faithfulness*, ed. William P. Brown (Louisville, KY: Westminster John Knox Press, 2004), 302–17; and "The Political Economy of Peasant Poverty," in "The Bible, the Economy, and the Poor," supplement 10, *Journal of Religion and Society* (2014): 34–60, provide solid exegetical exploration and grounding for Brueggemann's incisive statements about prophetic indictments.

imperial system of extraction that operated at a double level: tithes and offerings for support of the temple and high priesthood, and tribute to the imperial court.

The books of the New Testament were produced not by professional scribes in the service of rulers but by ordinary people—the descendants of the Israelites whose covenantal customs protected the common good of a mutually supportive village community, whose exploitation was protested by the prophets, from Elijah to Jeremiah. Brueggemann insists repeatedly that the previously standard individualistic and narrowly spiritual interpretations of the kingdom of God proclaimed by Jesus or the grace of God preached by Paul—detached from the concrete concerns of debts and daily bread—are distortions of the gospel message. He has an uncanny ability to discern how Paul's emphasis on the freely given grace of God generates communal generosity and sharing in the assemblies of Christ. Picking up on the recent recognition that Paul's mission was directly opposed to the Roman imperial order that siphoned off subject people's resources to the wealthy imperial elite, he explains how Paul was pushing what was in effect an alternative society, even an alternative economy.[4] Fulfilling "the law of Christ" meant bearing one another's burdens (Gal. 6:2), within the local community of sisters and brothers and in the collection for the poor among the saints in Jerusalem. Paul repeatedly exhorted the assemblies to withdraw as much as possible from dealings with the local imperial economy, "the [Roman] world" of supposed "peace and security" that was "passing away" (1 Cor. 7:29–31; 1 Thess. 5:1–11). In contrast to the vertical imperial extraction of resources, Paul pressed for the horizontal sharing of their meager possessions among subject peoples, working "for the good of all," as well as especially for "the family of faith" (Gal. 6:10).

The most explicit performance of an alternative economy in opposition to the imperial economy of extraction in Brueggemann's exposition of New Testament books is the practice of communal property that provided support for all in the assembly of Jesus loyalists in Jerusalem, in the early chapters of Acts (2:44–45; 4:32–37). He discerns that "there was not a needy person among them," echoing

4. Richard A. Horsley, "1 Corinthians: A Case Study of Paul's Assembly as an Alternative Society," in *Paul and Empire: Religion and Power in Roman Imperial Society* (Harrisburg, PA: Trinity Press International, 1997), 242–52.

the traditional regulation of debt cancellation in Deuteronomy 15:1–18. Certainly the earlier Israelite customs of mutual economic aid in village communities evident in the Mosaic covenantal laws in Deuteronomy and Leviticus stand behind the communal property in the Jerusalem community. Once we move beyond the individualistic reading of the New Testament texts, as Brueggemann insists, the Mosaic covenantal customs can be discerned also at the center of the Gospel stories of Jesus' mission. This has been obscured particularly by the focus on isolated individual sayings of Jesus that has continued as standard in most recent treatments of "the historical Jesus," resulting in a domesticated individual teacher of individuals. But the Gospels present Jesus as a prophet like Moses and Elijah, working in village communities. And in the most sustained of his speeches, specifically the Sermon on the Mount/Plain and the dialogues in Mark 10, he performs renewals of Mosaic covenantal community in village social-economic life, including explicit citations of and multiple allusions to traditional covenantal teaching of mutual aid and cooperation.[5] As Brueggemann insists, particularly in exposition of key parables of Jesus, "you cannot serve both God and mammon" is the summary of the stark choice between renewal of cooperative covenantal community, in which people do not covet and defraud one another, and the greedy storing up of private treasures of the extractive imperial economy.

While New Testament interpreters have often emphasized the extent to which the later-produced letters compromised with the dominant order in various ways, Brueggemann finds that the Pastoral and Catholic Epistles continue to advocate that the assemblies embody an alternative economy of generosity. James in particular sharply condemns exploitative practices that deny the rights of laborers, and Brueggemann points to the parallel in today's predatory exploitation of people, particularly in credit and mortgage arrangements and union busting.

In significant ways, Brueggemann's analysis of the book of Revelation and its implications for today provide the compelling climax of his survey of money and possessions in the Bible. In contrast with the scholarly misunderstanding of "(Jewish) apocalypticism" as obsessed with the end of the world in "cosmic catastrophe"

5. Horsley, *Covenant Economics*, chaps. 7–8; Horsley, *Jesus and the Powers: Conflict, Covenant, and the Hope of the Poor* (Minneapolis: Fortress Press, 2011), chap. 6.

(Schweitzer; Bultmann), he recognizes that this is visionary prophecy of God's condemnation of Roman imperial power, particularly its extractive economy, and the anticipation of an alternative economy (Rev. 17–18; 19–22). The "contemporary analogue," declares Brueggemann, is the global capitalism that has become the dominant political-economic and even cultural power that can control even the strongest governments, the power that some now call Empire. That some had not received "the mark of the Beast" indicates that some Christ loyalists had been resisting the demands of the imperial order, although it had involved suffering for the sake of the gospel (13:11–17; 20:4). In the contemporary analogue, Brueggemann insists, we can discern that the Empire of global capitalism is ultimately unsustainable, since it is destroying the very earth on whose resources it depends and is devouring the people it has subjected who increasingly have no money left to buy the commodities on whose sale it depends. Resistance is possible and an alternative economy is possible and both are indeed happening, usually in local cooperation. But both resistance and an alternative require refusal to participate in global capitalism—that is, obedience to the covenantal commandment against coveting, to come full circle. In effect, Brueggemann, like John on Patmos, is delivering a prophetic call to "come out of her, my people!"

Richard Horsley

PREFACE

The purpose of this book is to exhibit the rich, recurring, and diverse references to money and possessions that permeate the Bible. While we might conventionally assume, as we do in practice, that economics is an add-on or a side issue in the biblical text, an inventory of texts such as I offer here makes it unmistakably clear that economics is a core preoccupation of the biblical tradition. It is sufficient for this volume, I judge, to make that extended inventory of references to money and possessions available and visible, without needing or being able to exposit fully all of the texts. If I have offered a fair exhibit of these texts, then the reader can continue the interpretive work of making judgments about the meaning and relative importance of each text. I have along the way, of course, made interpretive judgments about texts. But the main work in that regard is up to the reader.

The title of the book reflects the sober Presbyterian series in which the book is placed. Were it elsewhere, it might properly be titled "Follow the Money" or "It's the Economy, Stupid." In writing the book I have, in ways that have surprised me, come to the conclusion that the Bible is indeed about money and possessions, and the way in which they are gifts of the creator God to be utilized in praise and obedience. In such a frame of reference, money and possessions are of course intensely seductive, so that they can reduce praise to self-congratulations and obedience to self-sufficiency. Whatever is to be made of this expansive inventory of texts, it is clear that the economy, in ancient faith tradition, merited and received much more attention than is usual in conventional church rendering.

I have found the writing of this book to be a difficult challenge on two counts. First, the biblical material on the theme is rich, diverse, and plentiful, so that I have had to be somewhat selective about the texts upon which I have commented. It is of course true that other interpreters might well select different texts or make different interpretive moves about them. At times I have been almost overwhelmed by the richness of the material. It is my hope that readers will make the necessary allowances for that challenge and recognize that no selection or commentary is innocent or without vested interest.

The second difficulty for me is that the assignment has pressed me into making critical judgments about the New Testament, which I have never done before. Consequently I have had to rely more extensively on the work of other scholars, most especially the work of Luke Timothy Johnson, although I have made my own interpretive judgments.

I did not set out to make this book into a statement of advocacy. My task has been reportage about the texts. I have found, however, that the texts themselves pressed in the direction of advocacy. While there is great diversity among the texts, I have concluded that in their great sweep, the biblical texts on money and possessions pivot on "God and mammon" as a decisive either-or (Matt. 6:24; Luke 16:13). When that distinctive mantra on the lips of Jesus is transposed into economic interpretation, the large sweep of the text suggests a critical exposé of an *economy of extraction* whereby concentrated power serves to extract wealth from vulnerable people in order to transfer it to the more powerful. That extraction is accomplished by the predatory if legal means of tax arrangements, credit and loan stipulations, high interest rates, and cheap labor. The combination of these practices reduces vulnerable people to hopeless debt that in the ancient world led to a form of slavery, that is, debt slavery. That recurring predatory economy of extraction is countered in biblical testimony by an *economy of restoration* that pivots on debt cancellation. In the ancient economy of extraction, debt cancellation was unthinkable, as it would most certainly damage, if not destroy, conventional economic practices and arrangements. Much biblical testimony, however, suggests that the proponents of debt cancellation, with a passion fueled by faith in the God of abundance, did not flinch from that radical and deconstructive alternative. It is clear, moreover, that such a map of economics is descriptive in our own time, when an economy of extraction operates both internally in the United States and internationally, so that the vulnerable are increasingly left with hopeless debt that takes various forms of bondage. Thus the map of the economy consists in interaction and tension between the extractors and those vulnerable to such extraction. Extraction proceeds by tax policy, credit and loan provisions, interest rates and cheap labor; the vulnerable require debt relief if they are to participate in a viable socioeconomic life.

Given such an economic map that receives many variant articulations in the Bible, it is simply astonishing that the church has willingly engaged in a misreading of the biblical text in order to avoid the centrality of money and possessions in its testimony. The church has done so by focusing on individual destiny (and sin), by spiritualizing and privatizing evangelical testimony (among both liberals and conservatives), and by offering hopes that are otherworldly. A study of money and possessions makes clear that the neighborly common good is the only viable sustainable context for individual well-being. Commitment to the neighborly good exposes the lie of privatization and the flight from material reality in much popular "spirituality." The recovery of the economic dimension of the gospel of course will require a rearticulation of much that passes in our society for serious Christian faith.

The church has long been haunted by a dualism with a commitment to the "fruits of the Spirit" in interpersonal relations while "works of the flesh" are too readily embraced in public life. But the Bible eschews every dualism and asserts the materiality of creation over which God generously presides. That pernicious dualism has readily produced a religion that is disconnected from public reality and that has sanctioned predatory economic practices that go hand in hand with intense and pious religion. Thus the earlier robber barons were card-carrying Christians in good standing; and in our time the church is mostly silent in the face of a predatory economy that reduces many persons to second-class humanity. That deceptive misreading is aided and abetted by a lectionary that mostly disregards the hard texts on money and possessions.

It is my hope that this exhibit of textual materials might evoke in the church a greater attentiveness to *a keener critical assessment* of the extractive economy around us in which we are implicated and *a more determined advocacy* for an alternative neighborly economy congruent with and derived from the gospel we confess. It is clear enough that voices that may champion and legitimate such alternative policy and practice are minimal in our society; the voicing of such alternative urgently requires the recovery of the tradition of neighborly money and possessions that has been entrusted to us.

I have benefited from a number of generous companions, most especially Timothy Beal, Davis Hankins, K. C. Hanson, and Tod Linafelt. I am grateful to Patrick D. Miller, who long ago initially invited me to work on this theme, and to Samuel Balentine, editor of the Interpretation series, and especially to Ellen Davis, who have devoted uncommon attentiveness and unstinting diligence to the great improvement of my work. I have long enjoyed the good work of David Dobson and his staff at Westminster John Knox Press, most especially Julie Tonini, to whom I am most grateful.

I am glad to dedicate this book to Peter Block and John McKnight, both tireless champions of and advocates for the neighborhood. They continue to instruct me, even while I delight in their generous friendship.

Walter Brueggemann

CHAPTER 1

Introduction

A Material Faith

Any study of money and possessions in the Bible is confronted with a mass of data that is complex and diverse in a way that refuses any systematic summary. Indeed, one can find in Scripture almost anything on the topic one wants to find. E. J. Dionne, after attending a Republican rally with many appeals to Ronald Reagan by a great variety of Republican speakers, was moved to quip: "Republicans of all sorts can appeal to the authority of Ronald Reagan in the same way that all Christians of every sort can appeal to the Bible as an authority." All readers can find what they want in the Bible concerning money and possessions. It is impossible in any survey to notice or discuss every possible reference, so one's treatment of the subject is sure to be selective.

I

As a way to begin this particular selective discussion, I propose six theses concerning money and possessions in the Bible that will provide a general frame of reference for the textual particularity that follows. In light of these theses I will survey, in canonical sequence, a variety of texts that variously witness to the truth of these theses.

1. Money and possessions are gifts from God. "All good gifts are sent from heaven above." For that reason a proper response

to such gifts is gratitude: "Then thank the Lord, O thank the Lord, for all his love." This affirmation is grounded in the doxological confession that God is the creator of the world and all that is in it. The lyrical poetry of Genesis 1 attests that without God there is only chaos. It is the creator God who transforms chaos into a living, generative environment that is blessed and fruitful in a way that produces abundance. That Genesis narrative, echoed in the Psalms, singularly credits the Creator with all plant and animal life. In its doxologies, Israel knows that all commodities of value are derivative from the generativity of the earth and that money (gold and silver) is a social symbol of value that derives from created commodities. In the Old Testament, in an agricultural economy, the three great money crops are grain, wine, and (olive) oil.[1] These are the produce of a generative earth, and that produce could be and was converted into wealth that eventuated in social well-being, social power, and social control.

The insistence that possessions are gifts and not achievements or accomplishments is a decisive check in biblical faith on any temptation to imagine self-sufficiency or autonomy. When the gift quality of possessions is forgotten, one can imagine that one has made the produce one's self. This temptation is reflected in the illusionary claim of Pharaoh, the great cipher of self-sufficiency, whom God reprimands for his imagined autonomy:

> Thus says the Lord God:
> I am against you,
> Pharaoh king of Egypt,
> the great dragon sprawling
> in the midst of its channels,
> saying, "My Nile is my own;
> I made it for myself."
> (Ezek. 29:3)

Pharaoh could not remember that it was the other way around: the Nile had made him, and the Nile is a river wrought by the creator God. This gift quality is the most elemental claim the Bible makes concerning money and possessions. It is an exceedingly important claim in a society like ours that easily imagines it is self-sufficient

1. See Samuel L. Adams, *Social and Economic Life in Second Temple Judea* (Louisville, KY: Westminster John Knox Press, 2014), chap. 3.

in its unrestrained eagerness for more. When the giver of all good gifts is forgotten, the gifts themselves are sure to be distorted in destructive ways.

2. Money and possessions are received as reward for obedience. This claim that runs throughout the Bible voices a robust quid pro quo connection between obedience and prosperity. That connection is clearly voiced in Psalm 1, which functions as an introduction to the book of Psalms:

> Happy are those
> who do not follow the advice of the wicked,
> or take the path that sinners tread,
> or sit in the seat of scoffers;
> but their delight is in the law of the LORD,
> and on his law they meditate day and night.
> They are like trees
> planted by streams of water,
> which yield their fruit in its season,
> and their leaves do not wither.
> In all that they do, they prosper.
> (Ps. 1:1–3)

And then the psalm adds tersely: "The wicked are not so!"

Prosperity arises in the wake of obedience to Torah, because the creator God is not indifferent to human conduct. Thus the commandments of the Sinai Torah are disclosures or regulations for bringing one's life into sync with the ordered quality of creation that is not negotiable. Taken in the most healthy way, such obedience consists in the joy of being in sync with God and not a burden, because it is simply an acting out in real life of one's true life with God and delight in God's companionship. A life in sync with the purposes of God is a life that will flourish!

Of course such a connection between obedience and prosperity that is based on mutual trust can be hardened into hard-nosed bargaining in the form of works righteousness. In such a distortion of glad obedience, one may obey in order to prosper, or one may imagine that one is owed prosperity for obedience. But such a bargaining expectation abuses and distorts a love relationship of glad responsiveness. The old temptation of works righteousness in our society, moreover, has morphed into the form of hard-nosed calculation in a market ideology in which there are no free lunches and no glad gratitude but only payouts for performance and production.

The distortion of this claim is even more pernicious when the rhythm of obedience that leads to prosperity is reversed, as in the case of Job. In that distorted rendering, Job's adversity is reckoned by his friends to be a result of disobedience. The biblical tradition knows, in its wise honesty, that the simple sequence of obedience–prosperity is not a fully reliable one. There are enough undeniable exceptions to evoke doubt around the so-called issue of theodicy. Thus this thesis is a guiding assumption of biblical faith that affirms that human conduct matters to human well-being because the Creator is not indifferent to conduct. In some great part, human conduct chooses human futures. But a guiding assumption cannot be reduced to a close, rigid calculus.

3. Money and possessions belong to God and are held in trust by human persons in community. In church practice, it is this claim that stands behind all thinking about stewardship. As is evident in the odd narrative of Isaiah 22, a steward is the "master of the household" who is responsible for its proper management, a role assigned to the human couple in the Genesis creation narrative concerning having "dominion" (Gen. 1:28). The steward is not the owner but is accountable to the owner (see also the parables of Jesus: Matt. 20:8; Luke 12:42; 16:2–4). In biblical faith, what human persons "possess" is in fact held in trust by God, who is the legal, entitled owner. Thus the psalmist can gladly assent:

> The earth is the LORD's and all that is in it,
> the world, and those who live in it;
> for he has founded it on the seas,
> and established it on the rivers.
> (Ps. 24:1–2)

The whole earth is the creation that belongs to the Creator who "has the whole world in his hands." This means, of course, that the stewards, all those who hold possessions in trust, are accountable for their use and management. When their possessions are well managed, they flourish, to the credit of the Creator. When they are mismanaged long enough, they may be withdrawn from the steward who has distorted the intent of the Creator-owner.

That reality of "held in trust" is readily forgotten. Thus in 2 Samuel 3:12, the wily general, Abner, sends a message to David:

"To whom does the land belong?" Abner is urging David to seize the land that is under the control of Saul. He has no notion that the land belongs to YHWH. Implied in his question to David is an invitation to David that if David wants the land, that is, if he wants to rule, he can do so and Abner will help him do it. More broadly, this was a risky assumption in ancient Israel about ownership of the land. Over time, Israel (and especially its kings and moneyed class) could imagine that the land could be held and used with impunity. Thus Ahab in the narrative of Naboth's vineyard (1 Kgs. 21). But as history eventuated, it became clear that the land finally belonged to YHWH, and Israel lost the land through its mismanagement. In the New Testament, the same risk of mismanagement is reflected in the parable of Luke 12:16–21, in which the main character is saturated with first-person pronouns, imagining that it all belonged to him. But of course as the narrative ends, his mismanaged "ownership" and autonomy are exposed as false.

4. Money and possessions are sources of social injustice. When possessions are held in trust, they may be well managed according to the will of "the owner," that is, for the sake of the neighborhood. But when possessions or money are viewed as "mine" without accountability, then they may be deployed in destructive ways at the expense of the common good.

The tradition of Deuteronomy is insistent that money and possessions must be managed in the practice of justice, that is, for the good of the entire community. That tradition further insists that Israel, in covenant with God and compelled by Torah, is to handle possessions and money differently from all others, so that economic resources are subordinated to the common good, that is, for the well-being of the neighbor, most particularly the neighbor without resources. Deuteronomy is clear that this is the mandate of the Creator-owner of worldly goods. As a result, the tradition makes a close connection between *remembering God* as owner and *doing neighborly justice*. Conversely, *forgetting God* is closely linked to the practice of *exploitative injustice*:

> In the pride of their countenance the wicked say, "God will not seek
> it out";
> all their thoughts are, "There is no God."
> . . . .
> They lurk in secret like a lion in its covert;

> they lurk that they may seize the poor;
> they seize the poor and drag them off in their net.
>
> They stoop, they crouch,
> and the helpless fall by their might.
> They think in their heart, "God has forgotten,
> he has hidden his face, he will never see it."
>
> (Ps. 10:4, 9–11)

Thus remembering God is not an intellectual act; it is a practical act of managing money and possessions differently.

And, of course, it is a common and recurring theme in the prophets that economic injustice and exploitation will in the end bring destruction and loss of one's possessions:

> "Alas for you who heap up what is not your own!"
> How long will you load yourselves with goods taken in pledge?
> Will not your own creditors suddenly rise,
> and those who make you tremble wake up?
> Then you will be booty for them.
> Because you have plundered many nations,
> all that survive of the peoples shall plunder you—
> because of human bloodshed, and violence to the earth,
> to cities and all who live in them.
>
> (Hab. 2:6–8)

The initial "alas" is traditionally rendered as "woe," that is, "big trouble coming!" The mismanagement of money and possessions is here identified by the terms "pledge" and "credit," which will be readily reduced to "booty" and "plunder," that is, to great economic upheaval. The practice of exploitative economics, culminating in "human bloodshed" and "violence," finally will bring trouble. The creator God will not tolerate unjust management of money and possessions. Nor will "your own creditors," who will, so the poet anticipates, "suddenly rise." The prophetic tradition is uncompromising concerning the linkage between mismanagement, suffering, divine indignation, and eventual loss.

5. Money and possessions are to be shared in a neighborly way. A core theme of biblical faith is that economic practice and policy must be ordered to serve the common good. The term "neighbor" means other members, that is, all members of the community. All

members of the community are entitled to the wherewithal for a viable life of security, dignity, and flourishing. This core mandate amounts to a rejection of any notion that the economy is autonomous and without reference to society. Thus the religious discipline that is required is nothing less than neighborly economics:

> Is not this the fast that I choose:
> to loose the bonds of injustice,
> to undo the thongs of the yoke,
> to let the oppressed go free,
> and to break every yoke?
> Is it not to share your bread with the hungry,
> and bring the homeless poor into your house;
> when you see the naked, to cover them,
> and not to hide yourself from your own kin?
> (Isa. 58:6–7)

The final phrase, "your own kin," is more exactly "your own flesh," an insistence on solidarity of all the neighbors, and especially solidarity between those with resources and those without resources. That mandate from Isaiah is echoed in the more familiar words of Jesus concerning neighborly engagement:

> Then the king will say to those at his right hand, "Come, you that are blessed by my Father, inherit the kingdom prepared for you from the foundation of the world; for I was hungry and you gave me food, I was thirsty and you gave me something to drink, I was a stranger and you welcomed me, I was naked and you gave me clothing, I was sick and you took care of me, I was in prison and you visited me." Then the righteous will answer him, "Lord, when was it that we saw you hungry and gave you food, or thirsty and gave you something to drink? And when was it that we saw you a stranger and welcomed you, or naked and gave you clothing? And when was it that we saw you sick or in prison and visited you?" And the king will answer them, "Truly I tell you, just as you did it to one of the least of these who are members of my family, you did it to me." (Matt. 25:34–40)

The phrase "members of my family" (or "my brothers") may originally have pertained to members of the Jesus community. But surely its implication is that all persons belong to this community of need and attentive care.

6. Money and possessions are seductions that lead to idolatry.[2] The Bible attests that money and possessions are not inanimate objects. They are rather forces of desire that evoke lust and "love" in a way that compels devotion and eventually servitude. The Bible asserts that such commodities, notably silver and gold, are not innocent but are in fact addictive and compel loyalty that rivals loyalty to God. Thus Moses can warn Israel that the worship of such possessions can talk Israel out of covenantal faith:

> Since you saw no form when the LORD spoke to you at Horeb out of the fire, take care and watch yourselves closely, so that you do not act corruptly by making an idol for yourselves, in the form of any figure—the likeness of male or female, the likeness of any animal that is on the earth, the likeness of any winged bird that flies in the air, the likeness of anything that creeps on the ground, the likeness of any fish that is in the water under the earth. And when you look up to the heavens and see the sun, the moon, and the stars, all the host of heaven, do not be led astray and bow down to them and serve them, things that the LORD your God has allotted to all the peoples everywhere under heaven. . . . So be careful not to forget the covenant that the LORD your God made with you, and not to make for yourselves an idol in the form of anything that the LORD your God has forbidden you. (Deut. 4:15–19, 23)

That seductive power is narrated in the story of the golden calf in Exodus 32, in which Israel can imagine that it was the *calf (bull!) of gold* that secured their emancipation from Egypt. It does not require much imagination to transpose the bull of gold to the icon of Wall Street, with its "bullish" markets, to see the allure of money that may distort neighborly covenantal relationships. Thus the narrative of Daniel can portray the self-destructive idolatry of Belshazzar and his court:

> Under the influence of wine, Belshazzar commanded that they bring in the vessels of gold and silver that his father Nebuchadnezzar had taken out of the temple in Jerusalem, so that the king and his lords, his wives, and his concubines might drink from them. So they brought in the vessels of gold and silver that had

2. See Jacques Ellul, *Money and Power* (Downers Grove, IL: Inter-Varsity Press, 1984).

> been taken out of the temple, the house of God in Jerusalem, and the king and his lords, his wives, and his concubines drank from them. They drank the wine and praised the gods of gold and silver, bronze, iron, wood, and stone. (Dan. 5:2–4)

The unnecessary repetitions of the narrator intend to mock the scene of extravagant self-indulgence that culminates in worship of the precious objects. We should not imagine, as the narrator did not imagine, that such extravagance was an innocent kind of prosperity. It was rather a seduction into complacent self-aggrandizement that led, in the narrative, to the demise of the power of Belshazzar. The seductive fascination with "gold and silver" culminates in the verdict of Paul in 1 Timothy 6:10: "For the love of money is a root of all kinds of evil, and in their eagerness to get rich some have wandered away from the faith and pierced themselves with many pains."

There may indeed be other theses that could be formulated on our topic, but these are the ones that have seemed clear to me.

II

I observe further that each of these theses in fact voices a clear contradiction to the conventional wisdom of the ancient world and that in our own time each of them contradicts the uncriticized wisdom of market ideology.[3] I am aware as I write that I do so in the midst of a market ideology (in which I am implicated) that occupies almost all of our imagination, and that readers will be situated in a similar way. It is this force of contradiction at the heart of the Bible that makes our study so demanding and difficult and which for the same reasons makes it urgently important. Thus:

1. To view money and possessions as gifts from God contradicts market ideology in which there are no gifts, no free lunches; there are only payouts for adequate performance and production.

2. To view money and possessions as reward for obedience is too readily transposed into the reward system of the market, so that

3. See Gerald Berthoud, "Market," in *The Development Dictionary*, ed. Wolfgang Sachs, 2nd ed. (New York: Zed Books, 2010), 74–94. Naomi Oreskes and Erik M. Conway write of "market fundamentalism" in *The Collapse of Western Civilization: A View from the Future* (New York: Columbia University Press, 2014), 37.

those who are productive should receive all the rewards that the system has to offer, even though the rewards often go not to the productive but to the well advantaged and the well connected. Such a distortion of biblical teaching results in the unproductive (the poor, the old, etc.) being excluded and left behind without merit or voice.

3. To view money and possessions as a trust from God contradicts the pretension of market ideology that imagines, not unlike Pharaoh with his Nile, that "my money is my own; I earned it and can do with it what I want."

4. To view money and possessions as a source of injustice is to contradict the easy assumption of the market that autonomous wealth is not connected to the community and so is not located in a venue where issues of social justice can even surface. Market ideology imagines that such autonomous wealth brackets out justice issues, so that what we get in our society, instead of transformative justice, is at most "charity" that does not acknowledge the huge sociopolitical leverage of wealth that is readily deployed against those without resources.

5. To view money and possessions as resources to be shared in a neighborly way contradicts the market assumption that there are no neighbors; there are only rivals, competitors, and threats. When neighbors are redefined and recast in this way, predatory strategies of wealth against them are taken as legitimate. Acknowledgment of neighbors makes predatory practices illegitimate.

6. To view money and possessions as seductions that lead to idolatry contradicts the market view that money and possessions are inert and innocent neutral objects. The thesis might invite us to reconsider the quasireligious passion of a consumer economy that is propelled by insatiable desire, in which we never have enough money or enough of the possessions that money makes possible. As any serious church leader knows, the one and only thing that is off-limits for comment or critique is the money system and its military support that undergird the illusionary well-being of our society.

Thus on all counts my own study of this subject has required me to think more clearly and more honestly about the way in which the testimony of Scripture is a deep misfit and an acute inconvenience in our society, with its tacit economic assumptions. It is my hope that the reader will, from this study, not only have more information about the data of biblical teaching but also see, as I have attempted to see, that the claims of the Bible amount to a deep critique of common practice and a summons to engagement with that common practice.

III

My task of introducing the topic requires of me one other introductory foray. The Bible is relentlessly material in its focus and concern. It refuses to let its passion be siphoned off into things spiritual, a matter of intense concern given the current rage about "spiritual" and "spiritual but not religious." Everywhere the Bible is preoccupied with bodily existence.

1. Creation faith as voiced in Genesis, Isaiah, the Psalms, and belatedly in Colossians is celebrative of the world as a world God has declared to be "very good." It is a real world of food and work and sexuality, all of which are understood to be under the rule of God's intent for all creatures. The commandments of Sinai are not arbitrary regulations that fall out of the sky. They are discernments of how the world works and what it means to be in sync with the ordering of creation that is not negotiable. Any flight from bodily creation is a distortion of this faith.

2. The Bible of necessity articulates God as a bodily agent, as one who has eyes, ears, mouth, face, hands, and arms.[4] Israel does not imagine God to be an unformed spiritual force, but an agent who occupies the space of the world and the drama of history.

3. The world as creation culminates, in Christian confession, in the Word that has become flesh in Jesus of Nazareth. Thus the link from creation to incarnation assumes that Christian faith will be acutely focused on the bodily life of the world. Jesus' several miracles of healing, feeding, and casting out demons consistently have as their outcome the restoration and rehabilitation of bodily life in the world, a gift given to bodily persons who have lost their capacity for a viable bodily life in society.

4. The human person, characterized in the Old Testament as a *nepeš*, is a body that is breathed on, engaged and empowered by the gift of God's spirit (*rûaḥ*):

4. See Benjamin D. Sommers, *The Bodies of God and the World in Ancient Israel* (Cambridge: Cambridge University Press, 2009).

> When you hide your face, they are dismayed;
> when you take away their breath [*rûaḥ*], they die
> and return to their dust.
> When you send forth your spirit [*rûaḥ*], they are created;
> and you renew the face of the ground.
>
> (Ps. 104:29–30)

And because the human person is a body, there is characteristically a concern for security, for food, and for home. This in turn means that the Bible talks relentlessly about economics, about the management and distribution of life resources so that all the neighbors can live an "abundant life." As a result the Bible is inimical to the sentiment heard by so many courageous preachers, "Stick to religion and stay away from politics and economics." This faith is intensely committed to bodily life in the world and so is preoccupied with social goods, social power, and social access.

5. The bodily reality of creation, the bodily characterization of God, the Word become flesh in Jesus of Nazareth, and the bodily reality of the human person means that the Bible is acutely concerned with the body politic. There is no private faith, no private intimacy with God, but only life as a participating member in the body politic with all the political and economic reality that pertains.

6. As a result, when the biblical tradition comes to think about the future (popularly, "life after death"), it does not speak about going to heaven to be with one's loved ones. It speaks rather of "a new heaven and a new earth," a new city, a new social reality. And so the creeds faithfully echo with their culminating anticipations:

> "I believe in . . . the resurrection of the body; and the life everlasting" (Apostles' Creed).
>
> "We look for the resurrection of the dead, and the life of the world to come" (Nicene Creed).
>
> More than that, the church prays, after the manner of Jesus, that the will of the Father God will be done "on earth as it is in heaven" (Matt. 6:10).

We live in a society that would like to bracket out money and possessions (politics and economics) from ultimate questions. The Bible insists otherwise. It insists that the issues of ultimacy are questions about money and possessions. Biblical testimony invites a serious reconsideration of the ways in which our society engages or does not engage questions of money and possessions as carriers of social possibility. The gift-giving God intends an abundant life for all creatures (John 10:10). That abundant life, however, includes all the neighbors, human and nonhuman. That inclusiveness requires a recharacterization of the body politic as an arena for the performance and embodiment of the will of the creator God, a will that contradicts much of our preferred, uncriticized practice.

CHAPTER 2

Israel's Core Narrative

No Coveting!

The final utterance of God in the awesome confrontation at Mount Sinai is this: "You shall not covet" (Exod. 20:17). It is as though this fearsome God has saved the sharpest zinger for this final statement. This terse prohibition seems an appropriate pivot point to the core narrative of ancient Israel that was repeatedly reiterated in many variations in Israel. The narrative begins in the wondrous creation lyric of Genesis 1 that culminates in Sabbath (Gen. 2:1–4). It sweeps through the ancestral narratives of Genesis, the emancipation from Egypt, the brief narrative of wilderness sojourn, the defining confrontation at Sinai, and more travel to the edge of the land of promise. James Sanders has noticed that the normative text of the Torah (Pentateuch) does not bring Israel into the land of promise but only to the entry point.[1] We might imagine with Michael Fishbane that the narrative account is from "Adamic" humanity to "Mosaic" humanity, that is, from creation to Sinai.[2] If we trace this movement *from Adam to Moses* we may suggest that the core story is a story about coveting. At least this is one possible rendering that serves our topic of money and possessions.

1. James A. Sanders, *Torah and Canon* (Philadelphia: Fortress Press, 1972), has seen that the canon of Torah stops short of land entry in order to serve the postexilic community of Judaism as it anticipated reentry into the land of promise.

2. Michael Fishbane, *Sacred Attunement: A Jewish Theology* (Chicago: University of Chicago Press, 2008), 119.

This tenth commandment refers to an originary attitude of desire, of being propelled in ways we do not understand to desire what is not properly our own, so that desire becomes a powerful, seductive force that skews one's life. The commandment suggests that it is the stuff that the neighbor has (wife, house, anything) that evokes the seductive energy of desire. It requires, moreover, no great imagination to see that our current consumer society is much propelled by such desire that is in part natural but also is in some great part manufactured.

The history of desire surely runs, in Christian tradition, all the way from Augustine to Adam Smith. Augustine is the great theologian of desire; he himself felt and noticed the compelling power of objects that become seductive and distorting of life.[3] He recognized that our true desire is for God, but that distorted desire focuses on many lesser objects that interrupt a proper desire for God. In the modern world, Adam Smith, in his analysis of "sentiment," noticed the way in which human persons can be propelled by wants; he observed further that such wants can be intentionally managed or manipulated.[4] Thus the history of coveting, in the memory and tradition of ancient Israel, is the story of proper desire and distorted desire that causes a confusion of proper desire and distorted wanting. It is a story that continues among us.

I

The tenth commandment, however, is misunderstood when it is taken, as it often is, as though it simply concerns an attitude of envy. Thus the tenth commandment is sometimes taken as very different from the other nine because the other nine clearly concern action, while this tenth one concerns attitude. The misunderstanding occurs because the term "covet" in truth concerns not only an

3. See the dense study of Augustine's analysis by Timo Nisula, *Augustine and the Functions of Concupiscence* (Leiden: Brill, 2012).

4. Adam Smith, *The Theory of Moral Sentiments* (1759; repr., Oxford: Clarendon Press, 1976). With an altogether different set of intentions, see also Jonathan Haidt, *The Righteous Mind: Why Good People Are Divided by Politics and Religion* (New York: Pantheon Books, 2012). Both Smith and Haidt long after him focus on emotive force in political and economic decisions, emotions that lie beneath and before the work of reason.

attitude of *wanting* but also an action of *taking*. Thus it concerns, like the other nine commandments, actual behavior. The prohibition concerns the acquiring of what belongs to another. The combination of *wanting (desiring)* and *seizing (acquiring)* produces an acquisitive system of money and possessions that is self-propelled until it becomes an addiction that skews viable social relationships so that no one is safe from predatory eagerness.

The tenth commandment, moreover, suggests, on the one hand, that such wanting/taking is prohibited because it is contrary to the will of the God of Sinai. The God of the gospel does not intend that social life should consist in the unrestrained, addictive pursuit of commodities. But on the other hand, as always in the Bible, the practical expression of the divine prohibition is the presence of the neighbor.[5] The term "neighbor" occurs three times in this terse commandment, and it is the first usage in the Decalogue, as though this is the originary statement of a faith perspective that finally concerns the well-being of the neighbor. It is the reality of the neighbor that is the God-acknowledged check on addictive acquisitiveness. The neighbor is a line that must not be transgressed, because the neighbor is an undeniable social fact that will not go away. Acknowledgment of the neighbor, the neighbor's presence, and the neighbor's property is indispensable for a viable social order. As the tradition develops, moreover, special emphasis is placed on the vulnerable neighbors who are without guaranteed social rights or the protection of an effective advocate. Thus the tradition of Deuteronomy, the great neighbor manifesto, asserts: "You must not move your neighbor's boundary marker, set up by former generations, on the property that will be allotted to you in the land that the Lord your God is giving you to possess" (Deut. 19:14).

The same prohibition is expressed in the wisdom tradition:

> Do not remove an ancient landmark
> or encroach on the fields of orphans,
> for their redeemer is strong;
> he will plead their cause against you.
> (Prov. 23:10–11; see 22:28)

5. On the centrality of the neighbor, see Lenn Evan Goodman, *Love Thy Neighbor as Thyself* (Oxford: Oxford University Press, 2008).

Coveting is inimical to viable community. The prohibition in the commandment anticipates the capacity of the rich and powerful, with smart lawyers, to override the unprotected claims of the vulnerable. From the outset, Israel from Sinai has work to do in constructing an alternative economy in which desire is limited by neighbor and confiscation is limited by divine prohibition. The play on the term "redeemer" in Proverbs 23:11 refers to an effective social advocate. But of course theologically God, the Redeemer, is on the side of protecting the economic viability of the vulnerable.

II

Israel, of course, has no monopoly on the temptation to covet. The history of coveting begins already in the creation narrative:

> So when the woman saw that the tree was good for food, and that it was a delight to the eyes, and that the tree was to be desired to make one wise, she took of its fruit and ate; and she also gave some to her husband, who was with her, and he ate. (Gen. 3:6)

Claus Westermann has observed that this verse joins together two quite different ideas.[6] On the one hand, there is delight in sensual pleasure; the fruit was pleasing. The attraction was intensified by being prohibited. Westermann's judgment is that this in itself is not taken as unnatural desire. Attraction to pleasing sensual objects is natural. On the other hand, the desire to make one's self wise, that is, "to rise above one's self," to achieve "new possibilities of life," is the core temptation. It is the desire to transcend one's self by seizing what is not one's own that is the act of coveting. Such coveting is a refusal to accept the limitations of one's self and to imagine that such limitation (in this narrative God-given) can be transcended. This is the "Adamic man" of whom Fishbane writes.

In reading through the ancestral narratives, we may mention that Abraham, recipient of the promise of land, in Genesis 13 is magnanimous in treating with his nephew Lot. He is not covetous of land but permits Lot to choose what he will have:

6. Claus Westermann, *Genesis 1–11: A Commentary* (Minneapolis: Augsburg Publishing House, 1984), 249.

> Then Abram said to Lot, "Let there be no strife between you and me, and between your herders and my herders; for we are kindred. Is not the whole land before you? Separate yourself from me. If you take the left hand, then I will go to the right; or if you take the right hand, then I will go to the left." (Gen. 13:8–9)

By contrast, the sons of Jacob who are the brothers of Joseph surely are covetous of the status of privilege enjoyed by their younger brother (Gen. 37:18–19). In their enmity they sought to eliminate him.

III

The history of coveting finally comes to Pharaoh, who is the quintessential coveter in the imagination and memory of Israel. The note on famine in Genesis 12:10 indicates that Pharaoh already had an ample food supply. His nightmares in Genesis 41:1–7, however, evidence that Pharaoh is overcome with anxiety about food; he is frightened by the prospect of scarcity. There is surely some irony in the fact that the one with the most is the one who has dreams of scarcity. The narrative may indeed be about food. More likely, however, it is that Pharaoh himself was not yet "enough," did not control enough, and so had to take steps beyond his anxiety about his regime. His program of compensation included the designation of Joseph, a Hebrew, to administer a plan to overcome Pharaoh's anxiety and to ensure against any potential scarcity. Because Pharaoh already has a sufficient food supply, so sufficient that he could feed refugees from other places of famine, we may conclude that his anxiety was not informed by reality. It was rather propelled by an anxious resolve to be self-sufficient.

The report of Genesis 47:13–26 makes clear that there was no limit to Pharaoh's usurpatious policies. In three successive years, Joseph, on behalf of Pharaoh, reduces peasant agriculture to slavery as the crown comes to possess all of the land:

> Then Joseph said to the people, "Now that I have this day bought you and your land for Pharaoh, here is seed for you; sow the land. And at the harvests you shall give one-fifth to Pharaoh, and four-fifths shall be your own, as seed for the field and as food for yourselves and your households, and as food for your little ones." . . .

> So Joseph made it a statute concerning the land of Egypt, and it stands to this day, that Pharaoh should have the fifth. The land of the priests alone did not become Pharaoh's. (Gen. 47:23–24, 26)

The generous tone of Joseph seeks to hide the economic reality that the land and its produce have been seized from the peasants for Pharaoh.

Pharaoh did indeed covet his neighbor's field and found a way to acquire it for himself by placing the peasants in an unsustainable economic position as tenant farmers. The exodus narrative that follows from Pharaoh's side is a narrative of unrelieved desire for more. Thus the slaves, who are treated ruthlessly, are kept busy with the task of building more storehouses so that Pharaoh can store the surplus grain produced by his agricultural monopoly (Exod. 1:11). The picture given in the narrative is a kind of restless acquisitiveness that has no restraint at all but that simply must have more, no matter what. The confrontation in Exodus 5 gives voice to Pharaoh's endless urge to have more . . . more labor to make more bricks to build more granaries to store more grain to control more of the food supply (5:4–19). It is evident that such a policy of brutalizing acquisitiveness has no restraint due to the claims of the neighbor, because there were no neighbors on Pharaoh's horizon; there were only workers pressed for more productivity. Exodus 5 suggests a restlessness without limit, so that we may assume that there would be no Sabbath rest for anyone in Pharaoh's domain. Pharaoh is so unlike YHWH, who rested on the seventh day!

This picture of seething, coercive productivity is in stark contrast to the provision for Sabbath rest at the conclusion of the creation narrative (Gen. 2:1–3). One could conclude that it is the willful, limitless force of desire that has made Sabbath a socioeconomic impossibility in Pharaoh's world. Such desire on Pharaoh's part is destructive of human relationships, for the slaves are reduced to a commodity, no more of value than the bricks that they produce.

The exodus narrative, read as part of the history of coveting, is thus an emancipation from the economic domain of coveting that brutalizes and dehumanizes in the compulsion for more. It will not surprise as a result that the Sabbath looms large in the community of the emancipated.[7] Such Sabbath in time to come is not only

7. See Walter Brueggemann, "The God Who Gives Rest" (forthcoming).

disciplined rest. It is an active form of resistance against insatiable desire that regularly segues to brutalizing seizure.[8]

In the story of the departure of the slaves from the domain of acquisitive desire, it is reported that the Israelites did indeed take with them commodities from Pharaoh to which they were not entitled, thus also a form of possession:

> I will bring this people into such favor with the Egyptians that, when you go, you will not go empty-handed; each woman shall ask her neighbor and any woman living in the neighbor's house for jewelry of silver and of gold, and clothing, and you shall put them on your sons and on your daughters; and so you shall plunder the Egyptians. (Exod. 3:21–22; see 11:2; 12:35–36)

It is curious that this confiscation by the slaves of the possessions of Pharaoh is passed over without comment and certainly without any criticism. Perhaps from the perspective of the emancipated such appropriation is legitimate payback for the inordinate seizures of Pharaoh. The act indicates that Israel was not lacking interest in or disengaged from possessions, but had to act stealthily in the face of the overwhelming power and the confiscatory practice of Pharaoh. The emancipated were not left "empty-handed" in their departure!

IV

The emancipation of Israel from Pharaoh's Egypt was a departure from a regime of inordinate coveting. But the future after the departure was risky and not guaranteed. For good reason the emancipated slaves had an urging to return to the desire system of Pharaoh that had victimized them (Exod. 16:2–3). Since Pharaoh had monopolized all food, they were left with wonderment whether there was any viable alternative to the usurpatious system of Pharaoh. In Exodus 16, on the first leg of the trip of emancipation, the drama of risk and scarcity is acted out. They are now outside the domain of Pharaoh's monopoly. But outside the domain

8. See Walter Brueggemann, *Sabbath as Resistance: Saying No to the Culture of Now* (Louisville, KY: Westminster John Knox Press, 2014).

of monopolized commodities, they become, after much grumbling, the recipients of the inexplicable gifts of meat (16:13), bread (16:14–18), and water (17:1–7). It turned out, to their relief and surprise, that outside Pharaoh's regime, the domain of monopolized commodity, a sustainable life was possible. We may reckon the manna story as being the pivotal narrative that attests a viable alternative to the kingdom of inordinate desire. Gifts are given! The place of destitution turns out to be the locus of abundance. It turns out, to the surprise of the characters in the narrative, that there is indeed life, sustainable life, outside the kingdom of acquisitive desire. We may read the narrative and respond, "Who knew?" Who knew there was life in the wilderness? Who knew there was sustenance apart from possessions? Who knew YHWH was a provider who could and would outdistance the parsimonious provisions of Pharaoh? Who knew, indeed? The abundance of YHWH is the counterpoint to the coveting of money and possessions in the Bible!

The narrative of manna in Exodus 16 suggests three important points in our study of money and possessions. First, there is enough, but it must be shared:

> This is what the Lord has commanded: "Gather as much of it as each of you needs, an omer to a person according to the number of persons, all providing for those in their own tents." The Israelites did so, some gathering more, some less. But when they measured it with an omer, those who gathered much had nothing over, and those who gathered little had no shortage; they gathered as much as each of them needed. (16:16–18)

Second, the gift food must not be stored up. They tried that. In their anxiety about sustenance, they tried to imitate Pharaoh by hoarding. But it would not work. Bread given out of inexplicable divine generosity does not function according to Pharaoh's quotas of desire:

> And Moses said to them, "Let no one leave any of it over until morning." But they did not listen to Moses; some left part of it until morning, and it bred worms and became foul. And Moses was angry with them. Morning by morning they gathered it, as much as each needed; but when the sun grew hot, it melted. (vv. 19–21)

Third, the narrative ends with provision for Sabbath rest:

> Moses said, "Eat it today, for today is a sabbath to the LORD; today you will not find it in the field. Six days you shall gather it; but on the seventh day, which is a sabbath, there will be none."
>
> On the seventh day some of the people went out to gather, and they found none. The LORD said to Moses, "How long will you refuse to keep my commandments and instructions? See! The LORD has given you the sabbath, therefore on the sixth day he gives you food for two days; each of you stay where you are; do not leave your place on the seventh day." So the people rested on the seventh day. (vv. 25–30)

In such a marginal existence one might have expected a daily, unrelieved foraging for food in the wilderness. But the creator God who governs the wilderness has provided more than enough. Even the need for food does not require the zone of YHWH's governance to become an endless rat race for more. There is, of course, something hugely ironic in this narrative:

> Pharaoh's zone of much food is endlessly restless for more.
> YHWH's zone of precarious food allows for Sabbath rest and refuses to allow the gift bread of the wilderness to be recruited for the rat race of Pharaoh.

Sabbath is a refusal of the rat race of commodity acquisition; coveting is in contradiction to the alternative of Sabbath. Or better, Sabbath is the alternative to coveting.

Thus the issue is joined in a dramatic way: the unrelieved rat race for more that is propelled by anxiety about scarcity, or a measured, disciplined work stoppage even in the wilderness, because this is a zone of YHWH's abundance. Sabbath in such an environment is a refusal to join the chase for possessions that had become all-defining for Pharaoh. The emancipatory work of YHWH provides a genuine alternative to the insatiable acquisitiveness of Pharaoh. Manna is the shorthand gospel answer to coveting. It is an affirmation that the abundance from God is more than adequate. The abundance of God in the wilderness is not unlike the abundance of God in the garden of delight where the first couple lived. In the garden they would not trust that abundance, and so they were propelled by desire that was not in sync with their situation amid generous divine provision. Now Israel has the opportunity to respond differently. The great insight of the Genesis narrative is that even the garden of abundance is host to the hissing voice of seduction. For that reason, it will not surprise that in time to come, that same hissing voice of desire will continue to operate destructively in Israel. Indeed, already in this narrative some, in defiance of the Sabbath prohibition, nevertheless do go out to collect bread on the Sabbath!

V

Now there is a pause in the tradition for the meeting at Sinai. The textual tradition of Sinai is saturated with memories of Egypt-exodus. Thus at the outset in Exodus 19:4–6, it is clear that Sinai is an alternative to Pharaoh's Egypt. And when God begins to delineate the Ten Commandments, the first reference is to Egypt: "I am the Lord your God, who brought you out of the land of Egypt, out of the house of slavery" (Exod. 20:2).

The one who speaks is the Emancipator from the acquisitive society of Pharaoh. Indeed, one can make a case that the Ten Commandments by design are a counter and alternative to Pharaoh's governance.[9] One can find Pharaoh's Ten Commandments in Exodus 5; all of his commandments are for "more." The Sinai commandments are a prohibition of organizing life as a pursuit of possessions. They are guidelines for how to live well and faithfully outside Pharaoh's world, which is devoted to the pursuit of possessions. The commandments are a championing of reliable, durable relationships of trust as an alternative to the pursuit of commodity. And while the term "neighbor" is not used before the tenth commandment, it is clear that the commandments are rules for honoring and sustaining neighborliness. This is a commitment and possibility that are nowhere present in Pharaoh's acquisitiveness, for acquisitiveness precludes neighborliness.

9. See Walter Brueggemann, "The Countercommands of Sinai," in *Disruptive Grace: Reflections on God, Scripture, and the Church*, ed. Carolyn J. Sharp (Minneapolis: Fortress Press, 2011), 75–92.

The choice of faithful relationship over commodities is defining for Israel. The deep contrast between the two is eventually echoed in Augustine's teaching that we may *love* persons in relationship and *use* commodities, whereas Pharaoh would do exactly the opposite, to *use* persons and *love* commodities.[10] The fourth commandment, on Sabbath, is an attestation that disciplined regular work stoppage, the kind of work stoppage not permitted by addictive acquisitiveness, is indispensable for maintaining a world of relationships of fidelity and obedience.

An attempt to read the Ten Commandments with reference to our topic of money and possessions suggests that they are regulations for refusing the endless propulsion of wanting and taking. Thus the first commandment begins with reference to emancipation from Egypt, the land that stands in Israel's imagination as a metaphor for brutalizing coveting. And the second commandment is a loud warning against undue attention to commodities that beg for worship (Exod. 20:4–6).

The tenth commandment, "You shall not covet," is not as simple as it looks but rather comes as the culmination of a long history of coveting. The commandment reaches toward each of the players in the history of coveting:

It addresses *Adamic personhood*, the human creatures who already in the garden of abundance, in their inordinate desire, brought huge trouble for themselves. The commandment invites all such Adamic persons into the counterworld of Mosaic membership.

It addresses *Pharaoh* by a summary condemnation of his way of governance, thus anticipating a condemnation of all rapacious economic systems and practices that are driven by anxiety about scarcity into a frantic pursuit of more.

It has in its horizon *the neighbor*. It is the acknowledgment of the neighbor as a figure of dignity and respect that enunciates the curbing of greed. The respect for boundary of the neighbor leads eventually to the prayer "Forgive us our trespasses, as we forgive those who trespass against us." The

10. See Sandra Lee Dixon, *Augustine: The Scattered and Gathered Self* (St. Louis: Chalice Press, 1999), 142–47 and passim.

maintenance of proper and just boundaries guarantees a viable and peaceable society.

It attests *YHWH* as the giver of the commandment. YHWH is the God who forbids acquisitiveness that is destructive of historical possibility. The reason YHWH can prohibit such acquisitiveness is that YHWH governs in abundance from a stance of generosity. The manna narrative in which YHWH provides enough for all is Israel's great witness against scarcity.

In the canonical sequence of the core narrative of Israel, the Decalogue is followed by a subset of commandments called by scholars the Book of Covenant (Exod. 21:1–23:19).[11] It is likely that the collection was originally independent of the Decalogue; its present placement, however, permits us to consider it as a commentary on or interpretation of the Decalogue. The commandments in this collection are a mixed lot. Here I will refer to three of them:

1. In Exodus 22:21–24 the commandment warns against oppression of the vulnerable—immigrant, orphan, widow—the great triad of the marginal who are without resources:

> You shall not wrong or oppress a resident alien, for you were aliens in the land of Egypt. You shall not abuse any widow or orphan. If you do abuse them, when they cry out to me, I will surely heed their cry; my wrath will burn, and I will kill you with the sword, and your wives shall become widows and your children orphans.

Oppression is already known in Israel from Egypt; in Exodus 3:9 it is acknowledged that YHWH has seen: "The cry of the Israelites has now come to me; I have also seen how the Egyptians oppress them." Doing wrong to someone is known elsewhere in the Torah: "When an alien resides with you in your land, you shall not oppress the alien" (Lev. 19:33; emphasis added).[12]

Both terms, "wrong" and "oppress," concern economic pressure on those who cannot protect themselves. Such abuse will

11. See Dale Patrick, *Old Testament Law* (Atlanta: John Knox Press, 1985), 63–96, and Frank Cruesemann, *The Torah: Theology and Social History of Old Testament Law* (Edinburgh: T. & T. Clark, 1996), 169–200.

12. While translated differently, the Hebrew is the same as in our text.

evoke a cry of anguish and protest (on which, see Exod. 3:9). In this commandment, the accent is the assurance that YHWH not only is attentive to such a cry from the oppressed but will act vigorously in retaliation. This stipulation is an echo of the prohibition against coveting that provides for enforcement that is not voiced in the tenth commandment. Destructive action toward the neighbor evokes the anger of God.

2. In the next commandment, the concern is more explicitly economic, though the same is surely implied in 22:21–24 as well:

> If you lend money to my people, to the *poor* among you, you shall not deal with them as a creditor; you shall not exact interest from them. If you take your *neighbor's* cloak in pawn, you shall restore it before the sun goes down; for it may be your *neighbor's* only clothing to use as cover; in what else shall that person sleep? And if your *neighbor* cries out to me, I will listen, for I am compassionate. (Exod. 22:25–27; italics added)

Here it is the poor who are designated as the "neighbor" who is the victim of coveting. The abuse of the vulnerable poor is likely to have been legal. It concerns the ordinary process of loans with interest. In verse 26, the offense concerns collateral for a loan. With interest and collateral, the creditor of course has immense leverage over the poor who must borrow money at whatever rate the creditor offers. The process of loan, credit, and interest is here, as always, a completely asymmetrical transaction.

Except that in the imagination of Israel, such economic transactions are never simply between creditor and debtor. They also involve YHWH, who in verse 27 speaks in the first person. The cry of the neighbor over injustice evokes the attention of YHWH, as the cry of the slaves had mobilized YHWH in the exodus narrative (Exod. 2:23–25). YHWH will listen, that is, pay attention and become involved. The ground for such attentiveness is YHWH's compassion that extends to the vulnerable. The different responses in these two regulations are perhaps complementary. In the first (22:24), "I will kill you with the sword"; in the second (v. 27), "I am compassionate." The two together mean that YHWH's compassion is not innocuous but has forceful implications. Of course in neither case is it said how YHWH's decisive response would occur. But even without specificity, the divine self-assertion on behalf of the vulnerable makes YHWH a force in economic transactions. The practitioners of coveting, exemplified by Pharaoh, could imagine that the powerful can act against the powerless with impunity. But no, say the commandments. It is a prohibition of great weightiness.

3. In order that we should not romanticize the significance of the Sinai regulations, we may consider another statute in the collection. Exodus 21:20–21 occurs in a list of cases that concern damage settlements for injury:

> When a slaveowner strikes a male or female slave with a rod and the slave dies immediately, the owner shall be punished. But if the slave survives a day or two, there is no punishment; for the slave is the owner's property.

In this ordinance the concern is a slave who is injured by being beaten by the slave owner as punishment. The regulation makes a closely reasoned distinction that meticulously measures the severity of the punishment administered to the slave. If the slave dies immediately from being punished, the punishment has been too severe, and the owner must be punished. We notice, however, that no particular punishment for the slave owner is delineated, even in this severe case. On the other hand, if the slave does not die the same day but lives a day or two more, this indicates that the punishment has not been too severe, and so the owner is not punished. And then the regulation adds by way of conclusion: "The slave is the owner's property." That is the NRSV translation. The slave is a commodity or a possession. But the Hebrew is even more telling; the slave is the owner's "silver," that is, money. There is no doubt that this mercenary understanding of slavery operated in our own society much too long. Slavery could not be interrupted because the economy depended upon it. Brevard Childs comments: "It is sad to realize that this verse continued to provide a warrant for 'biblical teaching' on slavery throughout the middle of the nineteenth century in the United States."[13]

If we consider all three texts—Exodus 22:21–24; 22:25–27; and 21:20–21—it is easy enough to see that the prohibition of coveting evoked endless disputatious interpretation. The force of economic interest could cause rapacious economics to be perceived not as

13. Brevard S. Childs, *The Book of Exodus: A Critical, Theological Commentary*, Old Testament Library (Philadelphia: Westminster Press, 1974), 471.

coveting, but only as the cost of doing business. But the testimony of the absolute prohibition stands. It is, I propose, the core confession of Israel concerning money and possessions that are to be kept in the orbit of neighborliness intended by YHWH.[14]

VI

Israel is to be different. This is not Adamic personhood, but now the chosen are summoned to Mosaic personhood. But of course the claim for Mosaic personhood is never clean and unambiguous. If we read in the old narrative directly from Exodus 24:18 (the end of the Sinai meeting) to 32:1, it is clear that Moses' absence evoked great anxiety in Israel. Indeed, the absence of Moses the mediator signified in Israel the absence of God. Out of that anxiety and the need for a more palpable god, Israel requests that Aaron "make gods": "Come, make gods for us, who shall go before us" (32:1).

Aaron's response indicates that *divine power* is to be equated with *valued commodity*: "Take off the gold rings that are on the ears of your wives, your sons, and your daughters, and bring them to me" (v. 2). He makes a god of gold who is credited with the exodus emancipation: "He took the gold from them, formed it in a mold, and cast an image of a calf; and they said, 'These are your gods, O Israel, who brought you up out of the land of Egypt!'" (v. 4). The newly crafted god promises security and invites offerings and sacrifices: "They rose early the next day, and offered burnt offerings and brought sacrifices of well-being; and the people sat down to eat and drink, and rose up to revel" (v. 6).

The prehistory of this text is obscure and difficult, because bull worship may have been an alternative form of YHWH worship. However that may have been, as we have the narrative, the *calf (bull) of gold* is a rival and alternative to YHWH. Divine power is readily merged with or confused with self-generating money and possessions. The later prophetic tradition includes a commentary on gods that are made from money and possessions:

14. See Marvin L. Chaney, "'Coveting Your Neighbor's House' in Social Context," in *The Ten Commandments: The Reciprocity of Faithfulness*, ed. William P. Brown (Louisville, KY: Westminster John Knox Press, 2004), 302–17; and Rainer Kessler, *Debt and Decalogue: The Tenth Commandment* (Leiden: Brill, 2015).

> And now they keep on sinning
> and make a cast image for themselves,
> idols of *silver* according to their understanding,
> all of them the work of artisans.
> "Sacrifice to these," they say.
> People are kissing calves!
> (Hos. 13:2; italics added)

Or more programmatically, Jeremiah can describe the work of god making:

> A tree from the forest is cut down,
> and worked with an ax by the hands of an artisan;
> people deck it with *silver and gold*;
> they fasten it with hammer and nails
> so that it cannot move.
> (Jer. 10:3–4; italics added)

The prophet goes on to notice that such gods are immobile and impotent and cannot save:

> Their idols are like scarecrows in a cucumber field,
> and they cannot speak;
> they have to be carried,
> for they cannot walk.
> Do not be afraid of them,
> for they cannot do evil,
> nor is it in them to do good.
> (v. 5)

The response of YHWH, and subsequently of Moses, to the "made god" of Aaron is one of alarm and then violence (Exod. 32:7–20).

Aaron's action requires from Moses risky negotiation with YHWH, because YHWH does not look kindly on being displaced by commodity worship (Exod. 33:12–22). Divine forgiveness is required in order to begin again (34:9–10). In the new stipulations that follow from the new covenant of 34:10, there is this terse prohibition: "You shall not make cast idols."

Idols are products of valuable commodities that are transposed into objects of desire and worship. They are without passion; they command or prohibit nothing. They are easy gods that make no covenant and that have on their horizon no neighbor. They cannot practice fidelity and have no transformative power. The entire narrative of YHWH from creation through emancipation to covenant tells powerfully against such an illusionary practice of worship that is propelled by the manipulation of money and possessions and that has as an inescapable by-product antineighborly policy and practice. Thus the tenth commandment contra coveting is linked to the first two commandments on "only YHWH" and no idols; it is not a surprise, then, that the tenth commandment focuses on neighbor, the very focus that coveting characteristically eliminates.

When we reach the narrative report of Exodus 36–40, we are in another world that reflects a very different tradition. In Exodus 25–31, Moses had received detailed instructions from God for the construction of a tabernacle as a place that may consequently host the covenant-making God. In chapters 36–40, we are told that Moses enacted precise obedience to these commands. His obedience consists in the construction of an adequate holy place. For such a construction, he must have proper building materials. Chapters 35–36 are an accounting of the accumulation of the required materials for the tabernacle construction. Moses enumerates all that he will need for the project. The people respond to his inventory in a mood of great generosity: "And they came, everyone whose heart was stirred, and everyone whose spirit was willing, and brought the LORD's offering to be used for the tent of meeting, and for all its service, and for the sacred vestments" (35:21).

The outcome of their glad generosity is a rich offering of money and possessions:

> So they came, both men and women; all who were of a willing heart brought brooches and earrings and signet rings and pendants, all sorts of gold objects, everyone bringing an offering of gold to the LORD. And everyone who possessed blue or purple or crimson yarn or fine linen or goats' hair or tanned rams' skins or fine leather, brought them. Everyone who could make an offering of silver or bronze brought it as the LORD's offering; and everyone who possessed acacia wood of any use in the work, brought it. (vv. 22–24)

In chapter 36, moreover, the generous offering of Israel continues: The artisans "received from Moses all the freewill offerings that the Israelites had brought for doing the work on the sanctuary. They still kept bringing him freewill offerings every morning" (v. 3). Most remarkable, it is reported that the generous offerings were more than enough, more than could be used or even received:

> All the artisans who were doing every sort of task on the sanctuary came, each from the task being performed, and said to Moses, "The people are bringing much more than enough for doing the work that the LORD has commanded us to do." So Moses gave command, and word was proclaimed throughout the camp: "No man or woman is to make anything else as an offering for the sanctuary." So the people were restrained from bringing; for what they had already brought was more than enough to do all the work. (vv. 4–7)

This is one of the most amazing and most successful stewardship campaigns in the history of faith! The report is without interpretive comment. We are not told why Israel was so generous toward the Lord.

It is clear in any case that in the text Israel did not covet. Israel did not withhold or give grudgingly. This is the antithesis of coveting. The outcome of this generous outpouring, we learn subsequently, is the construction of a tabernacle that will be occupied by the glory of YHWH (40:34–38). In this priestly tradition, YHWH will not dwell in shabbiness or parsimony. Israel has prepared a place for the "beauty of holiness" in which money and possessions are devoted in singular ways to the splendor of God. Exodus 32, with its *anxious idolatry*, and Exodus 35–36, with its *unrestrained generosity*, albeit from a different interpretive tradition, present an unmistakable contrast between the *work of anxiety* that issues in self-made gods and the *work of generous self-abandonment*. Or one could judge that in both cases the people were generous. Except that in the first case, it is all self-propelled and self-making ultimacy out of what they owned. The material substance in the two narratives is the same: gold! But the gold is always situated in a narrative that determines its significance. In chapter 32, the gold is set in *a narrative of deep anxiety* and the response is an effort at self-securing. In chapters 35–36, the gold (and other precious possessions) are set in *a narrative of generous gratitude and expectation* that signals readiness for yielding to the God of the exodus. The two narratives about money and possessions compete for Israel's loyalty. These two narratives of anxiety and confident trust, moreover, continue to compete among us. The narrative of anxiety will seek to control God and oppress the neighbor. The narrative of trust, to the contrary, will yield to God, to the God who stands with and by and for the neighbor. The question of competing narratives looms large and durably in the imagination of faith. Those who generously brought their money and possessions to the God of emancipation and covenant had arrived at the assurance of the psalmist: "The LORD is my shepherd; I shall not want" (Ps. 23:1).

CHAPTER 3

Deuteronomy

The Great Either-Or of Neighborliness

By the time we reach the book of Deuteronomy, Israel's core narrative has brought us to the edge of the land of promise at the Jordan River. In canonical sequence, the book of Deuteronomy consists in speeches of instruction by Moses about how to live faithfully in the land of promise that they are about to enter. In the text, the land is said to be the "land of the Canaanites." It turns out, however, that "Canaanite" is not an ethnic term. It is rather an ideological term that with our themes connotes a predatory economy. Israel's new habitat is to be amid a predatory economy.

Moses' articulation pivots on two accent points. *Negatively* the land to be entered will be *seductive*. Israel will be drawn into Canaanite practices that will compromise and abrogate Israel's covenantal faith. Thus there are harsh warnings in the book and an imperative to "purge the evil" of such anticipated seduction. On the other hand, *positively*, the instruction of Moses is an insistence that the land to be entered is *transformable*. A resolved Israelite covenantal practice can mute and negate Canaanite practices so that the land takes on the character and quality of Israel's faith. For our theme, that possibility of transformation means that the economy can be transformed from one of *predation* to one of *covenantal neighborliness*. Thus the urgency of Moses is that Israel is warned against the *seduction* and summoned to *the transformative task*.

In critical study, the Mosaic placement of Deuteronomy is taken to be a fictive construct. It is conventional to date the appearance of Deuteronomy in the eighth century BCE, perhaps under the influence of Near Eastern covenant-treaty formulations. In that context, Deuteronomy stands at the headwaters of the "classical prophets" of the eighth–seventh centuries BCE, with their urgent accent on covenantalism. This linkage pertains especially to the prophetic traditions of Hosea and Jeremiah that are intimately related to Deuteronomy, but more broadly it relates to the entire corpus of prophetic speeches of judgment. In that context, it is recognized that Israel has gone amiss if not completely failed in its covenantal mandate under the impetus of the Jerusalem religious-economic elites. Thus the book of Deuteronomy is a summons to return to covenantal practices, including economic neighborliness. Insofar as Israel has fallen into predatory economics, it has placed its life in the land in jeopardy.

More recent critical study is inclined to locate Deuteronomy in the fifth century BCE, in the period of Persian domination. If placed there, it is in the wake of the loss of land and political independence, so that Judah has been reduced to a Persian province, and the elite, upon return to the land, remain under Persian control. In that context, Deuteronomy serves as a prospective guide for how to order the life and economy of Israel upon return to and recovery of the land of promise. Because life under Persia is experienced as "slavery" (in the form of taxation; see Ezra 9:8; Neh. 9:36), the reordering of the economy is urgent.

I

Thus the book of Deuteronomy may be read (a) canonically at the edge of the land of promise, (b) in the eighth century when Israel is jeopardized by compromise, or (c) in the Persian period when Israel ponders a restored community. In any or all of these scenarios, Deuteronomy is the great summons of either-or:

> See, I have set before you today life and prosperity, death and adversity. If you obey the commandments of the LORD your God that I am commanding you today, by loving the LORD your God,

> walking in his ways, and observing his commandments, decrees, and ordinances, then you shall live and become numerous, and the LORD your God will bless you in the land you are entering to possess. But if your heart turns away and you do not hear, but are led astray to bow down to other gods and serve them, I declare to you today that you shall perish; you shall not live long in the land that you are crossing the Jordan to enter and possess. (Deut. 30:15–18)

The *either* of "life and prosperity" concerns adherence to the torah, which in context means the torah of Deuteronomy. Thus the commandments of Deuteronomy are presented as prerequisite for life and the land, and many of these commandments concern money and possessions. The *or* of "death and adversity" is to compromise or abandon the covenantal distinctiveness of Israel and to conform to the regnant predatory economy. The either-or of Deuteronomy is, of course, cast as a religious issue of true God or false gods; attention to the text, however, makes clear that *religious claims* are deeply intertwined with *socioeconomic issues,* so that the decision of life or death before Israel (in any of these contexts) is a decision that concerns money and possessions. The move in the tradition from religious criticism to economic criticism anticipates the aphorism of Karl Marx:

> The criticism of heaven is thus transformed into the criticism of earth,
> The criticism of religion into the criticism of law, and
> The criticism of theology into the criticism of politics.[1]

Thus a warning against *false religion* in Deuteronomy entails a warning against *false economic practice*. The rhetoric of Deuteronomy is focused on the command to "love the LORD your God with all your heart . . ." (Deut. 6:5); this mandate, however, is accompanied by the tacit commandment to "love your neighbor" (Lev. 19:18), so that the either-or that concerns God also concerns money and possessions in a decision for or against neighborliness in economic policy and practice.

1. Karl Marx, quoted in David McLellan, *The Thought of Karl Marx: An Introduction* (New York: Macmillan, 1971), 22.

II

The book of Deuteronomy, as Martin Noth has shown, has a sustained propensity to contemporaneity indicated by the repeated "today."[2] Deuteronomy is a dynamic tradition of interpretation that seeks always to adapt to the covenantal tradition and reapply it to new circumstance. Already in Deuteronomy 1:5, it reports that Moses "expounded" the torah. He did not simply reiterate, but he added interpretation that served contemporaneity. At the very outset, the book of Deuteronomy puts us on notice that what follows is exposition. Further, in Deuteronomy 5:1–5, as Moses summons Israel to covenant (in the eighth or the fifth century), he asserts: "The Lord our God made a covenant with us at Horeb. Not with our ancestors did the Lord make this covenant, but with us, who are all of us here alive today" (vv. 2–3). The covenant made at Horeb/Sinai is not "back there"; it is very present tense.

The corpus of sermons and commandments that follow are to be understood as an upgrading of Sinai according to the continuing authority of Moses. What follows in Deuteronomy 5:6–21 is a reiteration of the Ten Commandments from Exodus 20:1–17. This is the baseline of the Sinai covenant assumed by Deuteronomy, from which all else follows. The corpus of commandments consists variously in expositions of the Ten Commandments. This has led some scholars to suggest that the commandments in Deuteronomy 12–25 follow roughly the outline of the Ten Commandments.[3] For our purposes of considering money and possessions, we might particularly focus on the tenth commandment, "You shall not covet" (Exod. 20:17; Deut. 5:21). As we have seen, coveting includes both *the desire* to have what belongs to another and *the seizure* of what belongs to another. The commandment of Exodus 20:17 is terse but clearly concerns "the neighbor." The only other use of "covet" (*ḥmd*) in Deuteronomy is in 7:25, which is a summons to obey torah:

2. Martin Noth, "The 'Re-presentation' of the Old Testament in Proclamation," in *Essays on Old Testament Hermeneutics*, ed. Claus Westermann, trans. James Luther Mays (Richmond: John Knox Press, 1963), 76–88.

3. S. A. Kaufman, "The Structure of the Deuteronomic Law," *Maarav* 1:2 (1978–1979): 105–58; Georg Braulik, "The Sequence of the Laws in Deuteronomy 12–26 and in the Decalogue," in *A Song of Power and the Power of Song: Essays on the Book of Deuteronomy*, ed. Duane L. Christensen (Winona Lake, IN: Eisenbrauns, 1993), 313–35.

> The images of their gods you shall burn with fire. Do not *covet* the silver or the gold that is on them and take it for yourself, because you could be ensnared by it; for it is abhorrent to the LORD your God.

This statement is of particular interest and importance because it brings together the second commandment on images and the tenth commandment on coveting, thus linking religious prohibition and economic critique so that the images of other gods are taken to be forms of legitimation for desire and seizure. What follows this prohibition of coveting is extraordinarily strong language indicating the urgency of this issue for the maintenance of covenantal identity:

> Do not bring an abhorrent thing into your house, or you will be set apart for destruction like it. You must utterly detest and abhor it, for it is set apart for destruction. (v. 26)

The heaping up of the terms "ensnare," "abomination," "abhorrent," "destruction" (*ḥerem*), and "detest" (the latter stated in intensive absolute infinitive form) attests to the urgency of this matter. The focus on "silver and gold" as commentary on coveting means that money and possessions are seen in this tradition to be very dangerous, because when Israel is ensnared in such desire and seizure, it will compromise its holiness (7:5–6) and so forfeit its life in the land of promise. Thus the book of Deuteronomy may be seen as an urgent summons to either-or that is urgent precisely because it must have seemed then (as now) so ordinary and commonplace to adjust to a predatory economic practice that it could happen without notice. Such adjustment and conformity are, in this tradition, life or death.

III

The material in Deuteronomy roughly divides into sermonic exhortations and commandments. The negative target of both sermons and commandments is "Canaanite" seduction that principally concerns debt, the reduction of needy neighbors to indebtedness whereby some acquire powerful leverage against others in the community. The threat of a debt economy is that it sets one class of society against another class and so violates the community of neighborliness to which Israel is committed. Thus it is important in reading the religious rhetoric of the text to recognize that the subtext everywhere concerns economic neighborliness. In the sermonic materials of Deuteronomy 6–11, we may notice in particular two powerful commentaries. In Deuteronomy 6 Moses asserts:

> When the LORD your God has brought you into the land that he swore to your ancestors, to Abraham, to Isaac, and to Jacob, to give you—a land with fine, large cities that you did not build, houses filled with all sorts of goods that you did not fill, hewn cisterns that you did not hew, vineyards and olive groves that you did not plant—and when you have eaten your fill, take care that you do not forget the LORD, who brought you out of the land of Egypt, out of the house of slavery. The LORD your God you shall fear; him you shall serve, and by his name alone you shall swear. Do not follow other gods, any of the gods of the peoples who are all around you, because the LORD your God, who is present with you, is a jealous God. The anger of the LORD your God would be kindled against you and he would destroy you from the face of the earth. (vv. 10–15)

The affluence of houses, cisterns, vineyards, and groves will take the edge off the tradition and eventually result in amnesia. What will be forgotten is the exodus tradition and the God of the exodus, the one who emancipated the slaves from the predatory economy of Pharaoh. The urgency is that Israel, even in its affluence, must remember that the world is governed by the God of emancipation who is the great opponent to antineighborly economics. And if Israel forgets that God and that governance, it may mistakenly come to think that the "Canaanite" option of predation is normal and acceptable. And Israel would disappear!

Later in the same chapter, the children are to be instructed in the narrative memory of the exodus: "Then you shall say to your children, 'We were Pharaoh's slaves in Egypt, but the LORD brought us out of Egypt with a mighty hand. The LORD displayed before our eyes great and awesome signs and wonders against Egypt, against Pharaoh and all his household'" (vv. 21–22).

The recital to be taught to the children is the safeguard against Israel disappearing into the anticovenantalism of "Canaan." Michael

Fishbane judges the concern of the text to be the crisis of socializing the younger generation into this vision of social reality:

> The teaching of the fathers in Deuteronomy 6:20–25 is an attempt to involve their sons in the covenant community of the future, and undoubtedly reflects the sociological reality of the settlement in Canaan. The attempt by the fathers to transform their uninvolved sons from "*dis*temporaries" to *con*temporaries, i.e., time-sharers, is an issue of supreme and recurrent significance in the Bible.[4]

The recurrent significance of this insistence against amnesia is that without memory and recital, money and possessions can be settled on pharaonic terms that feature the disappearance and rejection of the neighbor.

The same urgency is reflected in Deuteronomy 8:11–20, in which affluence leads to amnesia:

> Take care that you do not forget the LORD your God, by failing to keep his commandments, his ordinances, and his statutes, which I am commanding you today. When you have eaten your fill and have built fine houses and live in them, and when your herds and flocks have multiplied, and your silver and gold is multiplied, and all that you have is multiplied, then do not exalt yourself, forgetting the LORD your God, who brought you out of the land of Egypt, out of the house of slavery, who led you through the great and terrible wilderness, an arid wasteland with poisonous snakes and scorpions. He made water flow for you from flint rock, and fed you in the wilderness with manna that your ancestors did not know, to humble you and to test you, and in the end to do you good. Do not say to yourself, "My power and the might of my own hand have gotten me this wealth." But remember the LORD your God, for it is he who gives you power to get wealth, so that he may confirm his covenant that he swore to your ancestors, he is doing today. (vv. 11–18)

The new note sounded here is that such amnesia leads to a sense of autonomy and self-sufficiency, and that with reference to

4. Michael Fishbane, *Text and Texture: Close Readings of Selected Biblical Texts* (New York: Schocken Books, 1979), 81–82.

"wealth." The memory of exodus, wilderness, and manna assures that one's wealth will be regarded as a gift to be shared. The loss of such memory causes wealth to be regarded as one's own achievement and possession without regard to social context. It is important to notice that in the solemn warning of verses 11–20 two absolute infinitives are utilized that underscore the urgency of this instruction: "really forget . . . really perish." The matter of keeping one's life situated in the narrative of exodus, wilderness, and manna is urgent; without it, Israel will disappear into the predatory woodwork of "Canaan."

IV

The urgency of the sermons is given specificity in the commandments. If we follow the suggestion that the commandments track the sequence of the Ten Commandments, we may expect "do not covet" to be accented in the final part of the corpus of commandments, and so it is. It is also clear, however, that the accent on a neighborly economy is pervasive in the corpus and is not confined to its final verses. In what follows, I will detail the Mosaic teaching on money and possessions amid a practice of economics that evidences the predatory ways of coveting. The aim of the commandments is to subordinate the economy to the requirements of neighborly society so that debt and its economic leverage over the vulnerable are not defining for social relationships.

We may identify four texts that concern *offerings* through which material possessions are to be shared with the community of the vulnerable. The tithe is a specified amount of produce that is owed in an agricultural community to the landowner. Thus a tithe brought to YHWH's sanctuary is an acknowledgment that YHWH is the landowner, and not the one who occupies the land (see Ps. 24:1). In Deuteronomy 14:22–29 there are three provisions for the tithe:

- The tithe of grain, wine, olive oil, herds, and flocks (all the best agricultural produce) is to be eaten by the donor in the presence of "the LORD your God," that is, at the sanctuary. This is a curious provision; no doubt the requirement is that the donor will, by such eating, acknowledge the sovereignty of God who gives the produce. It is like being welcomed at a table to eat, all the while recognizing that the table belongs to another. The act is a gesture against any imagined autonomy by acknowledgment of YHWH as the producer of the crops and provider at the table.

- If the distance to the sanctuary is great, the produce can be cashed out for "silver" (money). The regulation makes clear that this is a required economic transaction that is not to be taken too romantically. The money (silver) is for whatever one wants, but in the presence of YHWH.
- In the third year, the tithe is offered not at the sanctuary but in the village, to be shared with the vulnerable: immigrants, orphans, widows, and also Levites. The purpose is to sustain those without resources, an act that will evoke God's blessing. All three of these actions tell against any notion that the tithe (owed money) is "mine." The tithe asserts YHWH's rule over Israel and over the land.

In the festival calendar of chapter 16, two of the three festivals are a vehicle for providing generous sustenance for the stranger. In the Festival of Weeks, the guest list is inclusive: "Rejoice before the Lord your God—you and your sons and your daughters, your male and female slaves, the Levites resident in your towns, as well as the strangers, the orphans, and the widows who are among you" (vv. 11–12).

In the Festival of Booths, there is a parallel inclusiveness (v. 14). In the summary statement, moreover, participation in the festivals to YHWH requires that one not be "empty-handed" (v. 16). The worshiper must bring a substantive offering, an act that attests the materiality of Israel's faith and that precludes any misunderstanding of Israel's worship as a spiritual act detached from questions of money and possessions and their faithful management. In the provision for Passover, the festival is securely placed in the narrative of the exodus. The unleavened bread, the bread of affliction, is a remembrance, "because you came out of the land of Egypt in great haste, so that all the days of your life you may remember the day of your departure from the land of Egypt" (v. 3).

In 16:12, moreover, the motivation for a generous offering is the exodus. Either directly or by implication, all of these festival celebrations draw Israel back into its narrative of emancipation in order to affirm that Israel's life, identity, and destiny are outside the domain of the coercive economy. The question of who has access to the produce of the community is an acute one. Here the answer is that all members of the community have access, enough to rejoice together and to be sated.

The accent of the either-or of Deuteronomy, however, is not preoccupied with cultic matters. It is focused on civic, social regulations that will keep covenantal life viable. This accent is in contrast to the priestly tradition of Leviticus that is largely preoccupied with cultic questions. Most important of all of these civic, social provisions is the regulation on debt in the Year of Release, that is, "remission of debts" in the seventh year.[5] The core regulation in 15:1 is terse and unqualified. It is a simple, defining recognition that debt does not have an ultimate role to play in the economy and that the community has a profound stake in the management of debt so that it does not become defining for the community. This is a remarkable provision that lies at the heart of forgiveness in biblical faith. As Patrick Miller has shown with reference to a text in Luke, forgiveness was primarily an economic matter before it became a theological agenda.[6] (It is with reference to that fact that some versions of the Lord's Prayer concern forgiveness of "debts.")

At the outset we may acknowledge the ever-recurring question of whether, in fact, such a practice was implemented in Israel. It is telling, indeed, that of all the requirements in the ancient Torah, it is this one that evokes such wonderment. Such anxious wonderment is recognition of how peculiar and how dangerous such a provision would be to the maintenance of an ordinary economy. My sense about such a question is that it is characteristically a desire to be reassured that ancient Israel really did not mean this or take it seriously. We do not know; there are many reviews of the suggested evidence for such a practice that are not decisive concerning the historicity of the regulation. Be that as it may, that it is in the tradition and that it was imagined and remembered is enough to see the ways in which debt was kept penultimate in a covenantal milieu, that is, in the memory of Exodus-Sinai.

5. See Jeffries M. Hamilton, *Social Justice and Deuteronomy: The Case of Deuteronomy 15*, Society of Biblical Literature Dissertation Series 136 (Atlanta: Scholars Press, 1992).

6. Patrick D. Miller, "An Exposition of Luke 4:16–21," *Interpretation* 29:4 (1975): 417–21.

Because the provision of verse 1 is stated so starkly and radically, we can see why it received, in the text, extended elucidation. Verses 2–3 delineate between "neighbor" and "foreigner." As we shall see in several places, the foreigner can be treated according to conventional economics, but not the neighbor, that is, a fellow member of the covenant community. It is for that reason that the wonderment, "Who is my neighbor?," looms so large in the tradition.

It is clear in what follows in the text that the initial provision concerned all debtors, but the focus of interest is on the needy, the ones likely to be burdened with insurmountable debt. Thus the needy are front and center in verses 4, 7, 8, and 11. Economic matters must yield to social reality; and the social reality is that if the needy are kept in debt, they cannot be viable neighbors. The regulation is clearly addressed to creditors. Israel's creditors belong in a vast company of creditors:

> For thousands of years, the struggle between rich and poor has largely taken the form of conflicts between creditors and debtors—of arguments about the rights and wrongs of interest payments, debt peonage, amnesty, repossession, restitution, the sequestering of sheep, the seizing of vineyards, and the selling of debtors' children into slavery. By the same token, for the last five thousand years, with remarkable regularity, popular insurrections have begun the same way: with the ritual destruction of the debt records—tablets, papyri, ledgers, whatever form they might have taken in any particular place . . . all revolutionary movements had a single program: "Cancel the debts, burn the records, and redistribute the land."[7]

This address to creditors as a summons, moreover, is not welcome. Moses urges that creditors should not be "hard-hearted or tight-fisted" (v. 7), a condition that is likely if money is understood apart from the infrastructure of neighborliness. The warning against being "hard-hearted" could be an allusion to Pharaoh in his acquisitiveness, for he is the quintessential agent with a hard heart.

The urgency of the regulation is indicated in the exposition by the utilization of seven absolute infinitive verbs. This is an intensification of the verb in Hebrew whereby the verb is repeated a second

7. David Graeber, *Debt: The First 5,000 Years* (Brooklyn: Melville House, 2011), 8.

time. Unfortunately it is impossible to render this in a recognizable form in English. Thus the infinitive absolutes:

Sure to bless (v. 4)
Really obey (v. 5)
Really give (v. 8)
Willingly lend (v. 8)
Give liberally (v. 10)
Really open (v. 11)
Provide liberally (v. 14)

This mass of seven intensive verbs, paralleled nowhere else in Scripture, as far as I know, is a measure of how important this provision is in the tradition:

> There will, however, be no one in need among you, because the LORD is sure to bless you in the land that the LORD your God is giving you as a possession to occupy, if only you will obey the LORD your God by diligently observing this entire commandment that I command you today. When the LORD your God has blessed you, as he promised you, you will lend to many nations, but you will not borrow; you will rule over many nations, but they will not rule over you.
>
> If there is among you anyone in need, a member of your community in any of your towns within the land that the LORD your God is giving you, do not be hard-hearted or tight-fisted toward your needy neighbor. You should rather open your hand, willingly lending enough to meet the need, whatever it may be. Be careful that you do not entertain a mean thought, thinking, "The seventh year, the year of remission, is near," and therefore view your needy neighbor with hostility and give nothing; your neighbor might cry to the LORD against you, and you would incur guilt. Give liberally and be ungrudging when you do so, for on this account the LORD your God will bless you in all your work and in all that you undertake. Since there will never cease to be some in need on the earth, I therefore command you, "Open your hand to the poor and needy neighbor in your land."
>
> If a member of your community, whether a Hebrew man or a Hebrew woman, is sold to you and works for you six years, in the seventh year you shall set that person free. And when you send a male slave out from you a free person, you shall not send him out empty-handed. Provide liberally out of your flock, your thresh-

> ing floor, and your wine press, thus giving to him some of the bounty with which the LORD your God has blessed you. Remember that you were a slave in the land of Egypt, and the LORD your God redeemed you; for this reason I lay this command upon you today. (15:4–15)

We are, in this regulation, at the heart of biblical teaching about money and possessions, a regulation that wealth is held provisionally and debt cannot become a permanent lever of the economy. The most radical teaching of the Bible on money and possessions concerns forgiveness of debts, for debt over time erodes neighborliness and makes viable social life impossible.

Two statements in the exposition of the commandment, when juxtaposed, become especially interesting. In verse 4 it is asserted that "there will be no one in need among you," that is, no one without resources who remains in debt. That is, the practice of this regulation will eliminate economic debts. The reason that there will be no needy is that the resources of the community are distributed, not according to personal property, but according to social solidarity. The rhetoric of verse 4 is juxtaposed to the more familiar statement of verse 11: "There will never cease to be some in need on the earth." Or more familiarly, "The poor you will always have with you."

This is not a statement of resignation, as it is often taken to be. It is rather an underscoring about why this provision must be practiced with faithfulness. Thus verse 4 promises that poverty can be overcome; verse 11 asserts that continual attentiveness to the poor and needy is urgent. They can never be left in a vulnerable state, but are entitled to protection and a viable life in the community. The grounding for this urgent regulation, of course, is a remembrance of the exodus (15:15).

VI

Given the centrality of debt forgiveness in Deuteronomy as a way to think about and manage money and possessions, we can identify five other texts in Deuteronomy that concern economic protection for the vulnerable in what must have been a predatory economy, whether Canaanite, eighth century, or fifth century:

1. *Deuteronomy 23:19–20.* This commandment prohibits charging interest on loans to a neighbor, that is, an Israelite. In verse 19 the term "interest" is used five times as a verb and a noun. The tradition knows, as vulnerable people always discover, that charging interest is an enormous leverage that moneyed forces use against unmoneyed people to reduce them to dependency that becomes a form of slavery. The distinctiveness of Israel shows up exactly in such a prohibition of economic exploitation of the vulnerable. The regulation connects this economic no-no with the well-being of the land. The earlier regulation of Exodus 22:25 identifies the "poor" as the subject of the commandment, an intent implicit here as well.

2. *Deuteronomy 24:10–13, 17.* Clearly related to exploitative interest on loans is the usurpatious practice of demanding collateral for loans. The initial prohibition concerns the process of receiving collateral ("pledge") from a neighbor (vv. 10–11). But verse 12 moves attention yet again to the poor, the ones without protection or resources in economic matters. The regulation provides that a "garment" (coat) taken as collateral can only be kept during the day, because the poor person will need it at night to keep warm. In verse 17 the target group is broadened to include orphans, widows, and immigrants as well. The daytime collateral returned at night offers the ludicrous picture of each day claiming collateral and every night returning it to the debtor. Imagine doing that each day and each night for a thirty-year loan! Surely the intent is to make collateral so inconvenient that it is not demanded in the first place. The limitation on collateral from the poor is given motivation in verse 18 with reference to the exodus deliverance. The God who commands this is the God of economic emancipation. Exploitative collateral is reminiscent of Pharaoh's rapacious economics, and it must be shunned in the alternative economy of Israel.

3. *Deuteronomy 24:14–15.* The target group is "poor and needy laborers," those at the low end of influence and leverage, most vulnerable to exploitation in the world of capital and labor. The tradition knows that withholding wages, even for a day, permits the use of money by the employed that rightly belongs to the laborers. Of course beyond that, there are now, as surely then, many forms of wage theft. The failure to pay on the day earned is not simply antineighborly. It will evoke a cry to YHWH, not unlike the initial cry of Israel to YHWH in Egypt (Exod. 2:23–25). That cry will cause YHWH to hold the exploiter to account. It is worth noting that

in this regulation, as in Deuteronomy 24:10–14, the limit of anti-neighborly collateral or withheld wages must end at "sunset." It is as though economic leverage is permitted (collateral and withholding wages), but at sunset in the rhythm of creation, all such leverage must cease in the practice of neighborliness (see Ps. 104:21–23). Economic leverage has severe limitations that are ordered in the rhythm of creation that cannot be safely disregarded.

4. *Deuteronomy 24:19–21.*Whereas the preceding regulations concerning interest, collateral, and withholding wages were designed to restrain exploitation, this regulation commends positive action toward the vulnerable. The threefold provision concerning grain (harvest), olive (oil), and grapes (for wine) concerns the familiar triad of money crops. Because these are money crops with potentially large commercial profit, one might expect that the growers would be sure to extract every possible measure of them.

But not in Israel! In Israel, unlike the "Canaanite" economy of squeezed commodities, these money crops must be managed in a neighborly way.[8] When the provision goes on to identify the neighbors, it reiterates the triad of the vulnerable—widows, orphans, immigrants—those without resources or legal protections in a patriarchal society. For good reason, Frank Cruesemann has termed this provision an early "social safety net" in which agriculture for profit is curbed by the presence and need of the neighbor.[9] In a predatory economy, the great anxiety is that someone will get something for nothing. The assumption of such a mantra is the privatization of wealth and the autonomy of the owner of such produce. This regulation, however, refuses such privatization and insists that such productive wealth has a social public dimension. Thus the law is a break with conventional privatized economics; that break, moreover, is specified by yet another reference to the exodus in verse 22.The sum of all of these regulations is the assurance that the emancipatory actions of the exodus remain in the work of the economy.

8. Suzanne Daley, "After Harvest, Spanish Town Fights over the Leftovers," *New York Times*, April 3, 2015, reports on the contemporaneity of the issue of leftover crops in the field. Mr. Diaz judges of leaving the leftovers for the needy, "It's certainly better than having people go on welfare." Mr. Constantin concludes, "There are good farmers here and bad ones. Some of them say, 'Leave it all on the ground. It is mine.'" That contemporary dispute concerning leftovers in the field suggests the poignancy of the requirement in our verses.

9. Frank Cruesemann, *The Torah: Theology and Social History of Old Testament Law* (Edinburgh: T. & T. Clark, 1996), 224–34.

5. *Deuteronomy 25:13–16.* The concluding regulation of the legal corpus of Deuteronomy concerns exploitative commercial practices specified by "two kinds of weights" and "two kinds of measures." Such practices give traders, merchants, and bankers enormous discretion about which weight or measure to use with which client. It may be readily inferred that one measure or weight would be utilized for one's friends, and another for the less-favored neighbors. It takes no imagination to transfer this regulation to our contemporary practice of exploitative interest rates and payday loans for the disadvantaged, to no-bid contracts for the well connected. Thus the provision insists upon social equity of an egalitarian kind, so that the privileged, entitled, and advantaged do not receive, as in a predatory economy, still further advantage. This regulation is reflected in the indictment of Amos 8:5–6, in which "deceit" is practiced against the poor and needy with exorbitant price arrangements. The Torah was a great protector against the toxic temptations of a predatory economy.

VII

While Deuteronomy offers the most programmatic statement of a neighborly-covenantal economy, the Torah elsewhere as well insists on such a sensibility. Thus in the earlier stipulations of the Covenant Code, similar provisions are voiced.

Exodus 22:21–27. Oppression of the immigrant, orphan, widow, and the needy is prohibited. The generic prohibition of verses 21–22 is made more specific in verses 25–27 concerning interest and collateral. These regulations clearly anticipate those in Deuteronomy: "The entire regulation reflects the tendency of the wealthy to manipulate the vulnerable classes through usury, especially when the social structure allows for such behavior. The early, pre-exilic context for the Covenant Code fits this type of scenario."[10]

Exodus 23:6–7. The regulation concerns justice for the poor in judicial matters. It is no surprise, then or now, that court rulings can be rigged by judges who are committed to moneyed interests

10. Samuel L. Adams, *Social and Economic Life in Second Temple Judea* (Louisville, KY: Westminster John Knox Press, 2014), 106.

and that the poor and immigrant are characteristically vulnerable in contests with those who know the ropes, as the poor and immigrants ordinarily do not. In the next verse (8), the regulation warns against bribery, an act that permits economic leverage to skew neighborly justice. The term "subvert" (*slp*) is used as well in Deuteronomy 16:19, where NRSV translates it as "distort." The tradition knows about the ways in which money corrupts neighborly practices of justice. It is but an extension of the abusive power of money noted in these verses to connect this regulation to the recent court ruling *Citizens United v. Federal Election Commission*. This Supreme Court ruling has permitted those with immense wealth to distort democratic processes in the United States by the undue impact of money that is on offer in exchange for preferential consideration on government policy. That usage of "distort" in Deuteronomy is capped by the sweeping summary statement: "Justice, and only justice, you shall pursue" (Deut. 16:20).

Clearly justice that is not perverted does not consist in social outcomes that can be leveraged by wealth. Rather justice is the maintenance of neighborliness that permits all members of the community to flourish without the distortion or subversion of economic leverage.

The regulation of Deuteronomy 15:1–18 concerning the periodic cancellation of debts is the capstone of economic reality in the community of neighbors. That practice, as Patrick Miller has shown, is the middle term in Israel's insistence on the "sabbatic principle" that is definitional for Israel concerning money and possessions.[11] The prescribed cycle of seven years that precludes being "hard-hearted or tight-fisted" has behind it the practice of Sabbath. It is to be noted in the Deuteronomic reiteration of the Decalogue (Deut. 5:6–21) that there is only one notable modification from Exodus 20. That change is in the Sabbath commandment of Deuteronomy 5:12–15, which introduces a new motivation for Sabbath keeping, namely, exodus emancipation. Sabbath is now construed as a regular weekly reperformance of Sabbath rest that replicates the exodus. In Sabbath rest, the community publicly asserts that its life is not defined by production, consumption, and possession,

11. Patrick D. Miller Jr., "The Human Sabbath: A Study in Deuteronomic Theology," *Princeton Seminary Bulletin* 6:2 (1985): 81–97.

but by the economic emancipation made possible by the lord of the exodus.[12] Thus the stricture of Amos 8 is that the greedy merchants are eager to have Sabbath end for the sake of more commercial exploitation. Clearly Sabbath is a resistance and alternative to the fatiguing commoditization of society.

Thus the seven-year cycle of debt cancellation has behind it the weekly Sabbath as a public, visible declaration against money as reality. That seven-year cycle, moreover, has in front of it the practice of Jubilee, that is, a fifty-year cycle of restoration of property and land to those who have lost them in the predatory transactions of the economy. The well-known Leviticus 25 is a collection of many different provisions that gives great complexity to the matter of Jubilee; but the general intention of the stipulation is unmistakable. Neighborliness trumps everything! It allows no charge of interest on loans (v. 36). Property shall be returned (v. 27). Most of all, persons in debt shall be respected and held in hock only temporarily. No permanent underclass!

> If any who are dependent on you become so impoverished that they sell themselves to you, you shall not make them serve as slaves. They shall remain with you as hired or bound laborers. They shall serve with you until the year of the jubilee. Then they and their children with them shall be free from your authority; they shall go back to their own family and return to their ancestral property. For they are my servants, whom I brought out of the land of Egypt; they shall not be sold as slaves are sold. You shall not rule over them with harshness, but shall fear your God. (25:39–43)

In verse 42 the double use of "servant-slave" (same word twice) insists that all "neighbors belong to the God who has emancipated them, and they cannot be drawn back into the predatory practices exemplified by Pharaoh. They cannot be reduced to debt slaves. The warning, "Do not treat harshly" is a contrast to Pharaoh's treatment of slaves with ruthlessness (Exod. 1:13–14). That same harshness of relentless predatory pressure is common against the poor in our current ruthless economy.

12. See Walter Brueggemann, *Sabbath as Resistance: Saying No to the Culture of Now* (Louisville, KY: Westminster John Knox Press, 2014).

It is impossible to overstate the defining force of the sabbatic principle of (a) *Sabbath*, (b) *Year of Release*, and (c) *Jubilee* that altogether reorient thinking about money and possessions. The "Canaanite" practices in ancient time and in our own time have become so widely accepted that to critique them or to propose alternatives is enormously difficult. That, however, is what the tradition of Deuteronomy and the sabbatic principle relentlessly do. For good reason, Jacob Milgrom has concluded that Leviticus 25 is "a total reversal of antichretic loan arrangements."[13]

It may be imagined that such a stance on money and possessions is sheer fantasy in the "real world." Such an act of imagination, however difficult and complex, continues to evoke and revivify courageous alternative imagination. Thus Sharon Ringe has shown that the tradition of Jubilee did indeed fund gospel imagination in the listening community around Jesus.[14] And even in our own time, the turn of the new millennium has featured major initiatives around Jubilee debt cancellation. It is impossible to overstate the importance of this continuing tradition for issues of the real economy in the real world. The tradition attests that such practices assure well-being in the land, whereas disregard of such practices guarantees land loss. Current attentiveness to care for the environment stands in important continuity with the Jubilee summons. Surely the predatory economy is causing among us "loss of the land."[15] In his programmatic essay on the history of debt, David Graeber concludes: "It seems to me that we are long overdue for some kind of Biblical-style Jubilee; one that would affect both international debt and consumer debt."[16]

It is for good reason that the urgency of the Torah tradition rings in the ears of Israel when Joshua and Israel cross the Jordan River to the land of promise:

13. Jacob Milgrom, *Leviticus 23–27* (New York: Doubleday, 2001), 2207–9, quoted by Adams, *Social and Economic Life*, 107. Adams, 108, regards the Jubilee as "more utopian vision than actual practice."

14. Sharon H. Ringe, *Jesus, Liberation, and the Biblical Jubilee: Images for Ethics and Christology*, Overtures to Biblical Theology (Philadelphia: Fortress Press, 1985).

15. See Ellen F. Davis, *Scripture, Culture, and Agriculture: An Agrarian Reading of the Bible* (Cambridge: Cambridge University Press, 2009), 92–94, 108–10, and passim.

16. David Graeber, *Debt: The First 5,000 Years* (Brooklyn: Melville House, 2011), 390.

> Only be strong and very courageous, being careful to act in accordance with all the law that my servant Moses commanded you; do not turn from it to the right hand or to the left, so that you may be successful wherever you go. This book of the law shall not depart out of your mouth; you shall meditate on it day and night, so that you may be careful to act in accordance with all that is written in it. For then you shall make your way prosperous, and then you shall be successful. (Josh. 1:7–8)

Joshua, after Moses, imagines exactly an economy in the land that counters the lethal practices of "Canaan."

CHAPTER 4

Joshua, Judges, 1–2 Samuel, 1–2 Kings

The Contest

These six "historical books"—Joshua, Judges, 1 and 2 Samuel, 1 and 2 Kings—constitute an interpretive retrospect on Israel's life in the land of promise. The sweep of this account is from the crossing of the Jordan into the land of promise (Josh. 3–4) to the destruction of Jerusalem in 587 BCE (2 Kgs. 24–25).[1] It is commonly agreed by critical scholars that the final form of this text is from the exile in the sixth century BCE. The material consists in an interpretive commentary on how it was that Israel lost the land of promise, that Jerusalem was destroyed, and that the last Davidic king and the leading inhabitants of Jerusalem were deported into Babylon. The crisis of 587 BCE raised huge questions about the status of Israel as God's chosen people and about the reliability of God toward Israel.[2]

I have titled this discussion "The Contest." It is an interpretive contest, as Gerhard von Rad has seen, between the old Torah

1. The final paragraph, 2 Kgs. 25:27–30, runs beyond that framing from land entry to destruction. That paragraph is in my judgment deliberately ambiguous and indeterminate. See Walter Brueggemann, "Heir and Land: The Royal 'Envelope' of the Books of Kings," in *The Fate of King David: The Past and Present of a Biblical Icon*, eds. Tod Linafelt, Claudia V. Camp, and Timothy Beal (New York: T. & T. Clark, 2010), 85–100.

2. If one allows for a bit of figurative imagination, I suggest that our contemporary social experience of something like the disaster of 587 BCE is in the event of the terrorist attacks of 9/11 that placed in question the deepest sense of security we have had and created a new awareness of vulnerability that posed deep questions of meaning.

tradition of Deuteronomy and the buoyant promissory tradition of the Davidic dynasty.[3] As we have seen, the Deuteronomic covenant made obedience to the Torah the condition of prosperous life in the land; by contrast, the promise of God to David offered an unconditional assurance of God's support for and protection of Israel. That contest is well articulated at the end of the Solomon narrative in 1 Kings 11:11–13:

> Therefore the LORD has said to Solomon: "Since this has been your mind and you have not kept my covenant and my statutes that I have commanded you, I will surely tear the kingdom from you and give it to your servant. Yet for the sake of your father David I will not do it in your lifetime; I will tear it out of the hand of your son. I will not, however, tear away the entire kingdom; I will give one tribe to your son, for the sake of my servant David and for the sake of Jerusalem, which I have chosen."

On the one hand, the Deuteronomic covenant requires that disobedience will cause YHWH to "tear the kingdom" from the Davidic house. On the other hand, the divine "yet" of verse 12 assures that YHWH will not "tear it" out of the hand of Solomon.

To be sure, this historical reflection is not preoccupied with issues of money and possessions. We will see, however, that money and possessions play a major role in this long historical review whereby Israel performs obedience or disobedience to the Torah, thus presenting money and possessions as a venue for the performance of faith or as a vehicle for obedience or disobedience. Thus money and possessions are situated in and defined by the narrative of Torah and promise.

I

In the book of Joshua, it is reported that upon entry into the land there was no more manna, the bread of heaven that had sustained Israel in its long wilderness sojourn: "The manna ceased on the day they ate the produce of the land, and the Israelites no longer had manna; they ate the crops of the land of Canaan that year" (5:12).

3. Gerhard von Rad, *Studies in Deuteronomy*, Studies in Biblical Theology 9 (Chicago: Henry Regnery Co., 1953), 74–91.

Israel now had to depend on the rhythms of agricultural production. In that circumstance Israel had to make decisions about faith and economics. Claus Westermann comments: "The bread of blessing now takes the place of the bread of saving. This transition involved one of the most difficult internal arguments in the history of Israel, in which the belief in the one Yahweh prevailed, who also has to be acknowledged and venerated as the giver of the blessing."[4] That transition permitted Israel to think about owning land with the prospect of self-reliance and the capacity to grow their own food.

The text makes no connection of the end of manna to the crisis of chapter 7. But we may suggest a connection: when Israel came into the land it was easier to imagine that it was self-sufficient, could exercise autonomy, and would not be so immediately dependent upon YHWH's sustenance. The terse verdict thus introduces chapter 7: "But the Israelites broke faith in regard to the devoted things: Achan son of Carmi son of Zabdi son of Zerah, of the tribe of Judah, took some of the devoted things" (7:1).

"Devoted things" were precious objects that were to be offered exclusively to God, the giver of the land. But one person from one identifiable family "broke faith" and took some valuable objects for himself. As we shall see, the verb "take" will play a prominent role in this exposition of money and possessions. No motivation is given for this act of Achan that amounts to covenantal disobedience. But the result of such an act is clear in this quick summary: "The anger of the Lord burned against the Israelites" (v. 1).

This is strict Deuteronomic theology: violate the covenant of YHWH and receive hard sanctions from YHWH. The account does not explain or question that calculus. It is an assumption of the narrative. In that frame of reference, Israel suffers a catastrophic defeat (v. 5). When Joshua laments to YHWH about the defeat (vv. 7–9), YHWH's answer is direct and succinct: "Israel has sinned; they have transgressed my covenant that I imposed on them. They have taken some of the devoted things; they have stolen, they have acted deceitfully, and they have put them among their own belongings" (v. 11). The reason for defeat is "acting deceitfully" by taking what belongs to YHWH and placing them among their own belongings. It is a misappropriation of funds!

4. Claus Westermann, *What Does the Old Testament Say about God?* (Atlanta: John Knox Press, 1979), 46.

The careful and tedious investigation of Joshua leads to the identification of Achan as the culprit, whom Joshua interrogates: "My son, give glory to the LORD God of Israel and make confession to him. Tell me now what you have done; do not hide it from me" (v. 19). Achan makes a full and ready confession to Joshua:

> It is true; I am the one who sinned against the LORD God of Israel. This is what I did: when I saw among the spoil a beautiful mantle from Shinar, and two hundred shekels of silver, and a bar of gold weighing fifty shekels, then I *coveted* them and took them. They now lie hidden in the ground inside my tent, with the silver underneath. (vv. 20–21; italics added)

In quick succession we get four verbs: "I sinned, I saw, I coveted, I took."

This remarkable confession is the pivot point of the narrative. The objects are a mantle, silver, and gold. Their appearance was enough to evoke desire. The key term "covet" (*ḥmd*) translates as desire that leads to seizure. It is worth noting that the verb "covet" occurs only one other time in this extended historical narrative that concludes in 2 Kings. It is in 1 Kings 20:6, wherein Ben-hadad, king of Syria, permits his servants to seize from the Israelite capital, Samaria, whatever they covet. He sends this message to King Ahab:

> "Deliver to me your silver and gold, your wives and children"; nevertheless I will send my servants to you tomorrow about this time, and they shall search your house and the houses of your servants, and lay hands on whatever *pleases* [*hmd*] them, and take it away. (vv. 5–6)[5]

Such "desire" is enough to evoke royal policy and permission in the case of Ben-hadad. The sin of Achan is exactly a violation of the tenth commandment, the seizure for self, propelled by desire, of what belongs singularly to God. Nowhere does the narrative of Joshua suggest a linkage between being in the land without manna and the desire for possessions. It is fair to wonder, however, whether living in the land immediately became the kind of seduction about which Moses had warned in Deuteronomy, that is, does the land

5. Where NRSV has "pleases," the Hebrew is "eyes desire."

and its "beautiful ornaments" evoke the very desire that leads to self-destructive disobedience? The effect of the action of Achan was a disaster not only for him, his family, and his tribe, but for the whole people Israel in the form of military defeat. The connection assumed by the narrative and its characters is that Torah obedience is a condition for safety in the land of promise.

The punishment assigned to Achan is the confiscation of his possessions "spread before the Lord." In addition to the mantle, silver, and gold that he had taken, his other property was also seized by Joshua: "Then Joshua and all Israel with him took Achan son of Zerah, with the silver, the mantle, and the bar of gold, with his sons and daughters, with his oxen, donkeys, and sheep, and his tent and all that he had, and they brought them up to the Valley of Achor" (Josh. 7:24).

Achan was as rich as Job (see Job 1:3)! We are not told how Achan came to his other possessions, whether he desired and seized them as well, or whether he already possessed them. If the latter is true, then his coveting is in a context where he already had great wealth. In that case it is clear, as we know, that having many possessions does not curb a compelling desire for more. Indeed it may be propulsion to add to possessions already in hand.

The end point of this narrative of desire that leads to seizure is that Israel's venue of disobedience and defeat is named the Valley of Achor ("Trouble"). We may notice that in Hosea 2:15 the prophet alludes to this narrative and in a direct reversal by YHWH the long-remembered Valley of Trouble is redesignated "a door of hope." In the book of Joshua, the valley offers not a hint of hope; it is rather a mark of deprivation wherein the desire for money and possessions distorts Israel's proper adherence to Torah.

II

In the book of Judges, the stereotypical theological formula is voiced in 3:7–10. The formula consists in four parts:

Doing evil
Angering YHWH enough to produce historical subjugation
Crying to the Lord in need
Raising up a deliverer

For our purposes, the most pertinent element in the formula is the first, doing evil: "The Israelites did what was evil in the sight of the Lord, forgetting the Lord their God, and worshiping the Baals and the Asherahs" (Judg. 3:7).

The standard formula concerns the worship of other gods, a religious seduction. We have seen in our discussion of Deuteronomy, however, that this conventional religious critique brings with it a tacit indictment of socioeconomic practice. Thus the worship of Baals and Asherahs means engagement as well in antineighborly economics. When YHWH is forgotten, the norm of a neighborly economy is readily disregarded. As elsewhere, we may not read the book of Judges with religious innocence, because its religious formulations are deeply embedded with socioeconomic practice.

Perhaps the most pertinent text for our topic is the narrative of Gideon. In 6:14–18 Gideon is recruited by YHWH as a military leader in Israel. When he wins a mighty victory for Israel over the Midianites, the Israelites propose that Gideon should initiate a royal dynasty: "Rule over us, you and your son and your grandson also; for you have delivered us out of the hand of Midian" (8:22).

Such an innovation in Israel must have been extraordinary; the request made to Gideon indicates a deep misgiving and uncertainty about the effectiveness of the rule of YHWH who was King in Israel. They wanted something more visible, reliable, and reassuring. They wanted more than the prospect that YHWH would evoke deliverers in times of need. They wanted what other peoples had, peoples who were not defined by the old traditions of covenant.

Faithful to the covenant tradition, Gideon refuses their overture: "I will not rule over you, and my son will not rule over you; the Lord will rule over you" (8:23). But then Gideon goes halfway toward the practice of other nations: "'Let me make a request of you; each of you give me an earring he has taken as booty.' (For the enemy had golden earrings, because they were Ishmaelites)" (v. 24).

The comment placed in parentheses in translation is an explanation of why Israel could have gold possessions in any case: they had seized it as war booty! The term is not used here, but Gideon clearly desired (coveted) the gold objects. Thus the tension between his refusal of kingship in verse 23 and his request for gold in verse 24 bespeaks the characteristic tension in Israel concerning wealth: on the one hand, the stringent covenantal insistence against such coveting (desire and seizure) and, on the other hand, yielding to the desire and regarding such seizure as ordinary and acceptable. The book of Judges exhibits Israel's deep ambiguity about the matter whereby Israel regularly departed from Torah and "did evil" and then just as regularly turned back to YHWH with a cry for help in time of distress. That ambiguity marks Israel's life in the land with no manna, no doubt the same ambiguity experienced by faithful people who live in a culture of consumerism with its attractive commodities that allure.

The readiness of Gideon to yield to such desire is matched by a willingness of Israel to comply with his request, so grateful are they for his leadership:

> "We will willingly give them," they answered. So they spread a garment, and each threw into it an earring he had taken as booty. The weight of the golden earrings that he requested was one thousand seven hundred shekels of gold (apart from the crescents and the pendants and the purple garments worn by the kings of Midian, and the collars that were on the necks of their camels). (vv. 25–26)

Gideon ends a rich man! With its request for a king and a dynasty, the text is a remarkable proposal for innovation in Israel.

From now on Israel will have an itch for a king, a form of permanent leadership that bespeaks concentrated wealth and power and a radical redefinition of money and possessions. The conviction reflected in the Achan narrative that such goods belong singularly to YHWH (and thus to the whole community) is on its way to yielding to a notion that goods belong to whoever amasses a concentration of power strong enough to seize what is desired. That itch toward monarchy has immense implications as we consider Israel's way with money and possessions. The narrative does not elaborate, but it notices in verse 27 that the ephod made from the booty, a priestly icon made of precious metals, became a "snare" to Gideon and his family. The same term, "snare," is used with reference to serving other gods in Deuteronomy 7:16 (see Exodus 23:33). In Exodus 34:12 and Judges 2:3, it is other peoples who could become a snare to Israel. Thus other peoples or other gods offer attractive alternatives to the demanding logic of covenant. More important, the term is used in Deuteronomy 7:25, a text I have cited, which links images of the gods and coveting gold and silver which together could ensnare Israel. In Judges 8:27 this same usage speaks of the fate of Gideon. His desire and request for precious metal that he received ensnared him, even though he lived to a peaceful death (8:32).

III

The itch for kingship and an alternative way with money and possessions (which is sure to come with concentrated social power) continued to build in Israel. Thus in Judges 21:25 the absence of a king is taken as the cause of moral chaos. The sorry and barbaric narratives at the end of the book of Judges cry out for kingship. That cry is, of course, continued in the memory of Israel and comes to fruition in Samuel. It is common to recognize two "sources" or two voices in 1 Samuel that respectively favor or resist kingship. Because the narrative is refracted through the lens of exile when all was lost, it does not surprise that the narrative may take a dim view of monarchy. In 1 Samuel 8, we are given a critical anticipation of what monarchy will be like when it comes to Israel. The description of monarchy (vv. 11–18) is framed in verses 5 and 20 with a desire to be "like other nations"; that is, in its quest for security Israel is willing to relinquish its special status and distinctive identity as a covenant people who recognize and rely only upon YHWH as king.

The anticipated human king, characterized in vv. 11–18, will be a "taker." It is the verb "take" that dominates the description. Monarchy will be a confiscatory regulatory agency that will tax the produce of the peasants—vineyards, olive orchards, grain, slaves, cattle, donkeys, and flocks—that is, every aspect of productive agricultural life. The monarchy will conscript the children of the peasants for military service and for work on royal projects and property, and for the enhancement of royal life. The monarchy, it is anticipated, will be a powerful force to extract wealth from peasants and redeploy it for the monarchy, for the royal bureaucracy, and for the royal entourage of the privileged who surround the throne.[6] Implicit in the description is the awareness that the old covenantal

6. That entourage included priests and scribes and is now characterized by scholars as the "urban elite." The extent of such a circle of influence and benefit is indicated by the food requirements of the court enumerated in 1 Kgs. 4:22–23.

traditions of neighborly economics that have protected against such predatory acquisitiveness will perforce be compromised in the interest of "national security."

Of particular interest is the introductory formula, "These will be the ways of the king" (8:11, so NRSV). The term used here is variously rendered in this verse as "ways," "customs," "practice." But in fact it is the Hebrew word *mišpaṭ* that is most often elsewhere translated as "justice" and translated in the Greek as *dikaioma.* The term suggests more than "way, custom or practice"; it asserts that the coming monarchy will regard confiscatory practice as justice, as the proper and right deployment of wealth and possessions. Monarchy will offer an alternative mode of justice that contradicts the old covenantal norm of neighborly justice. One may take the statement as an allusion to rapacious royal power such as Israel could have witnessed in the monarchies all around it. Or one may see it as a cunning awareness that as wealth and possessions are accumulated, one's notion of covenantal justice begins to atrophy, so that the neighbor, most especially the poor or vulnerable neighbor, is eliminated from a vision of justice. Thus economic justice is recognized to be supple and open to recharacterization according to one's capacity for accumulation. Peter Berger can judge that a society may hold two competing theodicies:

> It is, of course, another question whether the same theodicy can serve both groups [the privileged and the deprived] in this way [as world maintenance]. If so, the theodicy constitutes an essentially sado-masochistic collusion, on the level of meaning, between oppressors and victims—a phenomenon that is far from rare in history. In other cases, there may be two discrete theodicies established in the society—a theodicy of suffering for one group; and a theodicy of happiness for the other. . . . These two theodicies may relate to each other in different ways, that is, with different degrees of "symmetry."[7]

An articulation of two theodicies is exactly what we have in the text concerning monarchy. One theodicy based on the Sinai covenant concerns justice for all the neighbors. The other theodicy,

7. Peter Berger, *The Sacred Canopy: Elements of a Sociological Theory of Religion* (Anchor Books; Garden City, NY: Doubleday, 1969), 59–60. For a contemporary exposition of these two quite distinct practices of justice, see Matt Taibbi, *The Divide: American Injustice in the Age of the Wealth Gap* (New York: Spiegel & Grau, 2014).

here given articulation in Israel, consists in justice for those who are on top of the economic pyramid.[8] It is possible to see these competing theodicies remaining in tension through this royal history of Israel. The royal-urban establishment understands justice consists in *legitimate accumulation and concentration of wealth*, whereas the covenantal-prophetic tradition (here presented as antimonarchal) has in purview the *well-being of all the neighbors*. The latter tradition understands that the accumulation and monopoly of wealth in the hands of the few will lead to the disregard of the many who are vulnerable and will eventuate in wretchedness for the common good because such a concentration of wealth and power is unbearable. Thus the polemical description of monarchy ends with a cry for help: "And in that day you will cry out because of your king, whom you have chosen for yourselves; but the LORD will not answer you in that day" (8:18).

IV

In the unfolding drama of monarchy in Jerusalem, we can see that royal justice had its way and came to ultimate expression as the crisis of displacement when Jerusalem was destroyed. David, the first king of the dynasty, is for the most part not portrayed as an aggressive taker. Indeed there is much about him as a tribal chieftain who opposed establishment monopoly. Thus in 1 Samuel 22:2–3 he is the leader of an outlaw band that functions more or less like Robin Hood: "Everyone who was in distress, and everyone who was in debt, and everyone who was discontented gathered to him; and he became captain over them. Those who were with him numbered about four hundred."

The triad of distress, debt, and discontent concerned those who had been victimized by the exploitative economic forces that David resisted. He is remembered as a king who "administered justice and equity to all his people" (2 Sam. 8:15).

The anecdote of 2 Samuel 23:13–17, moreover, indicates that he was remembered as a king with a common touch for the people and not as an accumulator of predatory wealth.

8. "Pyramid" is a useful metaphor for the concentration of wealth and power; it appeals to the predatory economy of Pharaoh, champion of pyramids. See the apt use made of the image by Peter Berger, *Pyramids of Sacrifice: Political Ethics and Social Change* (Garden City, NY: Doubleday, 1976).

But of course there is evidence to the contrary. He ran afoul of the old covenantal tradition when he conducted a census, for a census has only two proper purposes, to construct inclusive tax rolls and to register manpower resources for the military (2 Sam. 24:1–2). This initiative on his part was regarded in the narrative as a sin against YHWH (v. 10), an affront recognized as such by Joab (v. 3). More specifically, in the well-known narrative of David, Bathsheba, and Uriah, David is the taker, for he takes the wife of another man, even though NRSV softens the rhetoric to "get her." The verb is the one used repeatedly in the anticipation of monarchy in 1 Samuel 8:11–18. The verb is used twice (no doubt quite intentionally) in Nathan's indictment of David. It is used first in 2 Samuel 12:4 in the parable wherein the rich man "took" the poor man's lamb. The verb is reiterated more directly in the actual indictment of David: "You have struck down Uriah the Hittite with the sword, and have *taken* his wife to be your wife, and have killed him with the sword of the Ammonites" (v. 9).

At best David is an ambiguous figure; but the ideology of taking is surely under way with him, whereby those with acquisitive power come to think it is legitimate (just?) to take more from the vulnerable and unprotected. Thus I suggest that we read the royal history of 1 and 2 Kings as an endless tension between two notions of economic justice. It is this same tension that continues to pervade our contemporary life, as our views of justice are filtered through money and possessions that cause neighbor issues to be viewed in various ways, each of which from a particular perspective is judged to be legitimate.

V

It is with Solomon, David's son, that confiscatory notions of economic justice are given full play. The opening narrative of Solomon's prayer and dream at the beginning of his reign present the issue of money and possessions clearly:

> GOD: "Ask what I should give you" (1 Kgs. 3:5).
> SOLOMON: Give me "an understanding mind to govern your people" (v. 9).
> GOD: "Because you have asked this, and have not asked for yourself long life or riches, or for the life of your enemies,

> but have asked for yourself understanding to discern what is right, I now do according to your word. Indeed I give you a wise and discerning mind; no one like you has been before you and no one like you shall arise after you. I give you also what you have not asked, both riches, and honor all your life; no other king shall compare with you" (vv. 11–13).

Solomon did not ask for riches; God will give him riches! It is this exchange at the outset of his reign that legitimates his enormous wealth that is to follow.

At the end of the Solomon narrative, we are told that Solomon's many alliances with "foreign women . . . turned away his heart" (1 Kgs. 11:1–3)! The narrative nicely protects the "innocent" and faithful Solomon until after he builds the temple, after which his regime became a center of concentrated wealth. If, however, we read the Solomon narrative with any sense of irony, we may recognize that the "innocence" and "wisdom" of Solomon are presented so that the reader may come to see that he is in fact reckoned not as innocent or as virtuous, but as an eager accumulator of wealth with an endless, covetous desire for more.[9] Three times the narrative articulates the conditional "if" of Torah obedience, reminding the reader that this paradigmatic king is in fact held to the standard of Torah justice, that is, to the neighborly management of money and possessions (1 Kgs. 3:14; 6:12; 9:4–7).[10] Thus the narrative of Solomon is presented as the great king who is a greedy accumulator who will eventually be judged by Torah requirements; that judgment by the covenantal tradition is adumbrated by the "if" that recurs in the narrative. Solomon's greed is called to account by Torah.

The narrative of Solomon's accumulation confirms that he possessed more than enough, but he always wanted more. This aggressive economic policy is evident in the construction of the temple that is a grandiose exhibit of his wealth. Thus everything is of gold; Solomon is the Midas of ancient Israel!

> The interior of the inner sanctuary was twenty cubits long, twenty cubits wide, and twenty cubits high; he overlaid it with pure *gold.*

9. See Walter Brueggemann, *Solomon: Israel's Ironic Icon of Human Achievement* (Columbia: University of South Carolina Press, 2005).

10. Ibid., 139–59.

> He also overlaid the altar with cedar. Solomon overlaid the inside of the house with pure *gold,* then drew chains of *gold* across, in front of the inner sanctuary, and overlaid it with *gold.* Next he overlaid the whole house with *gold,* in order that the whole house might be perfect; even the whole altar that belonged to the inner sanctuary he overlaid with *gold.* (6:20–22; italics added)

> So Solomon made all the vessels that were in the house of the LORD: the *golden* altar, the *golden* table for the bread of the Presence, the lampstands of pure *gold,* five on the south side and five on the north, in front of the inner sanctuary; the flowers, the lamps, and the tongs, of *gold;* the cups, snuffers, basins, dishes for incense, and firepans, of pure *gold;* the sockets for the doors of the innermost part of the house, the most holy place, and for the doors of the nave of the temple, of *gold.*
>
> Thus all the work that King Solomon did on the house of the LORD was finished. Solomon brought in the things that his father David had dedicated, the silver, the *gold,* and the vessels, and stored them in the treasuries of the house of the LORD. (7:48–51; italics added)

What purports to be to "the glory of God" was in fact an exhibit of royal wealth that called attention to Solomon as a winner in the great game of accumulation. It is to be noticed that Solomon is the son-in-law of Pharaoh and so imitates the confiscatory policy of Pharaoh that we have seen in Genesis 47:13–25, which ended in monopoly.

Beyond the success of temple accumulation, Solomon's confiscatory effectiveness is evident in his trade policies. Thus he managed a fleet of commercial ships that brought in wealth (9:26–28). He was an arms dealer and functioned as a middleman in commerce concerning horses and chariots (10:26–29). His entrepreneurial capacity assured that money flowed in from every direction, as his commercial influence was without limit. He collected internally by taxes and externally by tribute:

> The weight of *gold* that came to Solomon in one year was six hundred sixty-six talents of *gold,* besides that which came from the traders and from the business of the merchants, and from all the kings of Arabia and the governors of the land. King Solomon made two hundred large shields of beaten *gold;* six hundred shekels of *gold* went into each large shield. He made three

> hundred shields of beaten *gold;* three minas of *gold* went into each shield; and the king put them in the House of the Forest of Lebanon. The king also made a great ivory throne, and overlaid it with the finest *gold.* The throne had six steps. The top of the throne was rounded in the back, and on each side of the seat were arm rests and two lions standing beside the arm rests, while twelve lions were standing, one on each end of a step on the six steps. Nothing like it was ever made in any kingdom. All King Solomon's drinking vessels were of *gold*, and all the vessels of the House of the Forest of Lebanon were of pure *gold*; none were of silver—it was not considered as anything in the days of Solomon. For the king had a fleet of ships of Tarshish at sea with the fleet of Hiram. Once every three years the fleet of ships of Tarshish used to come bringing *gold*, silver, ivory, apes, and peacocks.
>
> Thus King Solomon excelled all the kings of the earth in riches and in wisdom. The whole earth sought the presence of Solomon to hear his wisdom, which God had put into his mind. Every one of them brought a present, objects of silver and *gold*, garments, weaponry, spices, horses, and mules, so much year by year. (10:14–25; italics added)

But of course even that was not enough, for the royal appetite for more could not be satisfied. Thus we are told of two more coercive efforts that assured more money and possessions. On the one hand Solomon managed a very effective taxation system whereby wealth was extracted from peasant agriculture (4:7–19). So lucrative was the practice that two of his sons-in-law, Ben-abinadab and Ahimaaz, functioned as revenue officers (vv. 11, 16).

On the other hand, among his cabinet officers was one Adoniram, "in charge of the forced labor" (4:6). This would have been the systematic draft already anticipated in 1 Samuel 8. The tradition is ambiguous about whether Israelites were forced into state service or whether it included only foreigners, but the clear intent of the narrative is that Solomon would stop at nothing in his insatiable desire for more money, more possessions, and more control (5:13–18; 9:22–23).

Thus we should not read the verdict, "turned away his heart" (11:3) naively as though this were simply a report on a bad marriage. Solomon's heart was not turned away simply about religious matters, that is, the worship of other gods. His heart was turned away from the neighborly covenant; life was reduced to the pursuit and accumulation of commodities at the expense of vulnerable neighbors.

It is of course possible to read this narrative as a critique of government that overreaches in its avarice. In our society, I judge that the weight of such a critique applies not primarily to government but to corporate ideology that, imitating Solomon's policy of maximization of profits, will stop at nothing in its drive for more. That avarice in our time of course spills over into government, so that government becomes a tool in the reassignment of wealth by extraction as lobbyists and free-spending super PACs create confiscatory policies free from protective regulation. But whether because of the coercive force of government or the seductive force of market ideology, the reduction of life to accumulation renders neighborhood as a nearly unthinkable social possibility.

It turns out, in Israel's telling, that such systemic avarice is unsustainable. In the short run the collapse of Solomon's regime is initiated, according to the narrative, by prophetic utterance. Ahijah the Shilonite (that is, from the old sanctuary and tradition of Shiloh) evokes a revolutionary possibility in an address to Jeroboam, who is himself implicated in Solomon's policy of forced labor (11:28–40). The narrative would have us believe that a "rumor of alternative" cast as a word from YHWH set in motion the rejection of Solomon's establishment.[11] The biblical narrative characteristically asserts that such utterance that subverts the system is laden with immense practical possibility, which is why "Solomon sought . . . to kill Jeroboam" (11:40). It is for this reason that every oppressive regime is nervous about poetic, artistic utterance.

That oracular intervention by Ahijah, however, came to fruition in a much more mundane way. In 1 Kings 12:1–18 we have a report of practical political resistance in the form of tax revolt in which the peasant community refuses to have its money and possessions extracted by the exploitative royal regime. The resistance is so vigorous and so dangerous to the throne that the king's agent, Adoram, is killed by mob action and the king has to flee for his life (12:18). This peasant rebellion against Solomon's policy of extraction is congruent with the old neighborly view of money and possessions that resists accumulation and monopoly. That rebellion, however, is not

11. For a fictional account of the power of rumor, see Andre Brink, *Rumors of Rain* (New York: Penguin Books, 1984).

triggered by religious or moral concerns, but by the bodily pain imposed by royal usurpation whereby income is transferred from peasant necessity to royal-urban surplus. Large consolidation of wealth cannot be sustained in the face of the combination of oracular possibility and felt bodily pain—not then, not ever!

In the long term, the entire royal history of 1 and 2 Kings is a playing out of the consequences of royal confiscation. Already in 2 Samuel 12:10, Nathan had declared to David the "taker": "Now therefore the sword shall never depart from your house, for you have despised me, and have *taken* the wife of Uriah the Hittite to be your wife."

What David had begun was dramatically magnified by his son Solomon in his insatiable hunger for money and possessions. His covetousness was in part disguised as piety in the form of temple construction. Peter Ackroyd has observed that in 2 Kings 24:13 and 25:13–17 it is exactly the temple equipment of Solomon that is taken way and "cut in pieces" by the Babylonians. Thus the temple vessels became a way of indicating "total destruction and loss": "The final effect is to stress that temple and vessels are brought to an end. There is no room for restoration."[12]

Thus history has a long memory, a memory performed by the Babylonians. The long sweep of the royal narrative makes clear that when Solomon's heart was "turned away" from YHWH by a religion of commodity, disaster would follow. It could not be otherwise, because the truth of the old neighborly tradition would prevail.

VI

Right in the middle of the royal recital of 1 and 2 Kings there is a narrative pause to assert that there is an alternative to the usurpatious practice of the royal elite. In 1 Kings 17–2 Kings 9 (plus chap. 13) the royal recital is interrupted by the narrative intrusion of Elijah and Elisha. These uncredentialed characters without pedigree perform an economic alternative in ancient Israel that is grounded in uncompromising theological conviction.[13] The better known of

12. Peter R. Ackroyd, "The Temple Vessels: A Continuity Theme," in *Studies in the Religious Tradition of the Old Testament* (London: SCM Press, 1987), 58, 53.

13. See Walter Brueggemann, *Testimony to Otherwise: The Witness of Elijah and Elisha* (St. Louis: Chalice Press, 2001).

the two, Elijah, is featured in two narratives that are best taken together. In 1 Kings 18, in the contest at Mount Carmel, Elijah is the great champion of YHWH in defiance of the royal cult of Baal. This is, on the face of it, a religious confrontation. If, however, we twin this narrative with that of Naboth's vineyard in 1 Kings 21, we see that *the religious contest of YHWH versus Baal has direct and immense economic implications*.

The narrative of Naboth's vineyard features a contest between two economic theories and practices. Naboth with his "ancestral inheritance" of land believes that the land is inalienably linked to his family, and he cannot by any means be denied ownership of his land. It is indeed inalienable because it is a specific land rooted in a genealogy and narrative and a deep assumption of faith.[14] By contrast King Ahab, together with his queen, Jezebel, proceeds with a very different theory of possession that is linked to Baalism, namely, that all property is a tradable commodity. Thus the market value of any goods overrides the traditional claims of family, clan, or tribe. The extremes to which Ahab and Jezebel are willing to go in order to seize the vineyard of Naboth (false witnesses and finally murder) attest to the unrestrained power of commodity to overcome every traditional barrier. In our own time it is the same power of commodity—expressed as "free market"—that is willing to override any tribal tradition that causes conflict between traditional value and the "development" of "underdeveloped economies." Elijah comes only late to the Naboth narrative to declare himself an advocate for the old covenantal tradition, and therefore he is rightly perceived by Ahab as "my enemy" (1 Kgs. 21:20).

The championing of neighborly justice in the face of royal indifference is the continuing work of Elisha in the narratives that follow those of Elijah. In 2 Kings 4, Elisha is remembered as a wonder worker who defied conventional arrangements of credit and debt and so restored a nameless widow to a viable economic life. The narrative offers no explanation nor even expresses curiosity about Elisha's capacity to produce abundance in defiance of the conventional economics of scarcity.

14. The tribal notion of the inalienable connection to the land as inheritance is related to the provision of the Jubilee year in which land is returned to its proper owner. That Torah provision is rooted in a very old theory of land possession that resisted land as commodity.

In the narrative of the healing of the Syrian general Naaman, accent rightly falls on the healing wonder that is narrated without explanation (2 Kgs. 5:1–27). At the end of the encounter, however, the healed general wants to pay for his healing with "a present" (v. 15). That is, he wants to treat the healing as a tradable commodity on which a price can be set; Elisha refuses the payment because he understands that healing is a relational transaction that cannot be reduced to a priced commodity. At the end of the narrative, Gehazi, Elisha's servant, thinks more like the general than like the prophet for whom he works. He seeks to extract a fee for the healing, for which he is severely reprimanded (vv. 25–27). Thus the subtext of the healing wonder is a debate about an abundant gift freely given or a tradable commodity wherein two theories of money clash, one informed by abundance and the other by an economy of scarcity.

In the narrative of 6:24–7:20, we are situated in a famine. As in the old world of Pharaoh, we are mindful that the crisis of famine recurringly is not about the absence of food but about the high price of food due to short supply. In this narrative, two vulnerable women are desperate because of the price of food that they cannot afford: "As the siege continued, famine in Samaria became so great that a donkey's head was sold for eighty shekels of silver, and one-fourth of a kab of dove's dung for five shekels of silver" (6:25).

The two women cannot afford food at such a price, and so they will die. The complex narrative, after dismissing the king as an irrelevance to the problem, exhibits the combination of the prophet Elisha and the "sound" caused by YHWH that evoked the abandonment of a great food supply by the Syrians (7:6–8) and the sharing of that food among the desperate Israelites. As a result, food became affordable: "So a measure of choice meal was sold for a shekel, and two measures of barley for a shekel, according to the word of the Lord" (7:16). All could eat! All could afford to eat! The narrative may be read as a discussion of how food should be priced, since it is a gift, or as a continuing tension between an abundance of food attested in the prophetic narrative and a scarcity of food presided over by royal parsimony.

At every turn in these narratives, a generative capacity for abundance is performed by Elijah and Elisha, whereas the kings (who remain nameless) operate on a business model, moving an understanding of money and possessions always in the direction of scarcity.[15] The royal parsimony about money and possessions seems always to want to tighten the money supply in the interest of control and protection of privileged surplus, whereas these prophetic characters regularly attest abundance. In the end, of course, the kings prevail, because this is royal history. But the memory of the alternative lingers in the imagination of Israel; in that generative imagination, the contest remains open and undecided.

It is, I suppose, no wonder that the kings who preside over a narrative of money and possessions grounded in a theory of scarcity always want to silence the prophets. The prophets are witnesses to an alternative economy that is grounded in an ancient narrative of covenant. Whenever the prophets attest to this ancient narrative of covenant, by utterance or by gesture, they prove unnerving to the royal enterprise that depends upon the control of money and the maintenance of privileged surplus. Thus Elijah is reckoned in royal perspective as a "troubler" in Israel (1 Kgs. 18:17) and as an "enemy" of the king (21:20). It is for good reason that the contest between *royal ideology* and the *covenantal-prophetic tradition* culminated very often in the silencing or elimination of the prophets. Thus Jezebel killed the prophets (18:4). Manasseh shed much innocent blood (2 Kgs. 21:16), an act recorded just after the mention of the prophets. And Jesus would grieve over Jerusalem, the royal citadel: "Jerusalem, Jerusalem, the city that kills the prophets and stones those who are sent to it" (Luke 13:34)!

The ground for such royal hostility toward the prophets is theological. But the presenting problem is recurringly economic. The royal enterprise, committed as it is to surplus at the expense of the peasants, will not tolerate strategies of abundance, for abundance tells against the "taking" justice of royal ideology in which everything and everyone is reduced to a commodity that can be bought and sold.

Before I finish with this contest, I will mention a happy, albeit late, exception to the rule of kingly surplus. King Josiah is remembered in the tradition as the perfect torah keeper: "Before him

15. On the minor status of kings in these prophetic narratives, see Walter Brueggemann and Davis Hankins, "The Affirmation of Prophetic Power and Deconstruction of Royal Authority in the Elisha Narratives," *Catholic Biblical Quarterly* 76:1 (January 2014): 58–76.

there was no king like him, who turned to the LORD with all his heart, with all his soul, and with all his might, according to all the law of Moses; nor did any like him arise after him" (2 Kgs. 23:25).

The narrative account of his reign does not tell of his economic stance. A prophetic oracle in Jeremiah 22, however, celebrates Josiah as a practitioner of covenantal economics. The prophetic oracle focuses on King Jehoiakim, son of Josiah, who is a predictable practitioner of predatory economics:

> Woe to him who builds his house by unrighteousness,
> and his upper rooms by injustice;
> who makes his neighbors work for nothing,
> and does not give them their wages.
> . . . .
> But your eyes and heart are only on your dishonest gain,
> for shedding innocent blood,
> and for practicing oppression and violence.
> (Jer. 22:13, 17)

In the middle of the poem that indicts the greedy king, the prophet turns for a contrast from son Jehoiakim to his father, Josiah:

> Did not your father eat and drink
> and do justice and righteousness?
> Then it was well with him.
> He judged the cause of the poor and needy;
> then it was well with him.
> Is not this to know me?
> says the LORD.
> (22:15–16)

King Josiah is a complete contrast to his predatory son, Jehoiakim. Josiah practiced "justice and righteousness." As we will see, this is a tag phrase in the prophetic tradition for economic covenantalism. More specifically, he did justice and righteousness for the poor and needy, thus interrupting royal surplus for the sake of neighborliness. The final line of verse 16 is most remarkable, whereby the poem equates the cause of the needy and poor with knowledge of YHWH. In his exposition of alternative economics, José Miranda links this assertion in Jeremiah to the affirmation of 1 John 4:20:

> It is of this love that 1 John 4:7–8 affirms that he who loves his neighbor knows God and he who does not love his neighbor does not know God. This is exactly the decisive teaching of Jer. 22:16 and of all the prophets:
>
> . . . A man who does not love the brother whom he can see cannot love God, whom he has never seen (1 John 4:20).[16]

Josiah did not succeed in his alternative practice. His location near the end of the royal history suggests that an alternative was available for Israel. The framers of this text, moreover, have no doubt that faithful enactment of a neighborly economy would have protected the well-being of the royal enterprise in Jerusalem. To do that, however, the Jerusalem establishment would have had to reverse its exploitative practice of surplus, something always possible, except when it is too late:

> Still the LORD did not turn from the fierceness of his great wrath, by which his anger was kindled against Judah, because of all the provocations with which Manasseh had provoked him. Then the LORD said, "I will remove Judah also out of my sight, as I have removed Israel; and I will reject this city that I have chosen, Jerusalem, and the house of which I said, My name shall be there." (2 Kgs. 23:26–27)

Josiah's covenantal stance, championed by Jeremiah, did not prevail. It persists in the imagination of Israel, nonetheless, available from time to time when the prophets do not need to be killed and when abundance extends to all the neighbors.

16. José Porfirio Miranda, *Marx and the Bible: A Critique of the Philosophy of Oppression* (Maryknoll, NY: Orbis Books, 1974), 63–64.

CHAPTER 5

1–2 Chronicles, Ezra, Nehemiah

Empire and Extraction

These four biblical books—1 and 2 Chronicles, Ezra, and Nehemiah—are situated in the Persian period, a period now judged by scholars to be immensely generative for emerging Judaism. The Persian period stretched from the rise of Cyrus in 540 BCE to the defeat of Persia by Alexander the Great in 333 BCE. During its two-hundred-year run, the Persian Empire controlled an enormous territory, of which Judea/Israel constituted what was likely a not very important province of the empire.

I

Much of the working of the empire as it impinged upon Judea/Israel is obscure, but some things are clear enough. Some parts of the Old Testament have a great stake in portraying the Persian Empire as a benign or positive force in the life of emerging Judaism. Thus Second Isaiah can anticipate Cyrus as God's messiah who will emancipate Israel from Babylonian control (Isa. 44:28; 45:1). The historical review of 1 and 2 Chronicles, moreover, happily culminates with the report that Cyrus issued a decree permitting Jews to return to Judea (2 Chron. 36:22–23). In addition, the Ezra–Nehemiah narrative portrays the Persian government as a forceful contributor to the building of Jerusalem and the temple. In this reading the willingness of Jews to accept the imperial oversight reflects the changed status of Jews without their own political identity as they made the hard journey "from politics to piety."[1]

While there were no doubt some positive aspects of the Persian permit that let Jews return home, it is also to be recognized that the Jewish tradition had a vested interest in such a positive portrayal of the empire as a way of winning support and favor for restoration. It is, however, a common critical judgment that such a positive portrayal of Persian governance ought to be treated with caution, if not suspicion. Thus Joseph Blenkinsopp can aver:

> It is implied, though of course not stated explicitly, that there was not much to choose between the Assyrians and their imperial successors, the Babylonians and Persians. . . . In spite of the pro-Persian sentiments in Isa. 40–48 and favorable allusions to the Persians' providential role in Ezra-Nehemiah, there is no reason to believe that their rule was significantly more benign than that of their Semitic predecessors. The allusion to military conscription, forced labor, and the requisitioning of livestock recall references elsewhere to the heavy burdens of taxation during the early Persian period (Ezra 4:13; 7:24; Nehemiah 5:4). One of the worst aspects of imperial policy under the Achaemenids was the draining away of local resources from the provinces to finance the imperial court, the building of magnificent palaces, and the interminable succession of campaigns of pacification or conquest, especially after the accession of Xerxes in 486 BCE.[2]

The key to understanding Persian governance with reference to our theme of money and possessions is that Persian interest in Judea/Israel was as a tax-collecting agency that secured income from the province to the benefit of the core government. It was, in the words of Roland Boer, "a strong extractive regime."[3] The work of extraction was not accomplished by direct intervention but by the appointment of locals who could function as governors and

1. I take the phrase from Jacob Neusner, *From Politics to Piety: The Emergence of Pharisaic Judaism* (Eugene, OR: Wipf & Stock, 2003).

2. Joseph Blenkinsopp, *Ezra–Nehemiah: A Commentary*, Old Testament Library (Philadelphia: Westminster Press, 1988), 307.

3. Roland Boer, *The Sacred Economy of Ancient Israel* (Louisville, KY: Westminster John Knox Press, 2015), 151.

oversee the tax-collecting enterprise. Samuel Adams articulates the political-economic process of the empire:

> They allowed different customs to flourish including cultic practices, and they encouraged local infrastructure projects and trading. In pursuing this course of strategic flexibility, the ruling authorities did not act out of compassion. While granting certain freedoms, these rulers also expected subject peoples to meet heavy taxation and tribute demands. To generate revenue, royal officials worked with local elites to harvest indigenous resources and collect taxes. This strategy led to hardship for many and power for the few with close ties to the royal bureaucracy. . . . The Persians expected regular streams of revenue, even from smaller provinces. This section also indicates that local leaders tried to win the favor of their Persian benefactors by guaranteeing the regular collection of taxes.[4]

The locals achieved a privileged and preferential status in the community by their capacity to receive favor from the empire by effective tax collection. The process of favoring cooperative locals has in our time been evident by the way in which the Soviet Union managed its large hegemony by the support of locals who cooperated and implemented the policies of the Soviet Union. And of course it is not different in U.S. foreign policy, which depends on "friendly" local governments and which manages, sometimes violently, to displace local officials who are not cooperative. Thus in one case Franklin Roosevelt affirmed of a foreign leader that he was an SOB, but added, "at least he is our SOB." So it goes with empires, and so it went with the Persian Empire with its rule over Judea/Israel.

This process that created an ambiguous attitude toward the empire concerned both its *selective benign support* and its *coercive capacity to extract wealth*. More than that, depending upon locals inevitably created social tensions among Jews, between the privileged elite empowered by Persia and the rest of the Jewish population who enjoyed no such support or recognition. The outcome of such a strategy set the many over against the few in the community.

4. Samuel L. Adams, *Social and Economic Life in Second Temple Judea* (Louisville, KY: Westminster John Knox Press, 2014), 131–32, 137.

Thus the socioeconomic situation of the Persian period features a complex triangle of social agents. There were (a) the Persian overlords, (b) agents who might be called "elite Jews," and (c) "lesser Jews." The elite Jews had much in common with "lesser" Jews, but they depended upon the favor of Persia. And there were, perforce, ordinary Jews who may have experienced Persian authority and local elite Jewish authority as a single common enemy because both were committed to the extraction of wealth.

The local elites, represented by Ezra and Nehemiah, were in an ambiguous situation between ordinary Jews and Persian power. On the one hand, this permitted them to have flexibility and options in economic practice. On the other hand, it must have left them always in an uneasy place, being never fully trusted by Persian authority or by their fellow Jews, who must have resented their collusion with the empire. The evidence that we have concerning money and possessions in the Persian period is situated in this complex social arrangement. It requires us to entertain categories of interpretation concerning money and possessions that are not usual for us in other parts of the biblical tradition.

That complex and tense mapping of social power is not, however, peculiar to this context. Thus in the New Testament narrative, we can see the same social mapping with tax collectors in the service of the Roman Empire. And surely the United States, with its imperial reach, regularly favors locals who are consistently resented by other locals. Thus on the one hand we may recall the fall of Ferdinand Marcos in the Philippines, who was a favorite of the U.S. government but nonetheless was dispatched by popular action; on the other hand, we remember the overthrow of Salvador Allende in Chile at the behest of the United States because he was not friendly toward U.S. economic policy. This general mapping of social power invites us to bring a kind of realism to our study of money and possessions in this literature.

We will take up in turn 1 and 2 Chronicles, and then Ezra–Nehemiah. It is no longer thought, as it was for a long time, that these two pieces of literature, 1 and 2 Chronicles and Ezra–Nehemiah, are intentionally linked and even possibly by the same hand. It is clear that the two literatures operate with very different assumptions and have very different purposes. For that reason they must be treated very differently.

II

The books of Chronicles are a rewriting of the history of royal Israel as it is given in 1 and 2 Kings. While omitting mention of the northern kingdom and its kings and its prophets, Chronicles follows the sequence of Jerusalem kings and departs from that Deuteronomic account only in ways that will serve the peculiar agenda of the traditionalists in the Persian period. It pushes the beginning of that history back further than did the Deuteronomist, clear back to creation (1 Chron. 1:1). It extends that history beyond the scope of the Deuteronomist by a conclusion that anticipates, with Persian authorization, restoration in the land (2 Chron. 36:22–23). Given this later ending, it is of defining importance that this literature occupies the final position in the Hebrew Bible, so that a prospect for return and restoration is the final word of hope in the canonical sequence of the Hebrew Bible.

The sustained tilt of this rewrite of 1 and 2 Kings is characteristically in the interest of the Jerusalem cult and the establishment and equipment of the Jerusalem temple. Beyond appreciation for and affirmation of the Jerusalem temple, this narrative makes few advances beyond the narrative of 1 and 2 Kings. It exhibits no interest, moreover, in external history and alludes to Persian hegemony, its context, only in the last paragraph. The outcome is the offer of narrative of Israel's history that is largely devoid of sociopolitical or economic interest. Instead it creates a "world of worship" that is dominated by architecture, beauty, and music.[5] It would seem, then, to be less than forthcoming about money and possessions. We may identify the following points concerning our theme.

1. In this account of David, he is in control of great wealth that he devotes to the cause of the temple. This is in contrast to the earlier account of David wherein the wealth and opulence of the temple is withheld until Solomon. Thus the Chronicler pushes that focus on money and possessions back into the time of David:

5. On a "world of worship," see Samuel E. Balentine, *The Torah's Vision of Worship*, Overtures to Biblical Theology (Minneapolis: Fortress Press, 1999), 235–54; Jon D. Levenson, *Creation and the Persistence of Evil: The Jewish Drama of Divine Omnipotence* (San Francisco: Harper & Row, 1988), 53–127; and Sara Japhet, *I & II Chronicles: A Commentary* (Old Testament Library; Louisville, KY: Westminster/John Knox Press, 1993), 45.

> With great pains I have provided for the house of the Lord one hundred thousand talents of gold, one million talents of silver, and bronze and iron beyond weighing, for there is so much of it; timber and stone too I have provided. To these you must add more. You have an abundance of workers: stonecutters, masons, carpenters, and all kinds of artisans without number, skilled in working gold, silver, bronze, and iron. Now begin the work, and the Lord be with you. (1 Chron. 22:14–16)

> Then David gave his son Solomon . . . the treasuries for dedicated gifts; for the divisions of the priests and of the Levites, and all the work of the service in the house of the Lord; for all the vessels for the service in the house of the Lord, the weight of gold for all golden vessels for each service, the weight of silver vessels for each service, the weight of the golden lampstands and their lamps, the weight of gold for each lampstand and its lamps, the weight of silver for a lampstand and its lamps, according to the use of each in the service, the weight of gold for each table for the rows of bread, the silver for the silver tables, and pure gold for the forks, the basins, and the cups; for the golden bowls and the weight of each; for the silver bowls and the weight of each; for the altar of incense made of refined gold, and its weight; also his plan for the golden chariot of the cherubim. (28:11–18)

> Moreover, in addition to all that I have provided for the holy house, I have a treasure of my own of gold and silver, and because of my devotion to the house of my God I give it to the house of my God: three thousand talents of gold, of the gold of Ophir, and seven thousand talents of refined silver, for overlaying the walls of the house, and for all the work to be done by artisans, gold for the things of gold and silver for the things of silver. (29:3–5)

The description of such extravagance is not greatly different from what we have seen concerning Solomon in 1 Kings—only now it is all with David. The narrative suggests that David's huge wealth came from conquest (see 18:6–11). That, however, is not of interest to the narrator. The narrator rather stresses that it was all given to the temple in preparation for Solomon's work. In this imaginative narrative report from the Persian period, the king and the people are said to be ready to devote their money and possessions to the cause of the temple; perhaps the narrative views the temple as a counterreality to the shabby world of reality in which they were to live.

2. The capstone of David's eager generosity toward the temple is his blessing of YHWH in 1 Chronicles 29:10–22. The doxological statement credits YHWH as the giver: "Riches and honor come from you, and you rule over all. In your hand are power and might; and it is in your hand to make great and to give strength to all" (v. 12). The king articulates the fidelity of the people toward YHWH: "O Lord our God, all this abundance that we have provided for building you a house for your holy name comes from your hand and is all your own" (v. 16). David petitions that Solomon will be faithful: "Grant to my son Solomon that with single mind he may keep your commandments, your decrees, and your statutes, performing all of them, and that he may build the temple for which I have made provision" (v. 19). But the centerpiece of his prayer is the well-known formula of verse 14, voiced as an act of humble submissiveness and gratitude: "For all things come from you, and of your own have we given you" (v. 14).

This is an acknowledgment that all of David's enormous largesse is a pure gift from YHWH. David's generosity toward the temple project is simply a return of some of YHWH's gift to YHWH. As Ralph Klein notes, David's utterance is an anticipation of Paul in 1 Corinthians 4:7: "What do you have that you did not receive?"[6]

When we focus specifically on money and possessions, however, we should not be excessively innocent about this royal exhibit of piety. Surely the king, beyond the restraint of the Chronicler, would have known that such great wealth does not simply fall into one's lap. Rather it is received through great effort, great shrewdness, and in this case great conquests via fierce boldness. Thus the formula may be one of innocent trusting piety. It may also be a case of deception or self-deception, a proclamation of innocence when one knows better. The prayer is a characteristic one of the well-off who give thanks for divine generosity and all their own good fortune, when in fact the good fortune is a result of wise management, favorable tax laws, and generous credit arrangements.

6. Ralph W. Klein, *I Chronicles: A Commentary*, Hermeneia (Minneapolis: Fortress Press, 2006), 538.

One may recognize that it is this verse on David's lips that has become one of the most familiar formulae used in Christian liturgy for the presentation of offerings, a poem by William Walsham How:

We give Thee but Thine own,
Whate'er the gift may be;
All that we have is Thine alone,
A trust, O Lord, from Thee.

May we Thy bounties thus
As stewards true receive,
And gladly, as Thou blessest us,
To thee our firstfruits give.

To comfort and to bless,
To find a balm for woe,
To tend the lonely in distress,
Is angels' work below.

The captive to release,
To God the lost to bring,
To teach the way of life and peace—
It is a Christ-like thing.

And we believe Thy Word,
Though dim our faith may be;
Whate'er for Thine we do, O Lord,
We do it unto Thee.[7]

The poem touches the appropriate bases of "Thy bounties," "stewards," "firstfruits." It goes on to anticipate the missional possibilities of such an offering to comfort, to do angels' work, to release from prison, to save the lost, to teach people, and do it all "unto Thee." I do not suggest cynicism about such an affirmation and do not doubt the words reflect genuine missional passion. Since our topic is money and possessions, however, we should not miss the potential element of self-deception in the rhetoric of gratitude and gift that may be in tension with the actual workings of the economy

7. William Walsham How, "We Give Thee but Thine Own," *The Presbyterian Hymnal* (Louisville, KY: Westminster/John Knox Press, 1990), 428.

that makes such generosity possible. After all, David, before the Chronicler transformed him into a steady church guy, was a worldly character who capitalized on whatever spoils he could acquire. Very often so are we. Thus the interface of *economics* and *liturgy* is not always simple and innocent. It may have been in the case of this reconstituted David. But maybe not!

3. Solomon's capacity for the opulence necessary for the temple has already been fully considered in 1 Kings, which this narrative reiterates. In the narrative of temple repairs under King Joash, there is a significant departure from the narrative of 2 Kings 12. In 2 Chronicles 24:9–10 there is a reference to the "tax" that Moses "laid on Israel," thus an appeal to a very old obligation to support work on the temple. This is the only time that the term rendered "tax" in NRSV is rendered in this way. Steven Tuell links it to the provision of a regular contribution required in Exodus 30:12–16 and 38:25–26, and Nehemiah is reported to have used a tax for temple service and maintenance (Neh. 10:32–33).[8] While the matter is far from clear, the narrative suggests that such "offerings" were a part of a regulated public economy.

Two references portray Solomon as realistic about the economic realities of international life. In 2 Chronicles 9:22–28 his economic prosperity and international leverage are reiterated: "He ruled over all the kings from the Euphrates to the land of the Philistines, and to the border of Egypt. The king made *silver as common* in Jerusalem as stone, and cedar as plentiful as the sycamore of the Shephelah" (vv. 26–27). His political reach is specific and extended to the traditional scope of "Greater Israel." He is, moreover, so wealthy that silver had become utterly common. The usage is a close parallel to the wording of 1 Kings 10:21: "Silver—it was not considered as anything in the days of Solomon." Such wealth evoked disdain for what many others might have greatly valued.

In 2 Chronicles 16:2–3 the narrative reports on the stratagem of the Jerusalem regime in which the Jerusalem king offers the Syrian king money to break an alliance with northern Israel in order to ally with Judah. This ploy is already reported in 1 Kings 15:19; it is not a new point here. It is of interest, however, that such political

8. Steven S. Tuell, *First and Second Chronicles*, Interpretation (Louisville, KY: Westminster John Knox Press, 2001), 194.

realism about the power of money on an international scale is unexpected in such a pious, cult-centered narrative. Perhaps the narrator would say that such international attentiveness is the cost of doing business. Thus for all the devotion to and investment in the temple, not all money went to support the temple. Some of it was expended on questions of national security. Perhaps that note is an acknowledgment that in the real world of Persian power, which imposed certain requirements, even "sacred economics" is not without realistic contexts.[9]

III

Whereas the narrative of 1 and 2 Chronicles is largely an imaginative construct that must have served to sustain a Jewish population that had lost its political identity, the Ezra–Nehemiah text is marked by a much more realistic portrayal of economic matters in the Persian period. We may identify four concerns that pertain to economic practice.

1. The restoration movement led by Ezra and Nehemiah was greatly supported by the Persian regime. Artaxerxes gave authorization for expenditure of imperial money for the rebuilding of Jerusalem:

> I, King Artaxerxes, decree to all the treasurers in the province Beyond the River: Whatever the priest Ezra, the scribe of the law of the God of heaven, requires of you, let it be done with all diligence, up to one hundred talents of silver, one hundred cors of wheat, one hundred baths of wine, one hundred baths of oil, and unlimited salt. Whatever is commanded by the God of heaven, let it be done with zeal for the house of the God of heaven, or wrath will come upon the realm of the king and his heirs. We also notify you that it shall not be lawful to impose tribute, custom, or toll on any of the priests, the Levites, the singers,

9. Thus the title of Boer's discussion, *Sacred Economy*, suggests an economy that revolves around the temple. But the practitioners of that economy dared to imagine that everything pertaining to Jerusalem, including national security, was sacred. The extension of the sacred works that way for every vigorous energetic ideology; see William T. Cavanaugh, *Migrations of the Holy: God, State, and the Political Meaning of the Church* (Grand Rapids: Eerdmans, 2011).

> the doorkeepers, the temple servants, or other servants of this house of God. (Ezra 7:21–24)

His decree included not only royal finance but also full acknowledgment of Ezra's authority and economic protection for the priests, Levites, and other temple officials. In Nehemiah 2:7–8, Nehemiah is permitted to write his own bill of particulars for his work of restoration that received the full backing of Artaxerxes.

In addition to these imperial grants, the Persian regime permitted the return and restoration of all the valuable temple vessels to Jerusalem, the very ones that Nebuchadnezzar had seized from the temple to carry away to Babylon (2 Kgs. 24:13; 25:13–17; Jer. 52:17–23):

> King Cyrus himself brought out the vessels that of the house of the LORD that Nebuchadnezzar had carried away from Jerusalem and placed in the house of his gods. King Cyrus of Persia had them released into the charge of Mithredath the treasurer, who counted them out to Sheshbazzar the prince of Judah. And this was the inventory: gold basins, thirty; silver basins, one thousand; knives, twenty-nine; gold bowls, thirty; other silver bowls, four hundred ten; other vessels, one thousand; the total of the gold and silver vessels was five thousand four hundred. All these Sheshbazzar brought up, when the exiles were brought up from Babylonia to Jerusalem. (Ezra 1:7–10; see 5:13–17; 6:5)

This restoration of temple vessels signaled generosity on the part of the Persians and a readiness to be seen as reversing the confiscatory policies of Babylon. The repetition of the inventory in these several lists has caused Peter Ackroyd to conclude that the recurring list of temple vessels first lost to Babylon and then restored by Persia is more than an incidental inventory. It is, in fact, a narrative strategy in order to assert continuity between the lost temple and the soon-to-be-restored temple, and thus a sign of the continuation of YHWH's commitment to Israel and to Jerusalem:

> The community which sought to re-establish itself after the exile, deeply conscious of its ancestry in faith, but also aware of the problem of continuity with that faith, made use of the theme of the vessels, as it made use of other themes, to make good the claim to be the true successor (perhaps thereby to invalidate the

> claims of others), to be directly linked with those who stood on the other side of the exilic gulf.[10]

It is clear that this program of restoration and rebuilding succeeded only because of the weighty investment of the Persians. The empire had a stake in aligning itself with local restoration, to which it pledged its economic support.

2. The investment of Persia in the restoration, however, was not disinterested generosity. Thus the interpretive temptation to portray Persian investment in the restoration as wholly positive is surely an overstatement. It turns out that the local Jewish officials were indeed beholden to Persian authority; more specifically, the restored temple establishment functioned as a tax-collecting agency for the empire. Thus in thinking about money and possessions in the Bible, one must not read it in the categories of innocent pietism with a simple rule of "make all you can, save all you can, give all you can"; rather one must attend as well to macrosystems of investment and taxation, of credit and loans. It is the power of the economic system that frames whatever may be said about personal economics. The Bible itself is never uninterested in larger issues of economic policy, most especially policies of extraction that skew neighborly possibility. The obscure wording of Ezra 4:11–16 expresses a reflection on the previous rebellion against imperial authority by withholding "tribute, custom, or toll," thereby diminishing royal revenue. The verses attest that the regular payment of the Jewish province to the imperial treasury was an expectation that would surely be honored by local Jewish officials who depended upon Persian authorization and favor. Thus the payment of taxes to Persia was a prerequisite for the enterprise of restoration. The exemption from taxation of the temple officials in Ezra 7:24 indicates that taxation of others in the community was routine. In Nehemiah 5:4, moreover, the "king's tax" was known to be burdensome: "We are having to borrow money on our fields and vineyards to pay the king's tax." The taxation helped to create a class of the indebted who were in the process of being left behind. The usurpatious demands of empire produced a disadvantaged class of the indebted in the province.

10. Peter R. Ackroyd, "The Temple Vessels: A Continuity Theme," in *Studies in the Religious Tradition of the Old Testament* (London: SCM Press), 60.

The pressure of taxation required by the demands of empire and performed by local officials on behalf of the empire created a most burdensome situation. In his two great prayers, Ezra alludes to the burden of imperial taxation. He alludes to the claim that because of sin, "we, our kings, and our priests have been handed over to the kings of the lands, to the sword, to captivity, to plundering, and to utter shame, as is now the case" (Ezra 9:7). He celebrates a "brief moment" when relief was given in the form of Persian assistance: "But now for a brief moment favor has been shown by the LORD our God, who has left us a remnant, and given us a stake in his holy place, in order that he may brighten our eyes and grant us a little sustenance in our slavery" (v. 8). But immediately Ezra reverses the rhetoric of "favor" (*ḥnn*) to speak again of enslavement: "For we are *slaves*; yet our God has not forsaken us in our slavery, but has extended to us his steadfast love before the kings of Persia, to give us new life to set up the house of our God, to repair its ruins, and to give us a wall in Judea and Jerusalem" (v. 9; italics added).

These verses suggest an odd vacillation that wants at the same time to affirm (a) the fidelity of God, (b) new life made possible by Persia, and (c) the reality of enslavement via taxation. The prayer ends with a petition for God's justice that is profoundly urgent in the face of continuing injustice in the economic domain.

This allusion to Persian requirements as "slavery" is voiced with even more pathos in Ezra's second prayer:

> Here we are, *slaves* to this day—*slaves* in the land that you gave to our ancestors to enjoy its fruit and its good gifts. Its rich yield goes to the kings whom you have set over us because of our sins; they have power also over our bodies and over our livestock at their pleasure, and we are in great distress. (Neh. 9:36–37; italics added)

Here the case is less ambiguous than in the first of these prayers. And the reason is explicit. Kings, that is, Persian kings, have power over us! The characterization of Persian control of "our bodies" and "our livestock" is likely reminiscent of the narrative of Pharaoh in Genesis 47:13–25 concerning Pharaoh's preemptive food monopoly. It is usual, following Second Isaiah, to think of emancipation from Babylon by way of Persian intervention as a "second exodus" (see 2 Chron. 36:22–23). In light of actual economic circumstance, such an interpretative riff is surely glib and constitutes a disregard of the coercive regulations of Persia. Thus we are able to see that the favoring of some of the elite Jews was an ambiguous affair. On the one hand, the restoration movement depended on imperial generosity. On the other hand, such imperial favor was accompanied by a carefully executed policy of extraction. The old text of 1 Samuel 8:11–18 had anticipated royal extraction in Israel. The experience of Israel from Solomon to Artaxerxes was one of extraction, a policy continued under the tax collectors of Rome. In our economy, moreover, the extraction of economic resource from the vulnerable for the enrichment of the powerful is a process that continues unabated. The collusion of government and the corporate economy in our time makes such extraction—with its concentration of immense surplus—an enormous impediment to any neighborly possibility.

3. We may identity two steps reported in the text that functioned as resistance to such an economy of extraction. Ezra and Nehemiah are notorious for their harsh action that broke up mixed marriages and that required the expulsion of foreign wives:

> "So now let us make a covenant with our God to send away all these wives and their children, according to the counsel of my lord and of those who tremble at the commandment of our God; and let it be done according to the law." . . . "Now make confession to the Lord the God of your ancestors, and do his will; separate yourselves from the peoples of the land and from the foreign wives." Then all the assembly answered with a loud voice, "It is so; we must do as you have said." (Ezra 10:3, 11–12)

> In those days also I saw Jews who had married women of Ashdod, Ammon, and Moab; and half of their children spoke the language of Ashdod, and they could not speak the language of Judah, but spoke the language of various peoples. And I contended with them and cursed them and beat some of them and pulled out their hair; and I made them take an oath in the name of God, saying, "You shall not give your daughters to their sons, or take their daughters for your sons or for yourselves. Did not King Solomon of Israel sin on account of such women? Among the many nations there was no king like him, and he was beloved by his God, and God made him king over all Israel; nevertheless, foreign women made even him to sin. Shall we then listen to you and do all this

> great evil and act treacherously against our God by marrying foreign women?" (Neh. 13:23–27)

The motivation for this harsh action has usually been assumed to be that it was to protect the purity of the "holy seed" (Ezra 9:2), thus a religious motivation. And no doubt this is in part correct. Samuel Adams, however, has proposed an alternative explanation that in my judgment has great merit. He suggests that endogamy, marriage within one's cultural subset, was to maintain tight control of ancestral property rights.[11]

Adams notices that this action pertains especially to families of leadership, among those who had considerable wealth (Ezra 9:2):

> This detail highlights the example set by powerful households and their complicity in allowing others to follow suit. The decision by such persons to intermarry would have meant potential forfeiture of property to outsiders, especially those who did not go into exile. Many of these "officials and leaders" had significant wealth, and Ezra's exclusivist party does not want to risk mingling their holdings with families that are not part of the faithful remnant. In support of an economic motivation behind these verses, the Hebrew root *'rb* appears in the phrase from Ezra 9:2, "Thus the holy seed has mixed itself . . . with those of other lands." This root often has an economic connotation . . . and therefore the notion of "corrupting" the holy seed probably included the idea of "mixing" property with undesirable persons. Because of this terminology, we cannot assume that the statement here is merely one of social separation, especially since the text cites additional economic factors.[12]

Adams notices that in Ezra 10:8, "This verse indicates that Ezra's rigid opposition to intermarriage represents the best means for the exilic community to maintain property for themselves."[13] The motivation for harsh expulsion was an effort to keep control of wealth and property to limit the benefits available to the Persian overlords; thus the policies of Ezra and Nehemiah responded to the intentions of Persian policy and practice.[14]

11. Adams, *Social and Economic Life*, 26.
12. Ibid., 26–27.
13. Ibid., 27.
14. Ibid., 28.

This is a new idea to me, as it will be to most conventional readers of these texts. It is, however, a most plausible explanation for what is otherwise an acute embarrassment in the text. In a discussion such as the present one that seeks to "follow the money," this explanation might fit the mantra, "If they say it is not about the money, it is about the money." Such an understanding of the action of expulsion would take some of the poison out of our interpretation, though it would not lessen the brutality of the action. It would also relate to our contemporary effort at quasi-arranged marriages to assure that legacy families stay related to other legacy families.[15] Thus Ezra and Nehemiah by such expulsions resisted having wealth preempted by outsiders, perhaps even by mixed marriages with well-connected Persian women.[16]

4. The other action of limiting an economy of extraction is embodied in Nehemiah 5, certainly the most important text on economics in this literature of the Persian period and arguably the most important text of our entire discussion. The narrative begins with a "great outcry," the same "outcry" sounded at the beginning of the exodus narrative (Exod. 2:23). Only now it is an outcry of Jews against other Jews. The outcry concerns a desperate need for food, not unlike the demand made to Joseph in Genesis 47:13–25. On the one hand, the desperate need is for money in the midst of a food shortage when food prices are high, a need that resulted in debts and mortgages. On the other hand, there is the matter of "the king's tax," a Persian tax no doubt extracted by local Jewish officials in the service of Persia. The outcry is not against Persia. It is against Jews who are willing to collude with the policies of extraction at the expense of other vulnerable Jews, a collusion not unlike that of Joseph with Pharaoh. The situation is one of economic despair and helplessness, with peasant Jews reduced to desperate need by taxes and mortgage rates: "Now our flesh is the same as that of our kindred; our children are the same as their children; and yet we

15. For example, a long while ago Stanley Hauerwas was provoking a Presbyterian company about the way in which one of its conference centers, Montreat, functioned to generate "arranged marriages" among proper church families. He opined that it is a purpose of such enterprises to make sure the young encounter appropriate mates for continuing family legacies, connections, and status.

16. On the model of and parallels with Persian familial practices, see Christine Roy Yoder, *Wisdom as a Woman of Substance: A Socioeconomic Reading of Proverbs 1–9 and 31:10–31*, Beihefte zur Zeitschrift für alttestamentliche Wissenschaft 304 (Berlin: Walter de Gruyter, 2001).

are forcing our sons and daughters to be slaves, and some of our daughters have been ravished; we are powerless, and our fields and vineyards now belong to others" (v. 5).[17]

The picture portrayed in the complaint is in a covenantal mode amid predatory circumstance. Such relentless practice can only result in permanent indebtedness. Roland Boer identifies debt as "an extractive economic device" that increases the wealth of the lender in three ways, all of which are at work in this narrative:[18]

a) It is "compulsion for labor" as "debt slavery" or "indentured labor."[19]
b) It ensures "that the flow of wealth runs from debtor to lender, which initially was the state and temple, but soon included landlords."[20]
c) Debt functions to ensure and reinforce the hierarchy "between landlord and peasant, between palatine or temple estate and laborer. In other words, debt is a feature of class difference and often class conflict. In light of all this, it is no surprise that the first demands of popular uprisings throughout history have been and remain: cancel the debts, destroy the records, reallocate the land."[21]

The only thing exceptional about this case in Nehemiah 5 is that the circumstance of powerlessness is brought to effective and

17. The phrase "our flesh is the same as that of our kindred" brings to mind the mandate of Isa. 58:7, also a Persian-period text, which urges its addressees "not to hide yourself from your own kin."

18. Boer, *Sacred Economy*, 158.

19. Ibid., 158; Boer on the force of debt cites Gregory C. Chirichigno, *Debt-Slavery in Israel and the Ancient Near East* (Sheffield: JSOT Press, 1993).

20. Boer, *Sacred Economy*, 161.

21. Ibid., 162. See also David Graeber, *Debt: The First 5,000 Years* (Brooklyn: Melville House, 2011), 8: "For thousands of years, the struggle between rich and poor has largely taken the form of conflict between creditors and debtors—of judgments about the rights and wrong of interest payments, debt peonage, amnesty, repossession, restitution, the sequestering of sheep, the seizing of vineyards, and the selling of debtors' children into slavery. By the same token, for the last five thousand years, with remarkable regularity, popular insurrections have begun the same way: with ritual destruction of the debt records—tablets, papyri, ledgers, whatever form they might have taken in any particular time and place. (After that, rebels usually go after the records of landholding and tax assessments). As the great classicist Moses Finley often liked to say, in the ancient world, all revolutionary movements had a single program: 'Cancel the debts and redistribute the land.'"

insistent voice. In the ancient exodus memory, the outcry of the slaves evoked a response from YHWH. Here it evokes a response from Nehemiah, the Jewish governor on behalf of Persia. The indictment Nehemiah issues against his fellow Jews is charging interest on loans to your own people, that is, other Jews. Nehemiah apparently appeals to old Torah requirements such as Exodus 22:25 and Deuteronomy 23:19–20. A quite remarkable feature of Nehemiah's reprimand of his fellows is that he includes himself in the unacceptable action that he now rejects: "Moreover I and my brothers and my servants are lending them money and grain. Let us stop this taking of interest" (Neh. 5:10).

The complaint and indictment eventuate in a powerful imperative: "Restore to them, this very day, their fields, their vineyards, their olive orchards, and their houses, and the interest on money, grain, wine, and oil that you have been exacting from them" (v. 11). The required action is in this verb, "restore." There is no elaboration or direct appeal to tradition. But the economic recompense proposed is not unlike the Jubilee year that constitutes a return of inalienable property, or like the Year of Release from debts (Deut. 15:1–15; Lev. 25). The scope of the restoration is expansive and focuses on the three great money crops: grain, wine, and oil. The restoration, moreover, is to be immediate: "this very day."

It is remarkable that the moneyed people whom Nehemiah addresses promptly agree to his urging: "We will restore everything and demand nothing more from them. We will do as you say" (v. 12). It is as though Nehemiah's summons and his characterization of what had become routine economic exploitation was a huge wake-up call to his contemporaries. It is as though they had been lulled into conventional practices of extraction by participation in the dominant economy that led in turn to amnesia about the distinctive Jewish provisions for an economy among neighbors. Nehemiah's summons was to remind them that they are not free, as Jews, to practice conventional extraction; they have a different identity and therefore a different mandate. The dramatic exchange between Nehemiah and his Jewish cohorts is an affirmation that neighborly relations ("flesh of flesh") override the pressure of an acquisitive predatory economy. The recognition of those in debt and the acknowledgment of the mandate of God converge to produce concrete alternative economic action. The drama culminates in an oath to adhere to an alternative economic practice that acknowledges others in the economy as legitimate neighbors and not simply as targets of exploitation. The narrative ends with the assent of the assembly and praise to YHWH, the God of "no interest" (v. 13). Such a doxological conclusion to an economic transaction is not normal. Perhaps the doxology is because, like the alienated son in the parable who had lost his way in an economy of self-indulgence (Luke 15:17), these economic players "came to themselves," affirmed their true identity as Jews, acknowledged the neighborly demands of the Torah, and ended in glad praise. The imperial economy of extraction had bewitched them; even Nehemiah was charging interest! He should have known better! And now, beyond the studied complexities of exploitation, they have come down to the simple place where they ought to be. No wonder they said, "Amen" (Neh. 5:13)!

An addendum to this dramatic turnaround is given in Nehemiah 5:14–19. Nehemiah contrasts his conduct with that of "former governors" who had "laid heavy burdens on the people," that is, had imposed heavy taxation. Unlike his predecessors, Nehemiah resisted such exploitative practices, which perhaps means he had withstood the demands of the empire. He did not use up his expense account but used the money to nurture an assemblage of Jewish officials. The self-affirmation and self-congratulations of Nehemiah as a generous and thrifty administrator is not unlike the ancient farewell speech of Samuel in 1 Samuel 12:3–5 in which Samuel declares himself innocent of all wrong, most particularly with reference to money matters. Nehemiah's vindication is presented in the repeated phrase "heavy burden" (vv. 15, 18) that refers to economic impositions. One may wonder if Nehemiah's generous table reached to the common folk or if it pertained only to "officials." We may give him the benefit of the doubt, but the matter is not certain. His final appeal, reiterated in 13:31, is not for public recognition. It is rather for divine acknowledgment, which may indicate that he is indeed propelled by genuine piety. In any case, this great chapter 5 makes clear that economics is no business as usual; money and possessions must be subordinated to the common good in a way that contradicts the easy practice of acquisition by way of exploitative debt.

CHAPTER 6

The Psalms

Torah, Temple, Wisdom

Given the richness and diversity of the Psalter, we are required to make choices and selections from that expansive inventory. My selections in what follows have been informed by the two introductions of Psalms 1–2, each of which anticipates a major trajectory in the Psalter: on the one hand, the Torah tradition; on the other hand, the royal tradition.

I

Psalm 1 introduces the Psalter with an accent on Torah obedience. The psalm affirms the "righteous" who passionately adhere to the Torah. It promises good outcomes for such Torah keepers, who are contrasted with the "wicked," who will come to a sorry end. The word pair righteous-wicked is usually expressed in moral terms. But the terms can also be rendered in judicial terms as "innocent" and "guilty." The latter translations are useful, as the terms concern those who enhance or inflict damage on the common good. Patrick Miller, in his probe of "Torah piety," has shown how "Torah" used in Psalm 1 (and in what follows from Psalm 1) is in the tradition of commandments in the book of Deuteronomy.[1]

1. Patrick D. Miller, "Deuteronomy and Psalms: Evoking a Biblical Conversation," in *Israelite Religion and Biblical Theology: Collected Essays*, Journal for the Study of

That tradition of commandments, as we have seen in chapter 3, accents the practice of neighborliness in the sphere of economics. Thus Torah piety is concerned with attentiveness to the neighbor; the righteous-innocent are those who live with attentiveness to the common flourishing of the neighborhood. Given this introductory psalm, I have selected two psalms that characterize, respectively, the righteous-innocent who adhere to the Torah, and the wicked-guilty who give no heed to Torah expectations.

1. *Psalm 112* provides a sketch of righteous-innocent people who "greatly delight in his commandments" (v. 1).[2] The psalm affirms the assumption of Psalm 1 that Torah keepers have good outcomes, a theme that pervades the tradition of Deuteronomy. What follows in Psalm 112 traces out both the actions of the righteous-innocent person and the futures that arise from such actions.

The righteous-innocent are "gracious" and "merciful" (v. 4). They "deal generously and lend"; they "conduct their affairs with justice" (v. 5). They "distribute freely"; they give to the poor (v. 9). It is of crucial importance that the actions of those commended pertain precisely to the economic sphere of life.[3] They practice an economy of generosity toward the neighbor, especially the poor and needy neighbor. The generic term for such action is "justice" that takes responsibility for the well-being of those without adequate resources. The phrase "deal generously" is the word we often translate "grace" (*ḥnn*), that is, without expectation of payback. The term "lends" (literally, "enables borrowing ") refers to economic transactions that do not include exploitative interest:

> V. 5 names the "marks" of a life that agrees with the covenant and is rooted in *sedeqah*. The righteous person donates and lends (cf. also v. 9). His business affairs he takes care of with integrity—without charging interest (cf. Lev 25:35ff.; Deut

---

the Old Testament Supplement Series 267 (Sheffield: Sheffield Academic Press, 2000), 318–36.

2. See the fine exposition of Psalm 112 with reference to wealth and riches by Phil J. Botha, "'Wealth and Riches Are in His House' (Psalm 112:3): Acrostic Wisdom Psalms and the Development of Antimaterialism," in *The Shape and Shaping of the Book of Psalms: The Current State of Scholarship*, ed. Nancy L. deClaissé-Walford (Atlanta: SBL Press, 2014), 105–28.

3. See Erich Zenger, "Geld als Lebensmittel? Über die Wertung des Reichtums im Psalter (Psalmen 15.49.112)," *Jahrbuch für Biblische Theologie* 21 (2006): 73–96.

15:7–11), without deceit. He deals according to *mispat*: according to the demands of God's law.[4]

The outcome of such practice is that one ends well-off:

with prosperous descendants
with wealth and riches
stable and remembered
unafraid of bad news (likely economic reverses)
exalted in honor

The portrayal is of one who has substance, staying power, and influence in the community. Of course there is something ideological in this picture that believes that good actions produce good outcomes. Beyond that, however, the psalm has a keen insight into what makes for human flourishing. The psalm attests that giving, sharing, and caring in generous ways creates well-being for all parties. That insight should not be dismissed as self-satisfied moralism but as discerning wisdom about the kind of actions and practices that enhance community. In this sketch of a generative Torah keeper, the picture in Psalm 112 matches the portrayal of YHWH in Psalm 111:

> He has gained renown by his wonderful deeds;
> the LORD is gracious and merciful.
> He provides food for those who fear him;
> he is ever mindful of his covenant.
> . . . .
> The works of his hands are faithful and just;
> all his precepts are trustworthy.
> (Ps.111:4–5, 7)

The Torah keeper acts in imitation of YHWH and does so by obeying the radical commandments of neighbor love given in Deuteronomy. In Deuteronomy 10:17–18, we have an inventory of the generous justice of YHWH, "who is not partial and takes no bribe, who executes justice for the orphan and the widow, and who loves the strangers, providing them food and clothing." And then

4. Hans-Joachim Kraus, *Psalms 60–150: A Commentary* (Minneapolis: Augsburg, 1989), 364.

promptly, in verse 19, Israel is enjoined to "love the stranger." In Psalm 112 the stranger, "the other," the one unlike the subject of the psalm, is the needy neighbor. YHWH engages the needy other; YHWH's Torah keepers do the same. A practice of money and possessions that keeps the neighbor front and center is advocated. Psalm 112 ends, almost as a throwaway line, with a glance at the wicked-guilty who refuse Torah and refuse neighbor. In the end, they are filled with uncontrolled fury as they discern that greedy self-regard at the expense of the neighbor is in no way to generate or guarantee a good future.[5] A clear discernment of who YHWH is in Psalm 111 is the clue to the generative economic ethic voiced in Psalm 112.

2. *Psalm 10* offers an intense counterpoint to Psalm 112 as it sketches out the wicked-guilty, those resistant to Torah obedience.[6] The wicked-guilty are characterized here in the words and perception of the exploited poor, who describe them for God's benefit:

> In arrogance the wicked persecute the poor—
> . . . .
> For the wicked boast of the desires of their heart,
> those greedy for gain curse and renounce the Lord.
> In the pride of their countenance the wicked say,
> "God will not seek it out";
> all their thoughts are, "There is no God."
> . . . .
> They think in their heart, "We shall not be moved;
> throughout all generations we shall not meet adversity."
>
> Their mouths are filled with cursing and deceit and oppression;
> under their tongues are mischief and iniquity.
> . . . .
> . . . they murder the innocent.
>
> Their eyes stealthily watch for the helpless;
> . . . .
> they lurk that they may seize the poor;
> they seize the poor and drag them off in their net.

5. Ibid., 365.

6. See Walter Brueggemann, "Psalms 9–10: A Counter to Conventional Social Reality," in *The Bible and the Politics of Exegesis*, ed. David Jobling, Peggy L. Day, and Gerald T. Sheppard (Cleveland: Pilgrim Press, 1991), 3–15.

. . . .
. . . the helpless fall by their might.
(vv. 2–10)

The psalm weaves in and out with two indictments. On the one hand, the wicked-guilty imagine *autonomy* and so are free to do what they want. On the other hand, they are *free to exploit the poor*. They are a living embodiment of Dostoyevsky's famous dictum, "Without God, everything is possible." The wicked-guilty live in a world without God, and so without Torah. Their capacity for unhindered greed is without limit.

Because they do not know or honor the judgments of the Lord ("out of their sight"; v. 5), their greed is committed in "innocence." As a consequence, their greedy ways are likely not direct violent actions but actions that are performed according to legal arrangements of taxes, loans, debts, and interest, all of which amount to a dragnet against the vulnerable who are without protection. More than that, they "prosper at all times" (v. 5). What they do works!

Or what they do works if the psalm could end in verse 11. But of course the psalm does not end there. In verse 12 the voice that has been describing the wicked-guilty now turns to urgent petition. By a series of imperatives, the voice of the vulnerable insists that YHWH should enter the economic fray on their behalf:

Rise up, O Lord; O God, lift up your hand;
do not forget the oppressed.
. . . .
Break the arm of the wicked and evildoers;
seek out their wickedness until you find none.
. . . .
O Lord, you will hear the desire of the meek;
you will strengthen their heart, you will incline your ear
to do justice for the orphan and the oppressed,
so that those from earth may strike terror no more.
(vv. 12, 15, 17–18).

The voice of the poor who speak in this psalm know that if economic reality consists only in creditors and debtors, the debtors are lost, because debtors have no legal or societal leverage against the ownership class. In this psalm, however, the poor speak and refuse to accept that there are only creditors and debtors. It is the insistence of this voice that there is a third party in economic transactions, namely, YHWH. The work of the psalm, the insistence of the exploited, is to mobilize YHWH into the economic fray; when YHWH is finally engaged, the map of money, possessions, and social possibility is radically revised. The powerful have done everything they can to eliminate YHWH from the economic calculus. When YHWH is eliminated, economics comes down to an unequal contest between creditors and debtors, between haves and have-nots.

But Torah piety in which these vulnerable voices are embedded refuses such a reductionism. The prayer of the poor is vigorous and uncompromising. But it is also vexed. It wonders why YHWH has been so long absent and negligent. And it reminds YHWH of YHWH's history of engagement:

> But you do see! Indeed you note trouble and grief,
> that you may take it into your hands;
> the helpless commit themselves to you;
> you have been the helper of the orphan.
>
> (v. 14)

Because YHWH is on the side of the orphan—those without an advocate in a patriarchal society—the psalm anticipates justice for the orphan and the oppressed (v. 18; see Ps. 68:5). The psalm culminates in verse16 with a ringing doxology that celebrates YHWH's governance over the nations and, by implication, over the economy.

The economics of this psalm are not difficult to grasp. What interests us, however, is the theological subtext upon which everything depends. The imagined autonomy of the exploitative powerful depends upon the elimination of YHWH from the economic sphere of life. Already in the ancient world of Israel there was a readiness to imagine that the economy is an autonomous sphere that is unrelated to the reality of YHWH. In the modern world, the establishment of the economy, specifically the market economy, as an autonomous zone has been vigorous indeed. That project, perhaps rooted in Adam Smith, gained great traction with Friedrich Hayek and Milton Friedman and became the legacy of Margaret Thatcher and Ronald Reagan, culminating in Gordon Gekko's verdict, "Greed is good." The nervy determination to eliminate YHWH from the economy is essential to unbridled greed with impunity. In fact, Enlightenment rationality and its by-product, market economy, have been at work on this elimination for a long time, because the notion of a God who limits greed in a substantive way may be dismissed as primitive or at best as intellectually embarrassing superstition. The result is the careful confinement of YHWH to private and interpersonal matters outside the public domain.

But of course, the voice of the poor, with its bodily sense of pain imposed by such greed, will never accept the elimination of YHWH from the scene. Thus in this psalm the poor seize the chance to pray YHWH back into the economy. That ancient impulse has come to contemporary expression in liberation theology, with its programmatic insistence on God's preferential option for the poor. That is exactly what is voiced in this psalm. God is the helper of the orphan! God is committed to justice for the orphan and the oppressed, so that the doxology of verse 16 is not simply a liturgical platitude. It is an insistence that the world and its economy be interpreted differently. The issue is joined in this psalm as it is joined in the modern world: Is the economy an *autonomous sphere* that has a life of its own? Or is the economy *a zone of community* presided over by the king of the nations for the sake of all? One does not need to be a primitive supernaturalist, one who has a naive notion of God's direct governance of the world, in order to affirm the latter. One need only accept that the Torah is a nonnegotiable norm for the practice of social relationships.

In Psalm19:7–10 we are offered a meditation on the generative power of Torah. In this horizon, the Torah is not simply a set of rules or prohibitions. It is rather a generative force for life that brings joy and well-being. The culmination of the meditation in verse 10 is stark and nonnegotiable:

> More to be desired are they [the ordinances] than gold,
> even much fine gold;
> sweeter also than honey,
> and drippings from the honeycomb.
>
> (v. 10)

The term "desired" here is *ḥmd*, the same term we have seen in Genesis 3:6 and in the tenth commandment, where it is translated "covet." Torah is more to be coveted than fine gold, sweeter than honey! The dramatic *either-or* of *gold/Torah* is an urgent decision about two ways in the world. One way is embodied among the wicked-guilty in Psalm 10, those who believe that "more" at the expense of the vulnerable neighbor is in order. The other way of Torah affirms the rule of YHWH in the economy and allows for the legitimacy of the orphan and the oppressed as viable participants in the political economy. If we read back from Psalm 10 to Psalm 112, we find in the latter a person of substantive means who has not bought in to the ideology of greed that is among us, expressed as unfettered market dealings. Rather this well-off Torah keeper has not let his "wealth and riches" talk him out of his passion for Torah justice. Thus Torah piety can imagine an alliance between *the needy poor* who refuse to be submissively silent in a context of exploitation and *the prosperous wealthy* who refuse to be defined by their wealth. Righteousness, the practice of generative neighborliness, recognizes an alliance of haves and have-nots that focuses not upon generous charity but upon justice. Thus Psalm 10 describes an economy devoid of justice; Psalm 112 commends conducting affairs with justice. Both psalms allude to YHWH: "The works of his hands are faithful and just; all his precepts are trustworthy" (Ps. 111:7).

Psalm 111:9 speaks all at once of "redemption" and "covenant." The poor require redemption; the well-off, bound in covenant, perform that emancipatory act of redemption for the indebted poor. Such action is the performance of YHWH in the real world of money and possessions.

II

A second introduction to the Psalter is provided in Psalm 2. Quite in contrast to Psalm 1, this psalm is focused on Zion, the king in Zion, and eventually the kingship of YHWH in Jerusalem. This trajectory in the Psalter features the Songs of Zion (Pss. 46, 48, 76, 84), the Davidic royal psalms (Pss. 2, 72, 89, 100), and the psalms of the enthronement of YHWH (Pss. 93, 96–99). The scope of the Jerusalem liturgy, reflected in these texts, is the whole of creation over which YHWH presides. While not neglecting the cruciality and centrality of Israel, its scale is one of cosmic, universal ordering for shalom. And because this trajectory imagines cosmically, it reflects on the character of YHWH, the God of Israel, among the gods. This liturgical tradition participates more readily in the great myths of Near Eastern culture and so can imagine YHWH along with the other gods.

1. *Psalm 82* is a dramatic act of daring theological imagination in which God—the real God, the God above all gods—holds court to adjudicate the god-claims of other, lesser gods. The high God accuses the lesser gods of practices of wickedness and injustice in collusion with the wicked whom we have seen in Psalm 10:

> How long will you judge unjustly
> and show partiality to the wicked?
> (v. 2)

The high God sets forth the expectations to which the other gods must respond:

> Give justice to the weak and the orphan;
> maintain the right of the lowly and the destitute.
> Rescue the weak and the needy;
> deliver them from the hand of the wicked.
> (vv. 3–4)

The mandate given the other gods is to be agents of restorative justice. These norms are here not said to be Torah, but their substance is very much what we have seen of Torah, namely, a passionate commitment to the weak, the orphan, the lowly, the destitute, and the needy. These vulnerable are currently in the grip of the wicked-guilty, and it is "God-work" to give justice, maintain right, rescue, and deliver. These two verses delineate, in Yahwistic perspective, what is required to qualify as "God." We may notice that not included in this inventory are the usual abstractions of Western thought concerning omnipotence, omniscience, and omnipresence. Rather what constitutes godness is transformative solidarity with the socially, economically vulnerable. These verses are profoundly radical because they recharacterize godness in a way that departs completely from more conventional theological categories. The godness of YHWH has to do with taking sides against the wicked, that is, the ones who imagine they are autonomous and so are free to prey on the vulnerable.

In verses 5–6 other candidates for "god" are judged and found wanting, and so are condemned to death:

They have neither knowledge nor understanding,
they walk around in darkness;
all the foundations of the earth are shaken.

I say, "You are gods,
children of the Most High, all of you;
nevertheless, you shall die like mortals,
and fall like any prince."

(vv. 5–7)

The condemned candidates for godness are stupid and inhabit the zone of chaos; they have no chance of acting in ways that would let them qualify as gods. As a result they are dismissed and sentenced to death.

The psalm ends in verse 8 with an appeal to the Most High, the God who presided over the adjudication of the other gods. This is the only real God, the one who has in purview the legitimate needs of the vulnerable. This final verse is a petition that echoes the petitions of Psalm 10:12. The ones who speak are exactly the poor and vulnerable from Psalm 10 who will pray no more to the failed gods who walk around in darkness and have no understanding of their true vocation as gods. The petition of verse 8 asks for judgment, that is, a court ruling of justice, for those who have been squeezed out of conventional economic practice. It is a core claim of the tradition that the High God has a particular attentiveness to those without money or possessions. It is this that distinguishes the Holy God, "Lord of hosts," from lesser gods who collude with the ideology and practices of the wicked-guilty. Thus when the Jerusalem liturgy celebrates YHWH as King of creation, it salutes a "lover of justice":

Mighty King, lover of justice,
you have established equity;
you have executed justice
and righteousness in Jacob.

(Ps. 99:4)

It is a long way from the heavenly throne of the High God to the earthly throne of the Davidic ruler in Jerusalem. But the connection between the two is already made in Psalm 2 with the formula, "You are my son." The Davidic king is "son of God" authorized to do God's work in the world. Thus it is recurring in the book of Psalms that Israel, in its liturgical reflection, can celebrate YHWH's kingship but can also celebrate human kingship in Jerusalem.

2. *Psalm 72* concerns the proper conduct of the human king as the regent of the God of justice in Psalm 82. It is surely significant that this is the only one of the royal psalms that has the superscription "of Solomon," or perhaps "pertaining to Solomon."[7]

For the most part this psalm is an exuberant anticipation of the prosperity, power, longevity, and abundance for Solomon and his dynasty, exactly the kind of affirmation we might expect in a stereotypical temple liturgy designed to accent the authority of the king. The scope of his rule is as broad and deep as creation:

> May he live while the sun endures,
> and as long as the moon, throughout all generations.
> May he be like rain that falls on the mown grass,
> like showers that water the earth.
> In his days may righteousness flourish
> and peace abound, until the moon is no more.
> (vv. 5–7)

The liturgy can imagine that all other kings will be subservient to him:

> May he have dominion from sea to sea,
> and from the River to the ends of the earth.
> May his foes bow down before him,
> and his enemies lick the dust.
> May the kings of Tarshish and the isles render him tribute,
> may the kings of Sheba and Seba bring gifts.
> May all kings fall down before him,
> all nations give him service.
> (vv. 8–11)

There is an anticipation of royal wealth, fame, and material abundance, all rooted in the fruitfulness of creation, all the way to our own singing about "amber waves of grain":

7. The only other psalm with a Solomonic superscription, Ps. 127, is not usually reckoned to be a royal psalm. The lack of such superscriptions for Solomon elsewhere undoubtedly accents its peculiar use in Ps. 72.

Long may he live!
May gold of Sheba be given to him.
May prayer be made for him continually,
and blessings invoked for him all day long.
May there be an abundance of grain in the land;
may it wave on the tops of the mountains;
may its fruit be like Lebanon;
and may people blossom in the cities
like the grass of the field.
May his name endure forever,
his fame continue as long as the sun.
May all nations be blessed in him;
may they pronounce him happy.

(vv. 15–17)

This extravagant rhetoric, however, is placed in antiphonal juxtaposition to a very different motif, namely, the obligation that the king has for the practice of economic justice. Thus the opening lines of the psalm concern precisely "justice" and "righteousness,"' as though to take a page from Torah piety. The object of such royal obligation, moreover, includes the usual suspects—the poor, the needy, and the oppressed:

Give the king your justice, O God,
and your righteousness to a king's son.
May he judge your people with righteousness,
and your poor with justice.
May the mountains yield prosperity for the people,
and the hills, in righteousness.
May he defend the cause of the poor of the people,
give deliverance to the needy,
and crush the oppressor.

(vv. 1–4)

The king is not only to enforce equity but is to undertake positive effective intervention in the economy by way of "deliverance" and punishment of those who oppress. The mandate is clearly parallel to the God-mandate of Psalm 82. Three times these verses utilize the term "righteousness," which connotes active transformative intervention on behalf of the neighbor.

A second like entry is voiced in verses 12–14, which again pivot on the poor, the weak, and the needy:

For he delivers the needy when they call,
the poor and those who have no helper.
He has pity on the weak and the needy,
and saves the lives of the needy.
From oppression and violence he redeems their life;
and precious is their blood in his sight.

The royal agenda is precisely to redress the "oppression and violence" that pervades social practice. Such "violence" refers to the systemic exploitation of the vulnerable who, without royal intervention, are victims of the predatory class.

It is not surprising that this mandate to the king would be brought into juxtaposition with the Torah prohibition against royal acquisitiveness (Deut. 17:14–20), the anticipation of royal acquisitiveness (1 Sam. 8:11–18), and the narrative testimony of 1 Kings 3–11 that portrays Solomon's self-aggrandizement. According to the testimony, Solomon's actual predation violated, even contradicted, the liturgical mandate he had received. If we parse these several texts together, it becomes clear that Solomon was not the king he was summoned to be, any more than the lesser gods were the gods they were summoned to be. The enormous extravagance of Solomon that we have considered makes clear that Solomon operated in a self-congratulatory way about the wondrous promises of Psalm 72 (vv. 5–11, 15–17), but without the intrusion of the mandates (vv. 1–4, 12–14). It is as though the royal enterprise simply cut out of the text—and placed out of purview—the parts of the royal mandate that disturbed royal ideology and inconvenienced royal self-sufficiency. But then, this is how an unchecked ideology of wealth can operate, as is evidenced in the market ideology of our society: simply omit the requirements and relish the authorizations!

The two parts of Psalm 72, the grand prospects (vv. 5–11, 15–17) and the mandates (vv. 1–4, 12–14), are set in juxtaposition. The text does not quite say that the prospects are conditioned by the mandates, but it is impossible not to read the text in that way. The Psalter can do an honest reprise on the fate of the royal economy. In Psalm 89, the liturgy celebrates the abiding unconditional promise to the David house:

I will establish his line forever,
and his throne as long as the heavens endure.
. . . .

> I will not violate my covenant,
> or alter the word that went forth from my lips.
> Once and for all I have sworn by my holiness;
> I will not lie to David.
>
> (vv. 29–35; see vv. 24–28)

But then, in an abrupt reversal, the psalm voices the dynastic experience of rejection, destruction, abandonment, and demise. It ends with a pathos-filled question addressed to YHWH:

> Lord, where is your steadfast love of old,
> which by your faithfulness you swore to David?
>
> (v. 49)

The psalm will not quite say so, but the inescapable inference to be drawn from the prophetic tradition is that *divine loyalty* to the Davidic house depended on the *economic mandate* given to Solomon in Psalm 72. In the end, even for the Davidic house there is no free lunch for the powerful. The divine promise sounds unconditional in the assurances of Psalm 89:33, an echo of 2 Samuel 7:15–16. In the end, however, even David's covenanted dynasty in Jerusalem discovered the conditionality of totally committed divine love. The uncompromising conditionality is that money and possessions and eventually greed and acquisitiveness must yield to the neighborhood. That mandate, so clear in Psalm 72, will not be outflanked, even by royal liturgy in its hyperbolic imagination. The royal imagination could not outflank the mandates any more than could the self-congratulations of the lesser gods in Psalm 82.

The Psalter ends in Psalms 145–150 with a loud exuberant doxology to YHWH for the overflow of abundance in all creation. In the end, it is YHWH who performs the required transformation of the neighborhood:

> . . . who executes justice for the oppressed;
> who gives food to the hungry.
>
> The LORD sets the prisoners free;
> the LORD opens the eyes of the blind.
> The LORD lifts up those who are bowed down;
> the LORD loves the righteous.
> The LORD watches over the strangers;

he upholds the orphan and the widow,
but the way of the wicked he brings to ruin.
(Ps. 146:7–9)

The "wicked," in context, are those who have created the unbearable circumstance for those named here as the object of divine attentiveness. It is YHWH who will govern in Zion:

The Lord will reign forever,
your God, O Zion, for all generations.
Praise the Lord!
(v. 10)

The substance of that divine governance is the restorative action of verses 7–9. That is how YHWH rules. YHWH rules according to a neighborly practice of possessions that can sustain neighborly life.

Each of the actions in verses 7–9 consists in restoration to full participation in a viable economy of abundance. That is what YHWH does. That is what the king is to do in Psalm 72; that is what the gods are to do in Psalm 82.

We know, however, that the great doxologies of Psalms 145–150 follow loss in ancient Israel. They reflect a later assertion after the forfeiture of city and dynasty. The creator God will make things right. But as Christopher Seitz has noticed, accent on the Davidic house has, in the Psalter as in the Book of Isaiah, subsided to the point of disappearance.[8] The Davidic house is crucial to the imagination of ancient Israel. In the end, however, it is the rule of YHWH that persists and prevails. Given the failed Davidic rulers who in their greed caused the demise of Jerusalem, YHWH will undertake direct rule: "*I myself* will search for my sheep, and will seek them out" (Ezek. 34:11; italics added).

The disappearance of the Davidic house in the Psalter is an immense cautionary tale. The neglect of the divine mandate (Torah summons to justice and righteousness) in regard to money and possessions, power and wealth, becomes an unsustainable policy and practice. The ordering of creation according to divine abundance, sung about in Psalm 72, will not be mocked, interrupted, or

8. Christopher R. Seitz, *Word without End: The Old Testament as Abiding Theological Witness* (Grand Rapids: Eerdmans, 1998), 150–67.

preempted by episodes of greedy acquisitiveness. Neither the gods in Psalm 82 nor the kings in Psalm 72 are permitted such gross miscalculation. The caution of the tale pertains to all concentrations of wealth that disregard the reality of the neighbor. As the dynasty disappears from Israel's hymnbook, so we can, over time, anticipate the disappearance of many concentrations of wealth that imagine guaranteed life without neighborly inconvenience.

III

For a fifth psalm, I have selected *Psalm 49,* a wisdom psalm. The wisdom psalms have much in common with Torah piety in their modest way of adhering to God's perceived will but ponder life in terms of all creation, for wisdom teaching is indeed "creation theology." Thus Psalm 49 might be seen as an extrapolation concerning both our trajectories of *Torah piety* and of *Jerusalem expansiveness.*

The psalm is a meditation upon wealth and what it does to human community. Verses 5–6 suggest a scene of social interaction between those who live arrogantly with their wealth and those who are victims of such inordinate wealth. The voice that speaks is one of wisdom that looks past the immediate economic crisis, deabsolutizes the claim and power of wealth, and foresees well-being in the sphere of divine fidelity beyond the dominance of such wealth:

> Why should I fear in times of trouble,
> when the iniquity of my persecutors surrounds me,
> those who trust in their wealth
> and boast of the abundance of their riches?

There is no doubt that concentrations of wealth may create frightening social circumstances for those left behind, the kind the Okies experienced in Steinbeck's *Grapes of Wrath:*

> I hear there's three hundred thousan' of our people there—an' livin' like hogs, 'cause ever'thing in California is owned. They ain't nothin' left. An' them people that owns it is gonna hang on to it if they got ta kill ever'body in the worl' to do it. An' they're scairt, and that makes 'em mad. You got to see it. You got to hear it. Purtiest goddamn country you ever seen, but they ain't nice to

> you, them folks. They're so scairt an' worried they ain't even nice to each other.[9]

It is this relentless threat from the wealthy in their great wealth that propels the psalm.

The wise, however, look longer and know more and can offer a reassurance beyond the present circumstance of unjust inequality. The assurance of verse 5 is reiterated in verse 16, offered to those who presently feel helpless before the power of great arrogant wealth: "Do not be afraid when some become rich, when the wealth of their houses increases."

The psalm counters this fear of the aggressively wealthy by attestation to the limit of wealth that the wealthy finally will face. It is death that makes such wealth penultimate and therefore not definitive. The reality of death is a sober note to the wealthy: You cannot take it with you!

> Mortals cannot abide in their pomp;
> They are like the animals that perish.
> (v. 12)

And then repeated for emphasis:

> Mortals cannot abide in their pomp;
> they are like the animals that perish.
> (v. 20)

The term rendered "pomp" in NRSV means "splendor," that is, the social visibility and grandeur made possible by wealth. Such splendor is unsustainable, so do not be overly impressed or overly awed by it. Death will equalize, and the rich have no durable advantage:

> Their graves are their homes forever,
> their dwelling places to all generations,
> though they named lands their own.
> . . . .
> Like sheep they are appointed for Sheol;
> Death shall be their shepherd;

9. John Steinbeck, *The Grapes of Wrath* (New York: Penguin Books, 1939), 265.

straight to the grave they descend,
and their form shall waste away;
Sheol shall be their home.

. . . .

For when they die they will carry nothing away;
their wealth will not do down after them.
(vv. 11, 14, 17)

The wealthy cannot buy security (ransom) from God, because it is not for sale. Thus all the frantic posturing of the wealthy to guarantee their status and assure their longevity is futile. The wealthy end up just like everyone else, with only a grave as a permanent dwelling place. The ultimate futility of wealth is inescapable.

The fate of Sheol is not a threat; Sheol is not a place of punishment. It is rather a place of weakness, dysfunction, and impotence where death rules and is the order of the day. Such weakness, dysfunction, and impotence are of course a contrast to their current capacity to have, do, and control everything.

But positively more can be said. The wise offer comfort to the victims of the wealthy by bearing witness to a trustworthy reality beyond the power of acquisitiveness. An extraordinary claim is made in verse 15: "But God will ransom my soul from the power of Sheol, for he will receive me."

Whereas "ransom" cannot be purchased in verse 7, here God will enact it. What is denied to the wealthy is given to the speaker of this psalm, surely who speaks for those who have been victimized by the wealthy. The one who speaks is one who trusts in YHWH and has confidence in YHWH beyond death. In verse 14, moreover, the wealthy have Sheol as their home, whereas in verse 15, God will redeem from Sheol. This affirmation is not a loud attestation about life after death. It is rather a conviction that God's fidelity persists in and through and after death, as money will not. Thus death is not simply the end of life. It is the power of negation already at work amid the economy. Karl Barth can say about our verse: "Death does not merely confront man with limitations of life which he has experienced all along. . . . Death is not only a place where man will be, but also a power which holds him in thrall (Ps. 49:15)."[10] Gospel hope, deeply based in the Old Testament, can, according to Barth,

10. Karl Barth, *Church Dogmatics*, III/2 (Edinburgh: T. & T. Clark, 1960), 590.

declare: "Those who believe in Jesus can no longer look at their death as though it were in front of them. It is behind them."[11]

So it is in verse 15 of Psalm 49. Clearly the psalm does not appeal to any such claim about Jesus. Rather it settles for the ultimate trustworthiness of God. This confidence in God is in sharp contrast to the double reference in verses 12 and 20 that dismisses the wealthy who will die "like the animals that perish," forgotten and without durable significance. Thus the psalm asks the ultimate question about hope. The ultimate hope of an acquisitive economy is to get more and to have the most. That ultimate hope, futile in the end, is a great disturber of the common good when the less resourced are left in vulnerability. The ultimate hope in the psalm, by contrast, is that the God of fidelity persists beyond our deathly choices and practices. Or as John Calvin had it:

> Our hope is in no other save in thee;
> our faith is built upon thy promise free;
> Lord, give us peace, and make us calm and sure,
> that in thy strength we evermore endure.[12]

The assurance to which Calvin attests was already granted to the psalmist. Calvin's words do not cater to the popular cult of life after death. They affirm that God gives peaceableness about the contested present that "we evermore endure."

It is of course possible to take this psalm as an effort at foxhole religion, at the last moment to transfer hope from money to God. But that is not its intent. It is rather an invitation to reflect, amid a swirling economy, on what is of durable value. The psalm is an opportunity to sort out true value from transitory well-being that is unsustainable. Both *Torah piety* that anticipates prosperity for Torah keepers and *Zion theology,* grounded in temple liturgy that anticipates the rule of YHWH over all creation, affirm that hope is found only in God, not in money or possessions, not in the grasping of the wicked who abuse neighbors or in the grasping of kings who disregard their mandate. For that reason the Psalter ends in wondrous doxology, as the faithful end in "wonder, love, and

11. Ibid., 621. I have been led to this discussion by Barth by James L. Mays, *Psalms*, Interpretation (Louisville, KY: John Knox Press, 1994), 194.

12. John Calvin, "I Greet Thee, Who My Sure Redeemer Art," *Glory to God* (Louisville, KY: Westminster John Knox Press, 2013), 624.

praise."[13] The alternative to "wonder, love, and praise" is perhaps control, alienation, and satiation. The wise psalmist knows that you cannot take it with you, so better to stop its pursuit. Psalm 49 knows that the sooner we disengage from the foolishness of acquisitiveness, the sooner we may be ransomed from the reach of the power of Sheol.

13. This triad is from Charles Wesley, "Love Divine, All Loves Excelling," *Glory to God*, 366.

CHAPTER 7

Proverbs and Job

Wise beyond Smart

For security and success in the economy, one must be smart. Being "money smart" includes knowing when to buy and when to sell, when to borrow and when to lend, when to owe and when to pay back loans, and whom to trust. It requires a careful sense of timing, a very sharp pencil, and some readiness for risk. Beyond that it necessitates an unencumbered realism about earning and investment that is not infected by any kind of sentimentalism or distraction from the single aim of security and success. Money smarts dominate the economy of our society with its huge concentrations of wealth; it is likely that on a much more modest scale the same was true in ancient times, as reflected in many biblical texts.

Being money smart, however, is not the same as being wise about money and possessions. The book of Proverbs is permeated with reflections about money and possessions, and the wisdom required to be safe, happy, and responsible about money. The difference between *being smart* and *being wise* is that for those with "smartness," money is a thing unto itself. For the wise, money is deeply contextualized. On the one hand, because wisdom reflection is creation theology, wisdom requires thinking about money in terms of how the world works as God's creation. Wisdom ponders how God has ordered the world, with its gifts, limits, obligations, sanctions, and possibilities, so that wisdom about money consists in being in sync with the realities of creation that cannot be outflanked or evaded. On the other hand, wisdom is the critical awareness that all of life (including money practices) is situated in a social fabric of neighborliness that cannot be disregarded. Thus being *in sync with the creator God* means to love God. Being *embedded in a social fabric* amounts to love of neighbor. As a result, money and possessions are contextualized by *love of God* and *love of neighbor*, two irreducible mandates that money smarts per se do not acknowledge or take seriously.

I

If we consider the final form of the canonical text of the book of Proverbs as an intentional unit, we may see that it is roughly framed at the beginning (1:7–19) and at the end (30:8–9) by two assertions about money.[1] At the outset in the opening poetry, the governing theme of the book is stated: "The fear of the LORD is the beginning of knowledge; fools despise wisdom and instruction" (1:7). Every aspect and dimension of life is brought into relation with and subordinated to a faithful acknowledgment of YHWH. Everything else is conditioned by that relationship of trustful obedience. Verses 10–18 of Proverbs 1 reflect on being seduced by bad company that will lead to destruction and self-destructive behavior. Christine Yoder links the text to an analysis of desire: "Desire for the right object(s) is constituent of human flourishing."[2] But when seduced by a "frenzy of possession," the fool places the community in jeopardy. The text voices a sharp contrast between wisdom and foolishness:

> The parent of Proverbs 1–9 offers a model of theological-ethical discourse that urges the embrace of a wholly different understanding of desire: desire for knowledge and God that is sweet in its unquenched intensity, desire that directs our gaze outward for understanding and convicts us of our accountability and responsibility to the world we see. . . . Such a relational portrait of what

1. On the canonical shape of the book of Proverbs, see Brevard S. Childs, *Introduction to the Old Testament as Scripture* (Philadelphia: Fortress Press, 1979), 551–59.

2. Christine Roy Yoder, "The Shaping of Erotic Desire in Proverbs 1–9," in *Saving Desire: The Seduction of Christian Theology*, ed. F. LeRon Shults and Jan-Olav Henriksen (Grand Rapids: Eerdmans, 2011), 157.

> it means to be wise challenges our cultural push for atomism, the view that every individual is a sovereign self, an unfettered agent who is by nature not bound to anything or any authority. Taking her stand in the heart of the city, wisdom calls us away from such folly, ushering us instead into a landscape of towering loves, fidelities, and profound responsibilities—a landscape that the ancient sages deemed ripe for human flourishing.[3]

The conclusion drawn in verse 19 concerns those who are "greedy for gain," who end in self-destruction: "Such is the end of all who are *greedy for gain*; it takes away the life of its possessors."

It is astonishing that money appears so soon in the agenda of wisdom. Greed arises from misdirected desire and ends in self-destruction. The phrase "greedy for gain" describes aggressive economics than regularly bespeaks predatory action. Such is the conduct of those who do not subordinate economic desire to relational reality.

At the end of the final form of the text of Proverbs, we have several series of numerical sayings (30:7–31). The first among them is 30:7–9, in which the wise person asks God for two things, only two things. The first word pair is "falsehood and lying"; we may take this word pair as a willingness to abuse the neighborhood for the sake of self-advancement. The speaker asks to be relieved of that practice. But it is the second word pair that interests us:

> Give me neither poverty nor riches;
> feed me with the food that I need,
> or I shall be full, and deny you,
> and say, "Who is the Lord?"
> or I shall be poor, and steal,
> and profane the name of my God.
> (vv. 8–9)

The prayer of the wise is to be delivered from wealth and from poverty, that is, to be made indifferent to money. And then to be granted "the bread of my portion," that which I really need, that much and no more. The speaker reflects in verse 9 on the dangerous consequences of wealth and of poverty. There is no safety in economic extremity:

3. Ibid., 162–63.

- The danger of wealth is that one may imagine one's autonomy without reliance upon YHWH, a temptation we have seen already in the warning on self-sufficiency in Deuteronomy 8:17 and then in Psalm 10:4, 6, 11.
- The danger of poverty is the temptation to steal, thus to violate the commandment (Exod. 20:15) and so betray the relationship with God. It is evident in recent studies that a sense of shortage and lack propels an almost obsessive urge to have more. Such an urge is of course abandonment of any thought that God will provide, as in Psalms 104:27–28 and 145:15–16. Characteristically the saying is terse; it is full enough, however, to see that any skewed economic condition will distort a relationship with YHWH. The twin distortions are obvious enough in our society, an imagined autonomy and self-sufficiency, a great temptation to steal. It is more than a little ironic in our society that the temptation to steal is highly visible among the "self-sufficient," in terms of tax evasion, insider trading, bribery, and various forms of corruption, all modes of theft that attest an insatiable hunger for more and an inability to recognize "enough."

Alongside Proverbs 30:8–9 we may notice 31:8–9 from a different literary collection. Here freedom from money leads to advocacy in the midst of economic inequality:

> Speak out for those who cannot speak,
> for the rights of all the destitute.
> Speak out, judge righteously,
> defend the rights of the poor and needy.

Now the instruction is not to be free from preoccupation with money but to be actively engaged in the unsettled economics of the community.[4]

There is, to be sure, no straight line from Proverbs 1:19 to Proverbs 30:8–9 and 31:8–9; the path from the one to the other is

4. In addition to 30:8–9 and 31:8–9, at the conclusion of the book of Proverbs attention should of course be paid to the poem on the "woman of 'substance'" in 31:10–31, a text greatly preoccupied with matters of money and wealth; on the text, see Christine Roy Yoder, *Wisdom as a Woman of Substance: A Socioeconomic Reading of Proverbs 1–9 and 31:10–13*, Beihefte zur Zeitschrift für alttestamentliche Wissenschaft 304 (Berlin: Walter de Gruyter, 2001).

through many independent collections of sayings with varying sentiments and judgments.[5] Taken as final form, however, we may suggest that the acquiring of wisdom is the slow, long-term move from *"greedy for gain"* to *trust in YHWH* who gives bread as is appropriate. Thus the generous abundance of the creator God contradicts both the autonomy of the wealthy and the greedy propulsion of the poor. Wisdom about money is, in the book of Proverbs, framed by the reality of YHWH who gives bread enough to sustain life. The journey to trust in YHWH is a journey from "atomism of the sovereign self" to the embrace of a wholly different understanding of desire.[6] Christine Yoder, moreover, notes "our cultural push toward atomism"; likely even in the ancient world there was a similar push, against which wisdom offers a mighty alternative.

II

That canonical envelope contains many diverse wisdom reflections on money and possessions that are no doubt filtered through a variety of socioeconomic interests.[7] For the most part, wisdom teaching is committed to the proposition that creation is ordered so that *deeds* produce *consequences*.[8] Given that frame of reference, we

5. Two books that are most helpful for our topic discuss each of the collections in the book of Proverbs in turn: Timothy J. Sandoval, *Money and the Way of Wisdom: Insights from the Book of Proverbs* (Woodstock, VT: Skylight Paths, 2008), and R. Norman Whybray, *Wealth and Poverty in the Book of Proverbs*, Journal for the Study of the Old Testament Supplement Series 99 (Sheffield: Sheffield Academic Press, 1990).

6. Yoder, "Shaping of Erotic Desire," 162.

7. Samuel L. Adams, *Social and Economic Life in Second Temple Judea* (Louisville, KY: Westminster John Knox Press, 2014), 184–89, offers a succinct summary on wealth and poverty in the book of Proverbs:

1. "Greed ultimately leads to failure."
2. "The preferability of wisdom over material wealth."
3. "Honest assessments of the plight of the poor and their vulnerability."
4. "The association of poverty with laziness and financial gain with industrious behavior."

8. The defining discussion is by Klaus Koch, "Is There a Doctrine of Retribution in the Old Testament?," in *Theodicy in the Old Testament*, ed. James L. Crenshaw (Philadelphia: Fortress Press, 1983), 57–87. Over against that tight calculus of "deeds and consequences," Gerhard von Rad, *Wisdom in Israel* (Nashville: Abingdon Press, 1972), 98–101, has identified a series of texts in which YHWH exercises freedom beyond the perspective of "deeds consequences."

can observe two recurring calculations that no doubt reflect a certain social location.[9]

1. The proverbial teaching is committed to a work ethic that commends diligence, that confidently expects *diligence* to lead to good material outcomes, and conversely that treats *laziness*—with its sorry outcomes—as an alternative to diligence. The world is ordered so that the diligent end up with a good measure of wealth, whereas the lazy end up poor:

> A slack hand causes poverty,
> but the hand of the diligent makes rich.
> (10:4)

> Like vinegar to the teeth, and smoke to the eyes,
> are the lazy to their employers.
> (10:26)

> Those who till their land will have plenty of food,
> but those who follow worthless pursuits have no sense.
> (12:11)

> The lazy do not roast their game,
> but the diligent obtain precious wealth.
> (12:27)

> In all toil there is profit,
> but mere talk leads only to poverty.
> (14:23)

> The way of the lazy is overgrown with thorns,
> but the path of the upright is a level highway.
> (15:19)

> Those who are attentive to a matter will prosper,
> and happy are those who trust in the LORD.
> (16:20)

9. The social location and economic interest of the sages of the book of Proverbs continue to be unsettled and in dispute. I find the perspective of Robert Gordis, "The Social Background of Wisdom Literature," in *Poets, Prophets, and Sages: Essays in Biblical Interpretation* (Bloomington: Indiana University Press, 1971), 104–96, to be representative and compelling.

> Do not love sleep, or else you will come to poverty;
> open your eyes, and you will have plenty of bread.
> (20:13)

It is evident that the notion of diligence shades over into moral-covenantal categories:

> Misfortune pursues sinners,
> but prosperity rewards the righteous.
> (13:21)

> To get wisdom is to love oneself;
> to keep understanding is to prosper.
> (19:8)

The move from "diligence" to "righteousness" is a crucial shift in categories whereby diligence and hard work are invested with moral significance beyond mere pragmatics. It is likely that in a community committed to a work ethic, the two can slip into one combination, so that hard work itself that is generative of wealth is perceived as a moral good.

These proverbs are variously utilized in our culture to condemn the poor, who are dismissed as lazy. The matter, however, cannot be reduced to such a simplistic interpretation, because the notion of "diligence" does not pertain simply to hard work; with it comes a social awareness about the well-being of the entire neighborhood and the moral capability to attend to the needs and possibilities of the community. When such proverbs are reduced to a simplistic indictment of the poor, it indicates that a *wise statement* has morphed into a *smart claim* that is indifferent to social context and to the will of the creator. Genuinely wise "diligence" is much thicker than mere "hard work."

2. A second aspect of "deeds and consequence" concerns precisely those who are "greedy for gain." Just as diligence and laziness have predictable outcomes, so also does "greedy for gain," with its predatory inclinations. We have seen the phrase in Proverbs 1:19. Twice more the observation occurs, first in 15:27:

> Those who are *greedy for unjust gain* make trouble for their
> households,
> but those who hate bribes will live.

The outcome of such greedy action is to disturb the household, clan, or village. The second line of the proverb suggests that among the actions of those "greedy for gain" may be bribery wherein those with sufficient resources may skew social order, balance, and well-being by pushing unfair advantage. While the phrase tilts toward violence, the violence may be political and economic and not necessarily direct bodily assault. It takes little imagination to connect this observation to super PACs and limitless political money to see that such an act is a mode of bribery, greediness for unjust gain that brings endless trouble on the household or the community.

The third occurrence of the phrase is in 28:16:

> A ruler who lacks understanding is a cruel oppressor;
> but one who hates *unjust gain* will enjoy a long life.

The first line of the proverb describes a powerful person who lacks wisdom ("understanding") and so may be money smart but understands nothing about viable communal life or governance. The second line, with its rejection of greed for gain, proposes an alternative way of governance, alternative conduct that produces very different outcomes for the society and for the ruler. The deed of refusing exploitative economics has as its consequence a long and peaceable life.

While the phrase is not used in Proverbs 22:28 and 23:10–11, the moving of ancient boundary markers in those verses is an example of being "greedy for gain." Such a practice disturbs old tribal and village arrangements and especially permits exploitation of orphans and widows who are without strong social protection. As in the narrative of Naboth's vineyard (1 Kgs. 21), the wise recognize that covenantal, neighborly social arrangements are exceedingly vulnerable to the force of unjust greed.

3. The contrasts that are characteristic of wisdom teaching—diligence/laziness, greed for gain/maintenance of viable order—everywhere suggest that decisive life choices about money and possessions must always be made in a social context that is impacted by such choices. Taken in social context, choices about money and possessions (land) are not about money alone; rather, they impinge upon the life and well-being of the entire community. We can observe the deep *either-or* of wisdom teaching by a series of "better sayings" that affirm that some decisions are much to be preferred to other decisions:

Happy are those who find wisdom,
and those who get understanding,
for her income is *better* than silver,
and her revenue *better* than gold.
(Prov. 3:13–14)

Take my instruction instead of silver,
and knowledge rather than choice gold;
for wisdom is *better* than jewels,
and all that you may desire cannot compare with her.
(8:10–11)

My fruit is *better* than gold, even fine gold,
and my yield than choice silver.
(8:19)

Better is a little with righteousness
than large income with injustice.
(16:8)

How much *better* to get wisdom than gold!
To get understanding is to be chosen rather than silver.
(16:16)

It is *better* to be of a lowly spirit among the poor
than to divide the spoil with the proud.
(16:19)

Better is dry morsel with quiet
than a house full of feasting with strife.
(17:1)

Better to be poor and walk in integrity
than to be crooked in one's ways even though rich.
(28:6)

These sayings do not, for the most part, indicate why one choice is better than the other, or in what way better than the other. The ground for "better," however, is everywhere implied in the better sayings. These sayings regularly contradict what might at first glance seem preferable if one is thinking only in terms of money smarts. But of course these sayings intend precisely to contradict such smart thinking. What is better is surely the choice that enhances more general human flourishing and that is more in sync with the way in which God has ordered that flourishing. Each choice in the better sayings brings with it a consequence or an outcome. The consequence of the commended choice is not better in terms of getting richer or more secure or more successful or more influential. The better outcome is about the flourishing of the community.

III

Wisdom teaching about money and possessions is not exhausted with "deeds-consequences," even when deeds and consequences are taken in a thick community-oriented way. It turns out, in wisdom perspective, that beyond any pragmatic practice of deeds and consequences, there are obligations that go along with wealth. Indeed, even in these wisdom sayings we can find something like God's preferential option for the poor, or if not "preferential," then at least God's even-handed regard and provision for the poor. It is startling to read in this context of the deep alliance of the Creator with the poor:

> Those who oppress *the poor* insult their Maker,
> but those who are kind to the needy honor him.
> (Prov. 14:31)
>
> Those who mock *the poor* insult their Maker;
> those who are glad at calamity will not go unpunished.
> (17:5)
>
> If you close your heart to the cry of *the poor*,
> you will cry out and not be heard.
> (21:13)
>
> Those who are generous are blessed,
> for they share their bread with *the poor*.
> (22:9)
>
> Do not rob *the poor* because they are *poor*,
> or crush the afflicted at the gate;
> for the LORD pleads their cause
> and despoils of life those who despoil them.
> (22:22)

> The righteous know the rights of *the poor*;
> the wicked have no such understanding.
> (29:7)

This teaching clearly means to interrupt and contradict any sense that money is a private thing for one's self alone. With their sense of community solidarity, the wisdom teachers understood that we are all in this together and that peace, order, and well-being depend upon social attentiveness to every element of the community. They could not have imagined that anyone would ever become wealthy or powerful enough to construct a privatized world apart from the community. They found wisdom in seeking out the needy by those with wealth. One can in these proverbs find antecedents to the verdict of the judge in the parable of Jesus: "As you did it to the least of these . . . , you did it to me" (Matt. 25:40). It is the Maker who guarantees the legitimate presence of the poor in the community, and the proper claim of the poor upon the community and upon those with adequate resources.

Two other proverbs nicely articulate the common stake and value of the poor who are, in the presence of YHWH, equal to the wealthy:

> The rich and the poor have this in common:
> the LORD is the maker of them all.
> (22:2)

> The poor and the oppressor have this in common:
> the LORD gives light to the eyes of both.
> (29:13)

In a "smart money" world, social differentiations count for a great deal. In the wise world of Yahwism, those differences count for nothing at all. The Creator refuses the discounting or overvaluing of any member of the community. Affirmation of YHWH's capacity for justice is framed in several proverbs as a function of YHWH's freedom. YHWH is not tightly held in a framework of deeds-consequences but can impact social arrangements in other ways as well; see Proverbs 16:1–2, 9; 19:14, 21; 20:24; 21:30–31.

The wisdom teachers become quite specific about practices of social justice toward the poor. Fair economic transactions require equitable scales and weights, so that commerce is fair:

A false balance is an abomination to the LORD,
but an accurate weight is his delight.
(Prov. 11:1)

Honest balances and scales are the LORD's;
all the weights in the bag are his work.
(16:11)

Diverse weights and diverse measures
are both alike an abomination to the LORD.
(20:10)

Differing weights are an abomination to the LORD,
and false scales are not good.
(20:23)

In a money economy where such social solidarity is not insisted upon, skewed measures against the poor are rampant. Thus on the day I write this, the *New York Times* reports on exorbitant car loans for the poor that yield at the same time confiscation of cars and the hopeless miring in debt from unbearable interest rates on car sales.[10] This specificity clearly indicates that wisdom teaching is not mere pragmatics; it is rather social realism that is framed in a world guaranteed by and presided over by the God of justice.[11]

IV

Having exposited the dangers and temptations of wealth, these same teachers nonetheless could affirm that wealth may be responsibly acquired if one participates in the economy in wise and responsible ways:

10. Shaila Dewan, "Police Use Department Wish List When Deciding Which Assets to Seize," *New York Times*, November 10, 2014. The so-called civic seizures are, Dewan reports, conducted arbitrarily according to the needs and wants of police officers, even when there is no conviction.

11. See H. H. Schmid, "Creation, Righteousness, and Salvation: 'Creation Theology' as the Broad Horizon of Biblical Theology," in *Creation in the Old Testament*, ed. Bernhard W. Anderson (Philadelphia: Fortress Press, 1984), 102–17. Schmid's important book *Gerechtigkeit als Weltordnung* (Tübingen: J. C. B. Mohr, 1968) remains untranslated.

> Some give freely, yet grow all the richer;
> others withhold what is due, and suffer want.
> A generous person will be enriched,
> and one who gives water will get water.
> (Prov. 11:24–25)

> Those who trust in their riches will wither,
> but the righteous will flourish like green leaves.
> (11:28)

In commending the responsible persons with wealth, the direct language of wealth is not often utilized. More likely the fruitfulness of wise and responsible lives is parsed in metaphor as "flourish like green leaves" (11:28) and "tree of life" (11:30). Perhaps it was unseemly to speak directly about wealth for the righteous; more likely the speaker wants to place wealth in a context of a full life of well-being that includes monetary wealth but also goes well beyond the mere accumulation of wealth.

It is impossible to summarize wisdom teaching or to arrange it into a neat scheme. But the intent of the accumulation of specific sayings is unmistakable. When money and possessions are situated in a world of God's justice, they will flourish, generate prosperity, and guarantee a good life. Such a possibility, however, is in profound tension with the way of money smarts that must have been a durable temptation in that ancient world as it surely is a living seduction in our world. We are, in our world, subjected to a constant barrage of summons to privatized wealth that sets the pursuit of wealth over against the well-being of the community. This summons to self-protection and self-sufficiency shows up in endless advertising, in banks and brokerage firms promising wealth and security, in political super PACs that skew the political process, in payday loans for the poor, in resistance to taxation for the common good. All of this, in the perspective of these proverbs, is a huge act of foolishness that can only have savage outcomes. There is a place for financial security in the horizon of wisdom teaching. It is not, however, to be secured at the expense of or withdrawal from the common good. In wisdom perspective, such actions over against the common good contradict the good order of creation and cannot succeed.

V

It is not usual to read the book of Job with reference to money and possessions.[12] When the book of Job is read as a counterpoint to the book of Proverbs, however, such a reading is evoked when we attend to the accent on wealth in Proverbs. As we have seen, Proverbs is deeply committed to a deeds-consequences program; certain deeds yield certain consequences. We have seen, moreover, that the framework of deeds-consequences in Proverbs is concerned with the material world. There is a continuing concern for money and possessions and for the influence, security, and status that go with money and possessions. Wisdom teaching is precisely concerned with the material particularities of life and how they may serve or not serve human flourishing. Thus when we come to the book of Job, we find an argument about the assumptions of Proverbs, assumptions about how choices—wise or foolish—will yield well-being and wealth . . . or not.

The argument that the book of Job has with the assumptions of Proverbs is tightly choreographed.

1. The book of Job begins tersely: "There was once a man in the land of Uz whose name was Job. That man was blameless and upright, one who feared God and turned away from evil" (Job 1:1).

The narrative then describes Job's inordinate wealth that permitted his family to enjoy the good life: "He had seven thousand sheep, three thousand camels, five hundred yoke of oxen, five hundred donkeys, and very many servants; so that this man was the greatest of all the people of the east" (v. 3).

The text does not specifically connect the verdict of verse 1 with the reported wealth of verse 3, but the connection is surely implied. Job had been wise, and so deservedly wealthy. The connection voiced by the wisdom teachers is in fact true in Job's case!

2. But of course the story turns on the abrupt and complete reversal of Job's fortunes. Given the cunning scheme of God and Satan to which Job has no access (1:6–12), we learn (as does Job) of Job's loss:

12. An exception is Gustavo Gutiérrez, *On Job: God-Talk and the Suffering of the Innocent* (Maryknoll, NY: Orbis Books, 1987), though even Gutiérrez does not go very far in a materialist direction in his reading of Job.

> One day when his sons and daughters were eating and drinking wine in the eldest brother's house, a messenger came to Job and said, "The oxen were plowing and the donkeys were feeding beside them, and the Sabeans fell on them and carried them off, and killed the servants with the edge of the sword; I alone have escaped to tell you." While he was still speaking, another came and said, "The fire of God fell from heaven and burned up the sheep and the servants, and consumed them; I alone have escaped to tell you." While he was still speaking, another came and said, "The Chaldeans formed three columns, made a raid on the camels and carried them off, and killed the servants with the edge of the sword; I alone have escaped to tell you." While he was still speaking, another came and said, "Your sons and daughters were eating and drinking wine in their eldest brother's house, and suddenly a great wind came across the desert, struck the four corners of the house, and it fell on the young people, and they are dead; I alone have escaped to tell you." (vv. 13–19)

The repeated refrain, "I alone have escaped to tell you," is a pounding reminder that the "wise" connection between deed and consequence has been broken and is not reliable. Job's piety is all "for nothing" (v. 9). Thus the dramatic contrast between a good life with *much wealth* (v. 3) and a good life and complete loss of *much wealth* (vv. 13–19) sets the stage for all that follows. The book of Job, however, pushes beyond the clarity of prose narrative into the deep probe of poetry that raises deep and hard questions about the ordering of social reality.

All of the participants in the drama—Job and his friends together—are deeply committed to the old sapiential conviction that the world holds and is morally reliable. The conflicted exchange between Job and his friends takes place within that assumption that is not doubted or abandoned.

3. Job's pathos-filled speech in chapters 29–31 continues to champion the ratio of merited wealth to which he remains committed. In chapter 29 Job describes his earlier life, before he had lost his wealth and his social standing. He attests to the generosity of God toward him and to the enjoyment of his wealth:

> When I was in my prime,
> when the friendship of God was upon my tent;
> when the Almighty was still with me,

when my children were around me;
when my steps were washed with milk,
and the rock poured out for me streams of oil!
(29:4–6)

He enjoyed his social standing and the deep respect that comes with a prosperous, well-lived life:

When I went out to the gate of the city,
when I took my seat in the square,
the young men saw me and withdrew,
and the aged rose up and stood;
the nobles refrained from talking,
and laid their hands on their mouths;
the voices of princes were hushed,
and their tongues stuck to the roof of their mouths.
(vv. 7–10)

The ground of his well-being and his social standing was in his sustained practice of righteousness expressed as social justice:

Because I delivered the poor who cried,
and the orphan who had no helper.
The blessing of the wretched came upon me,
and I caused the widow's heart to sing for joy.
I put on righteousness, and it clothed me;
my justice was like a robe and a turban.
I was eyes to the blind.
and feet to the lame.
I was a father to the needy,
and I championed the cause of the stranger.
I broke the fangs of the unrighteous,
and made them drop their prey from their teeth.
(vv. 12–17)

But all of that is now gone! All lost! The good man has experienced evil consequences:

But now . . . (30:1)
And now . . . (30:9)
And now . . . (30:16)

He has been overwhelmed by "now" that is acutely in contrast to "then." He has come to a sorry end, and we anticipate that in his grief he will have no more to say:

> I go about in sunless gloom;
> I stand up in the assembly and cry for help.
> I am a brother of jackals,
> and a companion of ostriches.
> My skin turns black and falls from me,
> and my bones burn with heat.
> My lyre is turned to mourning,
> and my pipe to the voice of those who weep.
> (30:28–31)

Except that he does have more to say! He mobilizes his energy to make one more self-defense. Now it is not about his property or about his grief concerning his property now lost. It is about his integrity, because the entire scheme of deeds-consequences depends on a visible integrity. Thus he recites the virtuous truth of his life:

> If I have walked with falsehood,
> and my foot has hurried to deceit—
> let me be weighed in a just balance,
> and let God know my integrity!
> (31:5–6)

The if–then structure of his testimony is an insistence on his virtue, and by implication his claim to a better outcome than he has received in his severe reversal:

> If . . . then (vv. 7–8)
> If . . . then (vv. 9–10)
> If . . . then (vv. 16–22)

His case is foolproof. His testimony concerns his wise management of his wealth resources for the sake of the community, with special attentiveness to those without resources. But of course he receives no answer. The sky is silent; the deeds-consequences system and the God who presides over and guarantees that system are unresponsive. He is left bereft. His unshaken confidence in his integrity has left him entitled to that which he has not received. The reversal of 1:13–19 has not been reversed. Job will wait until hell freezes over for a response, for he must have one.

4. Of course he eventually receives a response from God in the whirlwind. That voice, however, is completely indifferent to Job's calculus. YHWH has no interest in the argument of Job and will not engage it. The poetry of Creator-creation-creature soars well beyond any close calculus until the subject is radically and deeply changed. The wording of 42:6 leaves open several interpretive possibilities, even though our English translations tend to eliminate such ambiguity. In the Hebrew wording, it is far from clear that Job docilely submits to YHWH.

5. Job is commended in the end for speaking "what is right" (42:7–8)! He has in the end refused to conform to the quid pro quo calculus of his friends, and he has refused as well to submit easily to the awesomeness of YHWH. He has, in the end, been willing and able to hold his own in a dialogic engagement with the creator God. And if he finally submits to YHWH in 42:1–6, he does so in what seems to be a cunningly ambiguous way.

And then abruptly, inexplicably, and without explanation, YHWH commits an astonishing act of generosity toward Job. The final paragraph, 42:10–17, is introduced by nothing more than a simple conjunction (*waw* consecutive). What follows is a genuine restoration:

> The LORD gave Job twice as much as he had before. . . . The LORD blessed the latter days of Job more than his beginning; and he had fourteen thousand sheep, six thousand camels, a thousand yoke of oxen, and a thousand donkeys. (vv. 10, 12)

To be sure, his full restoration consists in more than the restoration of his wealth; it includes the recovery of his family and the restoration of his treasured status in the community. For all of that, however, our attentiveness to money and possessions requires us to notice that there is a full and extravagant restoration of wealth:

> The scene returns to the intimate community of Job's brothers and sisters and "all who previously knew him." They bring him symbolic gifts: money—which will enable him to re-enter communal life—and jewelry—a signifier of value over and above use-value. YHWH also gives Job great wealth (v. 12). The gifts he

> receives from his family are homologous with the gifts he gives his daughters (vv. 13–15). Job gives them very useful inheritances along with their brothers as well as aesthetically-charged names that signify their value in excess of use-value. Their beauty, greater than any women in all the land, is enough to grab the attention of this terse narrative. Job's gifts to his daughters are unusual and ethically-charged since, according to ancient inheritance laws, daughters inherit only when there are no living male relatives. Their inheritances may free them from relying on their beauty and other means to secure their financial futures by procuring a hefty brideprice. The community in vv. 7–17 is beautiful and aesthetically-charged, extensive in horizontal and vertical relations, and enduring over four generations and 140 years (vv. 16–17).[13]

Thus read with an eye on the material (money and possessions), the book of Job consists in *wealth lost* and *wealth restored* in generosity. And between the two, a long dispute concerning merit and reliability. It is possible, I judge, that in the move from prologue to epilogue the book of Job may bring Job (and us) to a quite different perspective on money and possessions. In Job 1, the great wealth of Job is situated in a quid pro quo calculus of deeds and consequences. Job had "earned" his wealth by being "blameless and upright." But the divine speeches from the whirlwind make that arrangement of quid pro quo merit irrelevant. It will no longer do, in Job's world, to reason about the merit of wealth, as the book of Proverbs seeks to do. In the end, Job's wealth is a gift, signified by the gifts from his brothers and sisters, much more embodied in the generous restoration action of YHWH. Now Job's wealth is beyond merit; the old logic no longer pertains. Job is indeed "full of days" as he is full of wealth and full of social standing yet again. All is gift!

13. Davis Hankins, *The Book of Job and the Immanent Genesis of Transcendence* (Evanston, IL: Northwestern University Press, 2015), 222–23. As we consider the restoration of wealth and family to Job, we should not lose sight of the dissent of Emil L. Fackenheim, "New Hearts and the Old Covenant: On Some Possibilities of a Fraternal Jewish-Christian Reading of the Jewish Bible Today," in *The Divine Helmsman: Studies on God's Control of Human Events*, ed. James L. Crenshaw and Samuel Sandmel (New York: KTAV Publishing House, 1980), 202, who observes: "To Job sons and daughters are restored; but they are not the same sons and daughters." Fackenheim relates this to the loss of the children at Auschwitz.

The theological implications of this termination of life on the basis of merit are thick. Our focus on money and possessions, aside from other theological implications, concerns the transfer of money from the *logic of merit* to the *surprise of gift*, from precise *payback* to inexplicable *generosity*. And when Job's wealth is restored, Job himself is restored as a lively, influential member of society. So Hankins can identify a shift in perspective accomplished through the book of Job: "The most significant ethical aspect of the prose conclusion is its shift of focus from a subject-centered concern with Job's understanding, activities, and obedience, to Job's role in what constitutes and maintains the cultural, legal, and religious institutions of the community."[14]

Money has been redefined and reconstituted in terms of a larger common good that violates the more generalizing closer logic of proverbial wisdom. It is this transformation that moves Job from a calculating "smarts" about money to wisdom about money, a transformation accomplished by being on the receiving end of inexplicable generosity. I judge that Hankins is surely correct in affirming that the "new wisdom" of Job does not consistently fight against or displace the "old wisdom" of the book of Proverbs. There are indeed probes beyond the old system, probes that open to the surprising generosity of God. But these probes do not fully replace the old calculations, for even in the new blessedness of Job there is still the reciprocity of human gifts, the awareness of social status, and the joy of well-being. Wisdom is a big reach beyond smarts. But it never lacks realism about money and possessions, status and property.

VI

When we read Proverbs and Job with a focus on materiality, we can trace the several attitudes about money in the literature through Kierkegaard's *Stages of Faith*:[15]

1. The fool in Proverbs embodies Kierkegaard's "aesthetic" stage of faith, in which there is an absence of moral seriousness and a catering to a desire for commodity satisfaction.

14. Hankins, *Book of Job*, 223.

15. Søren Kierkegaard, *Stages on Life's Way* (New York: Schocken Books, 1967).

2. Job's friends and sometimes Job reflect the summons of Proverbs for "rewards for the righteous" that Kierkegaard termed "ethical." They are determined to live an ethical life, as is evidenced in Job's self-defense in Job 31. That ethical life, however, is contained within a quid pro quo of deeds and consequences. Thus Job, in his last utterance before the coming of the whirlwind, does not seek mercy, but only a court hearing:

> O that I had one to hear me!
> (Here is my signature! Let the Almighty answer me!)
> O that I had the indictment written by my adversary!
> Surely I would carry it on my shoulder;
> I would bind it on me like a crown;
> I would give him an account of all my steps;
> like a prince I would approach him.
>
> (31:35–37)

Here speaks the quintessentially ethical person!

3. By the time of the epilogue, however, that ethical force is completely shattered. Now there is no suggestion of merit. It is pure gift received, as Kierkegaard might say, in a "religious" posture. As the rhetoric of YHWH in the whirlwind stuns Job's self-defense, now the lavishness of YHWH overwhelms Job's moral scruple; he need no longer think about his ethical conduct or merit. Wealth is on free offer from YHWH, and Job, in a venue of Kierkegaard's "religious" stage, can trust himself and his community to the goodness of God. This is the dimension of divine freedom expressed as generosity, already present in the book of Proverbs, in the remarkable sayings identified by Gerhard von Rad.[16] The freedom of God runs well beyond the calculus of any conventional wisdom.

In the reading community of the church, it is easy enough to mount a critique of money and possessions cast in Kierkegaard's "aesthetic" terms. The church's preoccupation with sexuality is perhaps a dodge to keep from voicing that critique. But many of us do ponder money and possessions through the ethical performance of merit. The move from the ethical to the religious is a huge leap, perhaps only possible by engagement with the whirlwind. It is then possible to entertain "the possibility of a moral and material

16. Gerhard von Rad, *Wisdom in Israel* (Nashville: Abingdon Press, 1972). The texts von Rad has identified are Prov. 16:2, 9; 19:21; 20:24; 21:2, 30–31.

wholeness in life." The outcome, says Newsom, is one "in which the goodness of life in all its fragility is embraced."[17] A careful reading of Job will not allow the avoidance of fragility. On Job's good days, any sense of fragility may have been trumped by a sense of God's unutterable generosity. Such a sense is not easy to sustain; it is nonetheless the capstone of wisdom that rushes past every calculation. In that instant Job need not be smart about money. He need only be wise, wise enough to know that it is all a gift.

The appropriate response to such generosity is gratitude. Job's freewheeling delight in his newly given daughters is perhaps an expression of such affirmation; this conduct is in noticeable contrast to his cautious parenting in chapter 1. Job, however, can muster no specific word or gesture of gratitude. Perhaps it is too awkward for him, given his long reliance on merit. Or perhaps he still thinks of himself as entitled, and so need not be grateful. Or perhaps the writers of the book of Job have not yet figured out how to articulate that last move of Job toward gratitude that may still be forthcoming. That leap from ethical to religious may still be made by Job; we do not know yet!

17. Carol A. Newsom, *The Book of Job: A Contest of Moral Imaginations* (Oxford: Oxford University Press, 2003), 257.

CHAPTER 8

The Prophets

Wealth Ill-Gotten and Lost, Wealth Given Again

The prophets in ancient Israel constitute a great disruptive force in its life and economy. By daring, often outrageous poetic image and metaphor, they disrupt what had seemed to be a settled, well-ordered society. Prophetic utterance is clearly human speech that arises in concrete contexts among those deeply rooted in faith traditions who had both the capacity to discern social reality differently and the capacity for artistic articulation of that discernment. This human speech, moreover, is uttered with a claim of authority grounded in the character of God. Thus the authorizing formula, "Thus says the LORD," indicates that this human speech is uttered and perhaps heard as more than human speech.

I

This speech claims to voice the will, purpose, and intent of the God who has not been domesticated to the conventional social or economic order.

1. The prophets regularly appear in social circumstances where an organizing power exercises hegemonic control. Among the prophets of the eighth and seventh centuries BCE, that hegemonic control was exercised by the royal regimes in Samaria, capital city of northern Israel (see Amos 7:10–17), and much more powerfully by

the Jerusalem establishment that featured royal power enhanced by priestly and scribal functionaries. These hegemonic regimes fostered a kind of absolutism that was grounded in a claim of chosenness, so that visible power was supported by ideological posturing. The royal apparatus, north and south, sought to make a claim for legitimacy that refused any disruption and fostered a kind of self-sufficiency.

In the sixth century, by contrast, hegemonic control featured Babylonian governance, to be later displaced by Persian rule. These empires practiced domination and seemed guaranteed in perpetuity. Among the displaced Jewish population, such imperial control generated disappointment and despair, as the regimes appeared to be beyond disruption.

Both the royal regimes of Samaria and Jerusalem and the imperial regimes of Babylon and Persia were, in varying degrees, committed to economic extraction from the common population to produce surplus wealth for the governing elite, who had arranged the economy for their own benefit. Thus in eighth–seventh century Israel-Judah and in sixth-century Babylon and Persia, a kind of totalism was established that kept *a process of economic extraction* closely linked to *an ideological hegemony* that produced a closed sociopolitical system.

The emergence of the prophets in that context is a remarkable social phenomenon in which voices from elsewhere, from outside the totalism, sounded with immense authority that defied and displaced the authority of the regimes with the claim of authority of the creator God who rendered all other authority penultimate.[1] Thus prophetic utterance, with a claim to transcendent authority, voiced an alternative view of economics; the world they voiced featured YHWH, the Lord of the covenant and the guarantor of justice, as the true governor of all social reality, including the economy. The prophetic corpus offers a sustained critique of an economy of extraction that thrived in the kingdoms of Samaria and Jerusalem and in the larger imperial powers that displaced those kingdoms. On the one hand, such subversive speech countered the self-congratulatory governance of Samaria and Jerusalem. On the other hand, such intrusive speech countered the governance of empire that had resulted in despair for the Jewish population.

1. The best general study of the sociology of the prophets is Robert R. Wilson, *Prophecy and Society in Ancient Israel* (Philadelphia: Fortress Press, 1980).

2. When viewed as an interruption of totalism, it is not surprising that prophetic speech is characteristically poetic speech that abounds in playful imagery and metaphor. Settled political-economic power tends to converse in memos that are designed for control without slippage. In order to interrupt the tight world of memos, prophetic speech employs poetry that refuses the logic of hegemony and that generates imagined social possibilities that turn out to be deeply subversive.[2] Such elusive utterance refuses and resists every absolutism. This daring speech, however, does not suggest that it is lacking in social realism, for these prophetic voices evidence an acute practice of social analysis. It is not too much to say, I believe, that these poets rather consistently followed the money in a culture of extraction, for they knew that the ultimate intent of the creator God—expressed in the traditions of covenant—was for a neighborly economy. They knew, further, that performance of a just economy as a real social possibility represented an acute challenge to settled social power, an almost unthinkable alternative that required emancipated speech for its actualization. Thus prophetic utterance is speech that disrupts totalism, is grounded in divine alternative, and is voiced as emancipatory alternative.

3. The prophetic books consist, through a process of editing, of a collection of such utterances that are remembered and treasured and found always again to offer a fresh contemporaneity. We may imagine that such utterances were variously random and ad hoc as socioeconomic crises evoked them. But of course such random and ad hoc utterances, through the canonical process, have been intentionally ordered to give shape and body to the paradigmatic history of Israel. That paradigmatic history, which stands a bit distant from reportable history, consists in (a) the *destruction of Jerusalem* as the epitome of failed chosenness and the descent into the abyss of displacement, deportation, and loss, and (b) the promised *restoration of Jerusalem* and the anticipated homecoming of the displaced to their true homeland. This model of *displacement and restoration* has provided the pattern of the canonical ordering of the prophetic books:

> We can at least come to understand the value and meaning of the way in which distinctive patterns have been imposed upon the

2. See Walter Brueggemann, "Poems vs. Memos," in *Ice Axes for Frozen Seas: A Biblical Theology of Provocation*, ed. Davis Hankins (Waco, TX: Baylor University Press, 2014), 87–113.

> prophetic collections of the canon so that warnings of doom and disaster are always followed by promises of hope and restoration. . . . This centered on the death and rebirth of Israel, interpreted theologically as acts of divine judgment and salvation.[3]

Thus ordered and rendered, the ad hoc utterances now voice a paradigmatic constant that in Judaism concerns *exile and homecoming* and in Christian tradition has been transposed into *crucifixion and resurrection*, which concerns not only Jesus but also the life of the world.

This canonical pattern is evident in the several prophetic books as they characteristically begin in *harsh judgment* and end in *buoyant anticipation of recovery*. When this patterned canonical sequence is seen in terms of our theme of money and possessions, it comes to be expressed as (a) the harsh termination of the practice of economic extraction and (b) the prospect of a new economy that will be funded by divine generosity and practiced as neighborly justice. The entire process from *ad hoc particular utterance* to *canonical pattern* serves to connect divine purpose and actual concrete practice. That connection is uncompromisingly *subversive* of status quo hegemony and compellingly *anticipatory* of an alternative economic possibility outside the structures and strategies of hegemonic regimes.

II

A predominant theme of the prophetic corpus is the conviction that a predatory economy that permits powerful moneyed interests to prey upon the vulnerable peasant population is unsustainable. It is unsustainable when viewed from above, because the Lord of the covenant will not tolerate such practice. It is unsustainable when viewed from below, because a viable social order cannot endure such exploitative conflict and differential. Thus the theme of prophetic judgment is the declaration that an exploitative economy is unsustainable; it will fail and cause the disruption of social order,

3. Roland E. Clements, "Patterns in the Prophetic Canon," in *Canon and Authority: Essays in Old Testament Religion and Theology*, ed. George W. Coats and Burke O. Long (Philadelphia: Fortress Press, 1977), 49, 53.

social well-being, and social institutions.[4] Specifically, it will cause the loss of wealth among the predators who have ruthlessly taken what belongs to others.

It will be remembered that Solomon's united monarchy was disrupted by the tax revolt of 1 Kings 12:1–19. It will be remembered, moreover, that the policies of royal confiscation by the Omri dynasty in the north (Ahab) evoked harsh prophetic judgment against the dynasty (1 Kgs. 21:21–24). But neither regime seemed to learn from tax revolt or harsh prophetic condemnation. As a result, by the eighth century the economy had developed into an unbearable mismatch between the wealth of the *urban elites* in Samaria and Jerusalem and the *vulnerable agricultural peasants* who were reduced to near subsistence existence. By an appeal to Isaiah 5:8–10, D. N. Premnath terms this economic reductionism a process of "latifundialization" whereby the wealthy bought up increasing amounts of agricultural land, thereby denying the peasant population the capacity to live a viable economic life (see Gen. 47:13–26).[5] The wide and widening economic gap between the haves and have-nots evoked prophetic commentary and protest that declared such economic policy and practice unacceptable and unsustainable. We may cite from three eighth-century prophets:

1. Amos, reckoned to be the earliest of these poets, described the unseemly self-indulgence of the leisure class:

> Alas for those who lie on beds of ivory,
> and lounge on their couches,
> and eat lambs from the flock,
> and calves from the stall;
> who sing idle songs to the sound of the harp,
> and like David improvise on instruments of music;
> who drink wine from bowls,
> and anoint themselves with the finest oils.
> (Amos 6:4–6a)

The rhetoric smacks of extravagant expenditure of resources for amusement and indulgence. The inventory of lambs, calves,

4. See generally Claus Westermann, *Basic Forms of Prophetic Speech* (Philadelphia: Westminster Press, 1967).

5. D. N. Premnath, *Eighth Century Prophets: A Social Analysis* (St. Louis: Chalice Press, 2003).

wine, and finest oil suggests a careless consumerism. The critique is that such venal indulgence has narcotized the wealthy to the social implications of their actions: they "are not grieved over the ruin of Joseph" (v. 6b).

They do not have enough good sense to realize that such a style of life will lead to the "ruin" of the community. The extraction of wealth for self-indulgence blinds them to the destructive implications of the practices. The poignant conclusion comes with the prophetic "therefore" in verse 7:

> Therefore they shall now be the first to go into exile,
> and the revelry of the loungers shall pass away.

The "therefore" is an act of imagination rooted in the logic of deeds-consequences;[6] the poet judges that "revelry" of this kind will result in exile. The prophetic conclusion must have seemed outrageous to those who "innocently" used disproportionate measures of wealth for themselves at the expense of the peasant class that was never given access to such leisure investments. In 8:4–5 Amos describes dishonest commerce—false weights and measures—whereby the poor are cheated in the marketplace. His famous summons to "justice and righteousness" calls attention to the lack of such neighborly actions in an economy that is completely skewed by self-indulgence which has no regard for neighbors who are simply left behind by the privileged with their surplus wealth.

2. Isaiah bears witness to the distorted economy of Jerusalem that had come to be regarded as normal. Jerusalem, the center of the predatory economy, is condemned for its failure to care for all of its population:

> Your princes are rebels
> and companions of thieves.
> Everyone loves a bribe
> and runs after gifts.
> They do not defend the orphan,
> and the widow's cause does not come before them.
> (1:23)

6. The basic study is by Klaus Koch, "Is There a Doctrine of Retribution in the Old Testament?," in *Theodicy in the Old Testament*, ed. James L. Crenshaw (Philadelphia: Fortress Press, 1983), 57–87. On the prophets in particular, see Patrick D. Miller Jr., *Sin and Judgment in the Prophets* (Chico, CA: Scholars Press, 1982).

In a remarkable poem in chapter 2, the poet characterizes the people and the land in their failed practices:

> Indeed they are *full* of diviners from the east
> and of soothsayers like the Philistines,
> and they clasp hands with foreigners.
> Their land is *filled* with silver and gold,
> and there is no end to their treasures;
> their land is *filled* with horses,
> and there is no end to their chariots.
> Their land is *filled* with idols;
> they bow down to the work of their hands,
> to what their own fingers have made.
> (2:6–7; italics added)

The fourfold "full" is quite astonishing:

- full of soothsayers, a reference to predictive capacities to manage and manipulate the socioeconomic scene to certain advantage by penetrating the "mysteries" of holy power
- full of silver and gold, surplus wealth extracted from peasants
- full of horses and chariots, armaments to protect the surplus
- full of idols, self-constructed commodities of legitimacy

The convergence of wealth, arms, and religious icons permits the construction of a pretend society that is completely cut off from socioeconomic reality.

That social analysis is matched, in what follows in the poem, by the anticipation of the intrusion of the Lord of hosts who will, the poet imagines, move decisively and devastatingly against God's own chosen city. The pounding repetition of "against" situates God as an adversary of the chosen elite who have forfeited their status as the chosen:[7]

> For the LORD of hosts has a day
> against all that is proud and lofty,

7. This passage is of acute interest to me for a very particular reason. In September 2001, at the beginning of the semester, I was teaching a course on the book of Isaiah. By September 11 we had come to chap. 2; the class met just as we got news of the attack that day on New York and Washington, DC. The text, with its mention of high towers and fortified walls, seemed to the class and to me so immediately contemporary that it required almost no exposition on that occasion.

against all that is lifted up and high;
against all the cedars of Lebanon,
lofty and lifted up,
and against all the oaks of Bashan;
against all the high mountains,
and against all the lofty hills,
against every high tower,
and against every fortified wall;
against all the ships of Tarshish,
and against all the beautiful craft.
(vv. 12–16)

The poetry is not a prediction. It is rather an act of imagination; the poet invites his listeners to imagine the undoing of an economy that has failed to serve the population well and so has failed the intent of YHWH. The poem is an anticipation of the fate of the economy when seen in the purview of divine expectation. As a consequence, the Lord will "take away" all the extravagant consumer goods of the self-indulgent, socially indifferent elite (3:1, 18–23).

The dark side of such consumerism, inevitably, is the abuse of the poor, for the economy is misdirected away from its proper function:

The LORD enters into judgment
with the elders and princes of his people:
It is you who have devoured the vineyard;
the spoil of the poor is in your houses.
What do you mean by crushing my people,
by grinding the face of the poor? says the Lord GOD of hosts.
(3:14–15)

The poet offers a series of woes, the final one of which is voiced in 10:1–4:

Ah, you who make iniquitous decrees,
who write oppressive statutes,
to turn aside the needy from justice
and to rob the poor of my people of their right,
that widows may be your spoil,
and that you may make the orphans your prey!
What will you do on the day of punishment,
in the calamity that will come from far away?

> To whom will you flee for help,
> and where will you leave your wealth,
> so as not to crouch among the prisoners
> or fall among the slain?
> For all this his anger has not turned away;
> his hand is stretched out still.

The abuse of the needy poor is accomplished by legislation. The practice of greed is not simply in common consumer practice, but in arrangements of loans, interest, credit, mortgages, and taxes. It is this that "robs" the poor. The poet anticipates "calamity" that will come and cause flight that will entail the abandonment of wealth. You cannot take it with you, not only when you die, but also when you must flee for your life and travel light in the face of terror. The poet can imagine the erstwhile wealthy hiding in caves and holes when the threat comes (2:19–21). In such circumstance of unspeakable danger, "idols of silver" and "idols of gold" will be of no value. In an instant all the accumulated commodities will be worthless, and those who have accumulated them will be in jeopardy. The real threats are quite this-worldly in terms of military invasion. In poetry, however, the coming threat is from the holy God who finds the predatory economy unbearable—and will terminate it!

3. The prophet Micah offers two poetic units that imagine the total collapse of the regime that is dependent upon rapacious economic practices. In 2:1–2 the poet connects economic practice directly to the tenth commandment, on coveting:

> Alas for those who devise wickedness
> and evil deeds on their beds!
> When the morning dawns, they perform it,
> because it is in their power.
> They covet fields, and seize them;
> houses, and take them away;
> they oppress householder and house,
> people and their inheritance.

Powerful economic interests buy up and occupy the land of vulnerable peasants. In the next chapter, Micah characterizes the socioeconomic arrangements whereby the powerful—ruler, prophet, priest—collude in economic exploitation (3:9–11a). They do so on the assumption that as God's chosen people, all will be well. They imagine that chosenness gives a free permit to operate a regime of exploitative injustice:

> Yet they lean upon the LORD and say,
> "Surely the LORD is with us!
> No harm shall come upon us."
> (v. 11b)

The poet, however, knows otherwise and issues a mighty "therefore":

> Therefore because of you
> Zion shall be plowed as a field;
> Jerusalem shall become a heap of ruins,
> and the mountain of the house a wooded height.
> (v. 12)

Micah can envision a coming time when proud Jerusalem, in all its Solomonic splendor, will be razed to the ground. Micah has no need to mention the coming Assyrian army. That is all to be inferred. But his listeners could not have missed the point. In this perspective, the prosperous economy of the elites was a bubble soon to burst.

The matter has grown only more acute by the seventh century. Now the threat has morphed from Assyria to Babylon, but the crisis continues unabated. It is as though the practitioners of greedy exploitation are unable to change and so are fated to demise. We cite three prophets from the final days of the Jerusalem establishment:

1. Jeremiah was the prophet most acutely engaged with the issue of failure to obey Torah. The Deuteronomic "if" that states the condition of obedience to Torah figures in Jeremiah's judgment upon Jerusalem:[8]

> If you truly amend your ways and your doings, if you truly act justly one with another, if you do not oppress the alien, the orphan, and the widow, or shed innocent blood in this place, and if you do not go after other gods to your own hurt, then I will

8. On the provisional "if," see Walter Brueggemann, *Solomon: Israel's Ironic Icon of Human Achievement* (Columbia: University of South Carolina Press, 2005), 139–59.

> dwell with you in this place, in the land that I gave of old to your ancestors forever and ever. (Jer. 7:5–7)

In the next verses Jeremiah refers directly to the Decalogue and anticipates that disobedience will lead to displacement:

> Here you are, trusting in deceptive words to no avail. Will you steal, murder, commit adultery, swear falsely, make offerings to Baal, and go after other gods that you have not known, and then come and stand before me in this house, which is called by my name, and say, "We are safe!"—only to go on doing all these abominations? . . . Therefore I will do to the house that is called by my name, in which you trust, and to the place that I gave to you and to your ancestors, just what I did to Shiloh. And I will cast you out of my sight, just as I cast out all your kinsfolk, all the offspring of Ephraim. (vv. 8–10, 14–15)

That prose analysis is given poetic articulation in 5:26–28:

> For scoundrels are found among my people;
> they take over the goods of others.
> Like fowlers they set a trap;
> they catch human beings.
> Like a cage full of birds,
> their houses are full of treachery;
> therefore they have become great and rich,
> they have grown fat and sleek.
> They know no limits in deeds of wickedness;
> they do not judge with justice
> the cause of the orphan, to make it prosper,
> and they do not defend the rights of the needy.

The term rendered "scoundrel" is *rš'*, the "wicked" or the "guilty," that is, those who violate Torah and disrupt the common good. Their actions consist in confiscation, so that they "trap" human beings the way birds are trapped. And because of such actions, they have become "great and rich," "fat and sleek." The indictment concerns "foolish senseless people" (v. 21) who do not fear God (v. 24), who imagine they are free to do what they want. What they want (and must have!), moreover, is the control of a skewed economy so that vulnerable people are reduced to captured commodities. Thus the scoundrels are not outlaws, rogues; rather they are those who manipulate the economy in devious ways to their own advantage. The poet has no doubt that their great wealth is a result of their treacherous exploitation of those caught in their economic manipulations like helpless birds in a cage. It is wealth secured at the expense of the community!

Because the scoundrels (the guilty!) have no restraint, the inevitable outcome of their practices is injustice toward orphans and the needy whose legitimate rights in the economy are disregarded. It could have been otherwise. These same powerful people could have managed the economy to cause the vulnerable to prosper. But they did not, and so they are ready candidates for punishment and retribution. The argument is an appeal to Torah justice; but the specificity of the argument concerns the suffering of the vulnerable.

The failed king is indicted in the poetry of Jeremiah 22:13–15:

> Woe to him who builds his house by unrighteousness,
> and his upper rooms by injustice;
> who makes his neighbors work for nothing,
> and does not give them their wages;
> who says, "I will build myself a spacious house
> with large upper rooms,"
> and who cuts out windows for it,
> paneling it with cedar,
> and painting it with vermilion.
> Are you a king
> because you compete in cedar?

The woe pronounced against the king indicates that huge trouble is coming upon king and city. The indictment concerns *unrighteousness* and *injustice,* that is, the failure to enhance the common good for all the people of the realm. On the one hand, the king is guilty of economic extravagance in the form of large upper rooms, windows, and cedar paneling. On the other hand, the indictment concerns failure to pay workers; the self-indulgent showiness of the royal enterprise depends upon cheap labor. Adequate responsible governance, by contrast, is the practice of justice and righteousness for the poor, a practice credited here to Josiah, the father of the king. The king is a shabby contrast to his good father:

> But your eyes and heart
> are only on your dishonest gain,

> for shedding innocent blood,
> and for practicing oppression and violence.
> (v. 17)

In poetic idiom the prophet does a shrewd economic analysis and knows very well that low wages for cheap labor cannot be the basis for a viable society. Like so much of Jeremiah, these verses have an acute ring of contemporaneity for us, as we struggle in the midst of huge concentrations of wealth to raise the minimum wage to ten dollars an hour. The old and recurring temptation to ground *prosperity for some* in *the cheap labor of others* is enough, says the poet, to bring an enormous woe on the city.

2. The themes of Jeremiah are echoed by the minor prophet Habakkuk. It is astonishing that in the long history of Christian theology, Habakkuk 2:4 has been prominent because it highlights "the righteous [who] live by their faith," but no notice has been taken of the very next verse:

> Moreover, wealth is treacherous;
> the arrogant do not endure.
> They open their throats as wide as Sheol;
> like Death they never have enough.
> They gather all nations for themselves,
> and collect all peoples as their own.

The verse concerns trust in wealth rather than reliance on the vision noted in the preceding verses:

> If the fainthearted person does not trust the vision, if he considers it unreliable and thus refuses to walk in it, how much more will wealth prove deceitful to the one who seeks life by pursuing it? The arrogant man who reaches for wealth and power with insatiable, unbridled lust will not reach his goal. Thus the reliability of the vision is set over against the deceitfulness of wealth and power.[9]

It is mind-boggling to think how different the history of theology might have been if the Reformation accent on verse 4 had been connected to the substance of verse 5.

9. J. J. M. Roberts, *Nahum, Habakkuk, and Zephaniah*, Old Testament Library (Louisville, KY: Westminster/John Knox Press, 1991), 116–17.

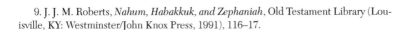

It is, moreover, no wonder that verse 5 is followed by a series of woes in verses 6–19 that detail the sure outcome of reliance on "treacherous" wealth:

- Big trouble to come on those who "heap up" what is not their own. The language concerns pledge (collateral), credit, booty, and plunder, culminating in violence (vv. 6–8).
- Big trouble to come on those who acquire "evil gain" (v. 9). The phrase "gain by violence" is the same phrase we have found in Proverbs.
- Big trouble to come on a town (Jerusalem in context?) built "by bloodshed," that is, by exploitative economic practices (v. 12).

The series of woes makes clear that public policy and practice not grounded in faith, not implemented by "the righteous," will lead to disaster. The continuing capacity of Christian interpretation to separate the theology of verse 4 from the materiality of verses 5–19 is an indication of how poorly the tradition has engaged the crucial economic dimension of the horizon of faith.

3. Because the prophet Ezekiel is a priest who is occupied with the holiness and glory of God, we may not at the outset expect him to be concerned with economic questions. But of course we must remember that the temple was very much an economic institution that was powerfully at work in the adjudication of money and possessions. We may notice two quite remarkable passages in which this priestly voice attends to the economy. In 18:5–18, the prophet traces three generations of "a man," likely a king. In all three cases—the righteous man (vv. 5–9), the unrighteous son (vv. 10–14), and the righteous grandson (vv. 14–18)—the prophet enumerates the three defining acts of righteousness.[10] First there is idolatry; second, sexual affront; third, economics:

> . . . does not oppress anyone, but restores to the debtor his pledge, commits no robbery, gives his bread to the hungry and covers the naked with a garment, does not take advance or accrued interest,

10. See Paul Joyce, *Divine Initiative and Human Response in Ezekiel*, Journal for the Study of the Old Testament Supplement Series 51 (Sheffield: JSOT Press, 1989), 138–40 and passim.

> withholds his hand from iniquity, executes true justice between contending parties . . . (vv. 7–8)

> . . . oppresses the poor and needy, commits robbery, does not restore the pledge, lifts up his eyes to the idols, commits abomination, takes advance or accrued interest . . . (vv. 12–13)

> . . . does not wrong anyone, exacts no pledge, commits no robbery, but gives his bread to the hungry and covers the naked with a garment, withholds his hand from iniquity, takes no advance or accrued interest . . . (vv. 16–17)

It is respect for and justice toward the neighbor in economic matters that receives the fullest exposition in each of the three cases; economic practice becomes one of the defining norms of life-giving righteousness. These three statements contain a surprising element of specificity about how money is managed equitably or not. Such equity in economics is decisive for the life of the righteous-innocent and the death of the wicked-guilty.

Perhaps most surprising of all is the indictment of Jerusalem in the long recital of chapter 16, in which the city is treated under the metaphor of Sodom. Given Ezekiel's preoccupation with "abomination" and his utilization of sexuality in a metaphorical way, we might expect Sodom would be indicted for sexual misconduct.[11] In fact, however, the guilt of Sodom is economic extravagance at the expense of the poor and needy: "This was the guilt of your sister Sodom: she and her daughters had pride, excess of food, and prosperous ease, but did not aid the poor and needy" (16:49).

It is this, says the prophet, that amounts to an abomination and that results in "removal." Given all the adrenaline used in the church on issues of sexuality, it is astonishing that we have not considered the economic sin of Sodom. Such neglect suggests the willful refusal of the church to recognize the centrality of economy for the practice of fidelity.

11. I do not suggest that the affront of Sodom in the narrative of Genesis 18–19 is one of sexuality, even though that is a popular assumption. The real affront of the narrative is wholesale violence. Thus the allusion to the narrative in Ezekiel may attest that "prosperous ease" and neglect of the poor in fact constitute an act of violence not unlike the violence of Sodom; see Isa. 1:10, where a parallel allusion to the Sodom narrative is voiced.

III

The rhetoric of the prophets in the sixth century after the destruction of Jerusalem continues to be concerned with matters of indictment and sentence for those who have violated Torah and sought to muster a life of prosperity through autonomy. Only now the rhetoric has been redirected; it no longer concerns Israel, who has been defeated. Now it addresses the arrogance of the nations who in their military success and economic prosperity imagine that they are self-sufficient and guaranteed to perpetuity. Their great affront, as Donald Gowan has noted, is their arrogance, which fails to recognize the limits on grandeur that are imposed by the reality of YHWH: "*Hybris* as we have defined its Old Testament sense is full rebellion against God; the effort to take control of the world and all of life and to do without any God but oneself."[12]

In the face of such imperial arrogance, the rhetoric of the prophets comes like a voice from elsewhere. Claiming to be rooted in the authority of YHWH the creator, the rhetoric breaks in upon the totalism of empire and anticipates the collapse and demise of empires in a way that is of course beneficial to Israel. Among the several dimensions of such demise, loss of ill-gotten wealth is noted. We may notice that in Isaiah 47:6 Babylon is condemned because it "showed no mercy." The entire covenantal-prophetic tradition is committed to the notion that mercy willed by YHWH sets a limit on predatory wealth. In the preexilic prophets, such mercy is toward the poor and needy. In the exilic texts, such mercy is toward vulnerable Israel. In both cases, mercy willed by YHWH precludes the seizure of wealth and the limitless, unrestrained practice of power. Such desire for wealth, say the prophets, is insatiable. Thus the prophetic word intrudes into regimes of self-sufficiency:

1. Jeremiah anticipates the demise of Babylon's predatory wealth:

> Come against her from every quarter;
> open her granaries;
> pile her up like heaps of grain, and destroy her utterly;
> let nothing be left of her.

12. Donald E. Gowan, *When Man Becomes God: Humanism and* Hybris *in the Old Testament* (Pittsburgh: Pickwick Press, 1975), 127.

Kill all her bulls,
let them go down to the slaughter.
Alas for them, their day has come,
the time of their punishment!
(Jer. 50:26–27)

King Nebuchadnezzar . . .
. . . .
has filled his belly with my delicacies.
. . . .
Babylon shall become a heap of ruins,
a den of jackals,
an object of horror and of hissing,
without inhabitant.
(51:34, 37)

2. Isaiah anticipates the complete reversal of Babylon:

Come down and sit in the dust, virgin daughter Babylon!
Sit on the ground without a throne,
daughter Chaldea!
For you shall no more be called
tender and delicate.
Take the millstone and grind meal,
remove your veil,
strip off your robe, uncover your legs,
pass through the rivers.
Your nakedness shall be uncovered,
and your shame shall be seen.
(Isa. 47:1–3)[13]

Like every such empire, Babylon had attached its religious passion to silver and gold:

Those who lavish gold from the purse,
and weigh out silver in the scales—
they hire a goldsmith, who makes it into a god;
then they fall down and worship!
They lift it to their shoulders, they carry it,
they set it in its place, and it stands there;

13. The imagery is one of slavery; thus the poem envisions a radical reversal of social roles in which the nobility of Babylon is abruptly reduced to slavery.

it cannot move from its place.
If one cries to it, it does not answer
or save anyone from trouble.
(46:6–7)

The gods of silver and gold never mandate mercy. But of course such gods cannot save. The regime that has chosen gold and silver to the neglect of mercy, a "lover of pleasures," cannot be sustained:

Now therefore hear this, you lover of pleasures,
who sit securely,
who say in your heart,
"I am, and there is no one besides me;
I shall not sit as a widow
or know the loss of children"—
both these things shall come upon you
in a moment, in one day;
the loss of children and widowhood
shall come upon you in full measure,
in spite of your many sorceries
and the great power of your enchantments.
(47:8–9)

3. Ezekiel can imagine the loss of wealth in Tyre, emblem of the great commercial city:

Your riches, your wares, your merchandise,
your mariners and your pilots,
your caulkers, your dealers in merchandise,
and all your warriors within you,
with all the company
that is with you,
sink into the heart of the seas
on the day of your ruin.
(Ezek. 27:27)[14]

You were in Eden, the garden of God;
every precious stone was your covering,
carnelian, chrysolite, and moonstone,

14. See the extensive and persuasive exposition of this text by Ellen F. Davis, *Biblical Prophecy: Perspectives for Christian Theology, Discipleship, and Ministry*, Interpretation (Louisville, KY: Westminster John Knox Press, 2014), 119–33.

beryl, onyx, and jasper,
sapphire, turquoise, and emerald;
and worked in gold were your settings
and your engravings.
. . . .
In the abundance of your trade
you were filled with violence, and you sinned;
so I cast you as a profane thing from the mountain of God,
and the guardian cherub drove you out
from among the stones of fire.
. . . .
By the multitude of your iniquities,
in the unrighteousness of your trade,
you profaned your sanctuaries.
So I brought out fire from within you;
it consumed you,
and I turned you to ashes on the earth
in the sight of all who saw you.
(28:13, 16, 18)

The future would, moreover, not be different for Egypt, which also stands under the threat of coming judgment:

A sword shall come upon Egypt,
and anguish shall be in Ethiopia,
when the slain fall in Egypt,
and its wealth is carried away,
and its foundations are torn down.
(30:4)

Arrogance that manages wealth against the common good will lead to loss!

IV

Both the eighth- and seventh-century prophets in Israel-Judah and the sixth-century prophets concerned with empires were vindicated by historical outcomes. The regimes of greedy confiscation did come to an end. Such regimes regularly turned out to be unsustainable, whether in Jerusalem or Nineveh or Babylon or Tyre. The old covenantal connection between *Torah obedience* and *prosperity* was true, even for regimes that knew nothing of Israel's Torah. The intrusive prophetic voices that regimes wanted to silence turned out to be truth tellers.

But there is more truth to be told! It is not often enough recognized that prophetic speech and therefore prophetic ministry is not fully defined by such warning, indictment, and anticipated demise. The canonical structure of the prophetic books provides that before they finish, the prophets segue to new possibility beyond demise and abyss. That new possibility comes as divine promise, as a resolve for restoration.[15] It is a promise that summons to ecstatic hope. One dimension of a promised future of well-being is the gift of new economic resources that will be completely in contrast to the present failed condition of despair and vulnerability. Prophetic anticipation concerns restoration of material well-being in the concrete sphere of lived history or, as we say, "on earth as it is in heaven."

The theme of restored wealth and well-being is recurrent; see Isaiah 54:11–13; Jeremiah 31:12; Ezekiel 34:13–14; 36:29; Haggai 2:7–9; Zechariah 14:14. The wealth promised to restored Israel is to be given to the faithful remnant that intends full Torah obedience. Thus while the new wealth is freely given by God (confiscated from the nations), it is to be given to a community of obedience.

The fullest, most important articulation of this future possibility guaranteed by divine promise is in the exultant poetry of Isaiah 60–62. These chapters promise a full and glorious restoration of Jerusalem as the site of YHWH's presence and as the restored home of the Jewish remnant. We may in particular notice two remarkable statements about the coming economy of Jerusalem. The poet imagines a great procession home once Israel has been freed from Babylonian restraint. The procession will include sons and daughters, all the heirs to the promise! Beyond that it will include abundance and wealth carried by a caravan of camels laden with precious metals, followed by flocks and herds, all the signifiers of money in that ancient economy:

> Lift up your eyes and look around;
> they shall gather together, they come to you;
> your sons shall come from far away,

15. See Claus Westermann, *Prophetic Oracles of Salvation in the Old Testament* (Louisville, KY: Westminster/John Knox Press, 1991), and Walter Brueggemann, *Reality, Grief, Hope: Three Urgent Prophetic Tasks* (Grand Rapids: Eerdmans, 2014), 89–128.

and your daughters shall be carried on their nurses' arms.
Then you shall see and be radiant;
your heart shall thrill and rejoice,
because the abundance of the sea shall be brought to you,
the wealth of the nations shall come to you.
A multitude of camels shall cover you,
the young camels of Midian and Ephah;
all those from Sheba shall come.
They shall bring gold and frankincense,
and shall proclaim the praise of the Lord.
All the flocks of Kedar shall be gathered to you,
the rams of Nebaioth shall minister to you;
they shall be acceptable on my altar,
and I will glorify my glorious house.

(60:4–7)

This is to be a showy procession! No reason for such abundance is voiced. No condition is stipulated. The destruction of Jerusalem had featured the confiscation of Jerusalem's wealth by military procedure. Now the process is reversed. Jerusalem will become a busy venue for commerce, so that trading centers and ports of entry will operate 24/7 to receive the lavish wealth that will pour in:

For the coastlands shall wait for me,
the ships of Tarshish first,
to bring your children from far away,
their silver and gold with them,
for the name of the Lord your God,
and for the Holy One of Israel,
because he has glorified you.
Foreigners shall build up your walls,
and their kings shall minister to you;
for in my wrath I struck you down,
but in my favor I have had mercy on you.
Your gates shall always be open;
day and night they shall not be shut,
so that nations shall bring you their wealth,
with their kings led in procession.

(vv. 9–11)[16]

16. The reference to the "ships of Tarshish" in v. 9 is likely an allusion to Tarshish in 2:16. The two references together are typical of the book of Isaiah, which can take an image of judgment in the early part of the book and retrieve it as a sign of hope in the

The imagery in 61:5–6 anticipates a renewal as the community that has been shamed before the nations now will be glorified and honored by the nations; "foreigners" and "strangers" will be cast as menial labor to free Israel for priestly performance and for the sheer enjoyment of wealth. More than a restitution of what was lost, now their wealth will be a "double portion," signifying the splendor of Jerusalem and the temple:

> Strangers shall stand and feed your flocks,
> foreigners shall till your land and dress your vines;
> but you shall be called priests of the LORD,
> you shall be named ministers of our God;
> you shall enjoy the wealth of the nations,
> and in their riches you shall glory.
> Because their shame was double,
> and dishonor was proclaimed as their lot,
> therefore they shall possess a *double portion*;
> everlasting joy shall be theirs.
>
> (61:5–7)[17]

It is all gift! It is all unearned wealth! The recovery is deeply rooted in fidelity on God's part; it is manifested fully and without embarrassment or explanation materially!

V

We may recognize that both the *stringent judgments* voiced by the earlier prophets and the *ecstatic anticipations* of the sixth-century prophets are cast as poetry. They are verbal (or written, in the case of Ezekiel) declarations that intend to contradict the world that is immediately in front of the listening community. Thus the *poetry of judgment* contradicts the congratulatory self-sufficiency, in turn, of Jerusalem and of the empires. That poetry asserts that unjust

latter part. Thus in Isa. 2 the ships of Tarshish signify arrogance; in chap. 60 these same ships concern the great wealth to be given to Jerusalem.

17. The "double portion" in chap. 61 may be an allusion back to 40:2, though the wording is different. More interesting is that the same term for "double portion" (*mišneh*) is used in Job 42:10 for YHWH's restoration of Job. That parallel may merit more study, for it suggests "twice as much" for restored Israel, even as it was for restored Job.

wealth cannot be sustained. The *promissory poetry* contradicts the despair of centralized extraction and asserts that such policy and practice will, soon or late, yield to the resolve of YHWH. It is all poetry. This emancipated rhetoric refuses establishment restraint and dares to link the material reality of life to the rule of YHWH, the very resolve that moneyed interests characteristically want to dismiss as fantasy.

These superb acts of imagination, in the traditioning process, have been woven into a sustained counternarrative, a narrative that runs counter to the dominant narrative of the Jerusalem elite or the dominant narrative of empire. This counternarrative refuses the obdurate *denial* of preexilic Jerusalem and imagines the inescapable failure of an economy of extraction. The counternarrative refuses, in like manner, the *despair* of the exilic community that could see no way out of the imperial grip.[18] This counternarrative thus pivots on the *loss* of ill-gotten, ill-managed self-sufficient wealth and on the *restoration* of wealth that will fund the abundant life intended by the God of Israel. These two accents on *loss and restoration* defy monetary realism, a defiance legitimated, in poetic discourse, by the God who wills and presides over an alternative economy.

In reading such a sustained act of imagination, we do not fully understand how the several poetic pieces, likely delivered in an ad hoc and random way, were woven into a coherent communal, canonical vision. Nor do we know how it was that these several poetic traditions could turn abruptly from the *poetry of loss* to the *poetry of possibility*. We can only observe that the poetry did become canon. We can see, moreover, that the *imagination of loss* was indeed transposed into the *imagination of restoration*. These two interpretive maneuvers are defining for the prophetic corpus. They may reflect shrewd discernment rooted in a deeply held ideology that refused the facts on the ground; or they may be the fruit of the Spirit who blows where it will. Or perhaps it is both! Whether *ideological courage* or *Spirit-led conviction*, or both, the outcome is a way to live differently in the world of money and possessions. Worship of this God is more than sacrifice that so easily became in Israel (as elsewhere) an act of commodity bargaining. Life in this covenant is more than commodity:

18. See Brueggemann, *Reality, Grief, Hope*, 89–128.

> For I desire steadfast love and not sacrifice,
> the knowledge of God rather than burnt offerings.
> (Hos. 6:6)[19]

Something decisive happens to money and possessions when they are held closely in the sphere of steadfast love and knowledge of God.

19. A note will suffice on the book of Daniel, which is not quite to be reckoned among the prophetic books. The kingdom in which Daniel functions as a civil servant is marked by its extravagant, exhibitionist wealth (see 3:1–7; 5:1–4). In the anticipated struggle among the kingdoms of the world, disputes over money and wealth were commonplace (11:8, 24, 43). But Daniel, the model Jew, would have no part in this dispute over wealth. He refuses the seductions of the wealthy kingdom (1:8–20; see 10:3). As a result of such resistance, Daniel maintains the purity of his Jewish identity. One of the outcomes of his refusal and resistance is that Daniel could see clearly and speak truthfully beyond the distortions of the kingdom. Without being seduced by the kingdom, he could counsel King Nebuchadnezzar: "Therefore, O king, may my counsel be acceptable to you: atone for your sins with righteousness, and your iniquities with mercy to the oppressed, so that your prosperity may be prolonged" (4:27).

Daniel understood, in his sustained, undefiled, and uncompromised Jewish identity, that governance and prosperity depend upon righteousness and mercy to the oppressed. He understood, amid an economy of extraction, that elemental Torah requirement upon which all power finally depends. For an instant, we are told, after his season of insanity, Nebuchadnezzar was persuaded of that summons to justice and truth: "Now I, Nebuchadnezzar, praise and extol and honor the King of heaven, for all his works are truth, and his ways are justice; and he is able to bring low those who walk in pride" (4:37).

CHAPTER 9

The Five Scrolls

Scripts of Loss and Hope, Commodity and Agency

The five festal scrolls (Megilloth) are not in any frontal way concerned with our theme of money and possessions. The five scrolls are variously arranged in different sequences, so the order is mutable. In each usage, of course, reasons are given for a particular order.[1]

Ruth: Feast of Weeks
Song of Songs: Passover
Ecclesiastes: Feast of Booths
Lamentations: the Ninth of Ab
Esther: Purim

These festivals mark major points in abiding memory, moments of loss, risks, and joy that belong to Judaism and are rooted more or less in known occasions. In the Christian canon, the five scrolls are distributed across the larger canon in an effort to locate them historically. In neither case—liturgical or historical—do we expect matters of money and possessions to be the defining issue of the scrolls. It is clear enough nonetheless that even when the literature has other agendas, biblical faith cannot and does not avoid the defining power

1. See Donn F. Morgan, *Between Text & Community: The "Writings" in Canonical Interpretation* (Minneapolis: Fortress Press, 1990).

of economics for all of life. Thus inevitably matters of money and possessions appear in these scrolls in compelling ways.

I

The story of Ruth is a delicate transaction between a have and a have-not. It is dominated by economic matters, but those matters are made more complex by the fact that the subtheme of sexuality pervades the narrative, so that the economic contact between Boaz and Ruth is set in a patriarchal society where the man, especially "a man of substance," can define the relationship when the person without resources is a woman (2:1). Thus have–have-not is reinforced by man-woman, but we must not permit the theme of sexuality and sexual power to cause us to disregard economic aspects of the narrative.

The problematic of the story is set in 1:9, where Naomi hopes for the "security" of each of her daughters-in-law: "The LORD grant that you may find security, each of you in the house of your husband" (1:9; see 3:1). The term rendered "security" is *mənûḥâ*, a restful safe place.[2] Phyllis Trible notes the risky and bold action of Ruth: "Her choice makes no sense. It forsakes the security of a mother's house for insecurity abroad. It forfeits possible fullness in Moab for certain emptiness in Judah. It relinquishes the familiar for the strange."[3]

Boaz is a very powerful actor, a prominent wealthy landowner. He is accustomed to giving direction to his workforce as well as giving decisive guidance to community elders. Thus his administration of field and threshing floor matter to the narrative. Of special interest is the fourfold use of "acquire" (*qanaḥ*):

> Then Boaz said, "The day you *acquire* the field from the hand of Naomi, you are also *acquiring* Ruth the Moabite, the widow of the dead man, to maintain the dead man's name on his inheritance." . . . So when the next-of-kin said to Boaz, "*Acquire* it for

2. Tod Linafelt, "Ruth," in *Ruth and Esther*, by Tod Linafelt and Timothy K. Beal, Berit Olam (Collegeville, MN: Liturgical Press, 1999), 10, notes that "security" is regularly an alternative to wandering. But not here; here Ruth must wander in order to find rest.

3. Phyllis Trible, *God and the Rhetoric of Sexuality*, Overtures to Biblical Theology (Philadelphia: Fortress Press, 1978), 172.

> yourself," he took off his sandal. Then Boaz said to the elders and all the people, "Today you are witnesses that I have *acquired* from the hand of Naomi all that belonged to Elimelech and all that belonged to Chilion and Mahlon. I have also *acquired* Ruth the Moabite, the wife of Mahlon, to be my wife, to maintain the dead man's name on his inheritance, in order that the name of the dead may not be cut off from his kindred and from the gate of his native place; today you are witnesses." (4:5–10; italics added)

Samuel Adams notes that the attention to the marriage in this narrative concerns economic matters:

> Economic motivations seem to drive the behavior of the "next-of-kin" (Heb. *gō'ēl*) in Ruth 4. . . . When Boaz announces to the next-of-kin that whoever exercises the right to purchase Elimelech's hereditary land will also "acquire" Ruth (4:5), this unnamed fellow declines: "'I cannot redeem it for myself *without damaging my own inheritance*. Take my right of redemption yourself, for I cannot redeem it'" (v. 6; emphasis added). . . . We cannot avoid the conclusion that inheritance concerns lie at the heart of both refusals.[4]

Both acquisitions are reckoned to be purchases. Because Boaz is generous toward Ruth and she "finds favor" with him, it is evident that his acquisition of a wife is not merely an economic matter. Boaz is also capable of generous fidelity that he extends toward Ruth. His generosity is explicitly material: "He gave me these six measures of barley, for he said, 'Do not go back to your mother-in-law empty-handed'" (3:17).

Ruth is contrasted with Boaz in every way. She has no field of her own. She goes to the threshing floor that she does not control. She is committed to gleaning, because she must secure by her own effort the wherewithal to live.

Tod Linafelt has pointed out that while Boaz is very much in charge in the public processes of chapters 2 and 4, Boaz is "clearly out of his element" in private with Ruth.[5] Thus the narrative finally cannot be reduced to an economic transaction between a have and a have-not, not even to a patriarchal transaction between a man

4. Samuel L. Adams, *Social and Economic Life in Second Temple Judea* (Louisville, KY: Westminster John Knox Press, 2014), 54.

5. Private correspondence. I am grateful to Tod Linafelt for his acute discernment of the economic issues in this narrative.

and a woman. In fact the narrative takes a surprising turn because the characters refuse to be stereotyped by economic or social roles. As a result, Ruth takes an initiative in chapter 3, and in the end the future is opened to this woman who began the narrative with no "security." She has indeed gained security! The narrative surely knows the force of economic reality; in the end, however, it will not let economic reality define the relationship of Boaz and Ruth that generates the future. That surprising generativity emerges because Ruth is a self-respecting agent in her own life and she takes responsibility for her future. At the same time, the narrative makes room for the mysterious but powerful work of YHWH that is recognized by the characters:

> NAOMI: "The LORD grant that you may find security" (1:9).
> BOAZ: "May the LORD reward you for your deeds, and may you have a full reward from the LORD, the God of Israel, under whose wings you have come for refuge!" (2:12).
> NAOMI: "Blessed be he by the LORD, whose kindness has not forsaken the living or the dead!" (2:20).
> THE WOMEN: "Blessed be the LORD, who has not left you this day without next-of-kin; and may his name be renowned in Israel!" (4:14).

We may judge that the flat power of money and possessions is relativized in the narrative in two ways: *the readiness of Ruth to be an active agent* in her own history, and *the hidden work of YHWH*, who does not conform to economic patterns of power. Good outcomes become possible when economic matters are subordinated to the deeper facets of dialogic transactions, human and divine.

II

The Song of Songs is preoccupied with love, sweet love. One would not expect economic issues to be voiced in such poetry. Nonetheless, in the climactic (!) statement of chapter 8, this exuberant love poetry alludes to the abandonment of wealth in the pursuit of love. The woman addresses her beloved:

> Set me as a seal on your heart,
> as a seal upon your arm;

for love is strong as death,
passion fierce as the grave.
Its flashes are flashes of fire,
a raging flame.
Many waters cannot quench love,
neither can floods drown it.
(8:6–7a)

And then she indicates the extreme measure of that love, a readiness to forgo all privilege for the sake of love:

If one offered for love
all the *wealth* of one's house,
it would be utterly scorned.
(v. 7b)

She sounds like a young woman of privilege who is prepared to renounce all of her trust funds that are conditioned by her marriage to the right kind of man. She will not be constrained by any such economic factor!

Her speech, however, is interrupted by the objections of her "brothers" who cast themselves as her male protectors in a patriarchal society:

We have a little sister,
and she has no breasts.
What shall we do for our sister,
on the day when she is spoken for?
(v. 8)

They view her as young, naive, and vulnerable. They propose to protect her by building guards for her, utilizing the images of wall and door:

If she is a wall,
we will build upon her a battlement of silver;
but if she is a door,
we will enclose her with boards of cedar.
(v. 9)

The wall will be silver; nothing is too good for their sister; it must be beautiful, and they think in terms of money. The door will be blocked by precious cedar, whereby, says Longman, "They will plug up her opening."[6] They will prevent her lover from having access to her. They aim to foil her passionate eagerness for her lover. They act as if she is being taken advantage of by her lover.

The question arises, why are her brothers so determined to block her overture to her lover? They clearly fear that she will lose or has lost her virginity. Since the brothers think in terms of wealth ("silver" as money, "cedar" as possession), and since she is prepared to scorn wealth, their objection clearly pertains to wealth, the loss or protection of wealth. In that ancient patriarchal world, the loss of virginity outside marriage is an act of shame; it is, moreover, shame that has economic consequences, because such a loss would mean the diminishment of value in the seeking of a bride-price (see Gen. 34:12, Exod. 22:16; 1 Sam. 18:25).[7] That is, she would be less valued by a potential husband and his family, which would, in turn, entail a loss of revenue for the bride's family.[8] The objection by her brothers then is not primarily moral or concerned for her vulnerability and the prospect of her being used or hurt. It is economic! They seek to protect their economic interest by assuring the virginity of their sister. They have reduced her sexuality to tradable commodity.

It is not a surprise that she responds to her brothers with refusal and resistance. She does not need or want their protection from her lover. She does not need a wall of protection because she is a wall; her breasts are "towers." She is no longer the vulnerable little girl they imagine her to be:

> I was a wall,
> and my breasts were like towers;
> then I was in his eyes
> as one who brings peace.
>
> (v. 10)

She takes up a new image, "vineyard."[9] She observes that the vineyard of King Solomon was worth many thousand pieces of

6. Tremper Longman III, *Song of Songs*, New International Commentary on the Old Testament (Grand Rapids: Eerdmans, 2001), 217.

7. As above, I am indebted to Tod Linafelt for this connection.

8. Samuel Adams, *Social and Economic Life*, 29–34, makes clear that the profit from the bride-price goes not to the bride but to her family, in this case to the brothers of the woman.

9. J. Cheryl Exum, *Song of Songs*, Old Testament Library (Louisville, KY: Westminster John Knox Press, 2005), 259–60, suggests that it is her lover who speaks these lines

silver. She grants that much to their economic concerns. But then she asserts that her vineyard (her fecund capacity) is worth much more than that. She answers their commodity concerns but insists that the sexual capacity is greater than their financial worry. She understands, as they do not, that love cannot be priced economically or reduced to commodity. Thus their economic preoccupation is swept aside, as she moves finally to summon her lover, unencumbered by the financial preoccupation of her brothers:

> Make haste, my beloved,
> and be like a gazelle
> or a young stag
> upon the mountains of spices!
> (v. 14)

The brothers had reduced erotic love to a commodity in a way that their sister resisted.

The temptation of her brothers may give us pause. The commoditization of sexuality is a durable temptation. In our time one thinks of course of the common vicious traffic in sex and the big business of recruitment of sex slaves. In more acceptable ways, however, the advertising industry—with reference to cars, beer, cosmetics, or almost anything else—is selling sex that is reduced to commodity, available for purchase with an assurance that such a purchase will bring happiness. The brothers assumed that a big price for their sister would bring them gain. Happily she refuses such commoditization of her genuine human passion.

III

The book of Ecclesiastes offers a voice of realism about money that is based on careful observation. Choon-Leong Seow suggests that the book reflects a commercial society from the perspective of the middle class:

> They are people of the middle classes who are trying to scale the social pyramid without sliding into poverty. They are people

claiming that she is his vineyard. This may be correct, but it does not impact the point made here.

> caught between the impulse to protect and conserve whatever they have (5:12–16; 11:1–2) and the desire to get rich (4:4–6). They are a people caught between the opportunities and risks of a volatile economy.[10]

This social location assures that they are aware of both the risks and the opportunities of the economy that is exceedingly slippery for vulnerable people. We may identify three major accents in this perception of money and possessions:

1. The ultimate judgment of the book is that money, along with wisdom (1:12–18), pleasure (2:1–11), and work (2:18–23), will end in futility ("vanity"). Money is a passing value that will not ultimately make safe. Thus the Preacher has observed abrupt economic reversal, even among those to whom wealth had been given:

> There is an evil that I have seen under the sun, and it lies heavy upon humankind: those to whom God gives wealth, possessions, and honor, so that they lack nothing of all that they desire, yet God does not enable them to enjoy these things, but a stranger enjoys them. This is vanity; it is a grievous ill. (6:1–2)

2. The making of money leaves one dissatisfied and restless, because one never has enough. Thus there is an "addictive pursuit of accumulation" that may take over one's life.[11]

> Again, I saw vanity under the sun: the case of solitary individuals, without sons or brothers; yet there is no end to all their toil, and their eyes are never satisfied with riches. (4:7–8)

> The lover of money will not be satisfied with money; nor the lover of wealth, with gain. This also is vanity. (5:10)

> All human toil is for the mouth, yet the appetite is not satisfied. (6:7)

10. Choon-Leong Seow, "The Social World of Ecclesiastes," in *Money as God? The Monetization of the Market and Its Impact on Religion, Politics, Law, and Ethics*, ed. Jürgen von Hagen and Michael Welker (Cambridge: Cambridge University Press, 2014), 152.

11. Michael Welker, "Kohelet and the Co-evolution of a Monetary Economy and Religion," in von Hagen and Welker, *Money as God?*, 101.

3. Remarkably, even given these acknowledgments, the Preacher also commends the full utilization and enjoyment of one's wealth while it is in hand as a gift from God:[12]

> There is nothing better for mortals than to eat and drink, and find *enjoyment* in their toil. This also, I saw, is from the hand of God; for apart from him who can eat or who can have enjoyment? (2:24–25)

> I know that there is nothing better for them than to be happy and *enjoy* themselves as long as they live; moreover, it is God's gift that all should eat and drink and take pleasure in all their toil. (3:12–13)

> It is fitting to eat and drink and find *enjoyment* in all the toil with which one toils under the sun the few days of the life God gives us; for this is our lot. Likewise all to whom God gives wealth and possessions and whom he enables to enjoy them, and to accept their lot and find enjoyment in their toil—this is the gift of God. (5:18–19)

> There is nothing better for people under the sun than to eat, and drink, and *enjoy* themselves, for this will go with them in their toil through the days of life that God gives them under the sun. (8:15)

> Go, eat your bread with *enjoyment,* and drink your wine with a merry heart; for God has long ago approved what you do. (9:7)

We may note in particular two rather enigmatic statements about money. In 7:12 money is compared to wisdom. Both are from God; both can be acquired. Both are an advantage. But the difference is that "wisdom gives life." The text does not say so, but the inference is that money—given by God, acquired, an advantage—cannot give life:

> Wisdom is as good as an inheritance,
> an advantage to those who see the sun.
> For the protection of wisdom is like the protection of money,

12. R. Norman Whybray, "Qoheleth, Preacher of Joy," *Journal for the Study of the Old Testament* 23 (1982): 87–98, proposes "joy" as a defining theme for the book.

> and the advantage of knowledge is that wisdom gives life to the one
> who possesses it.
>
> (7:11–12)

In 10:19 money is categorized along with feasts and wine as sources of well-being:

> Feasts are made for laughter;
> wine gladdens life,
> and money meets every need.

Except as Seow has shown, the statement about money is ambiguous.[13] The statement might be translated, as with NRSV, "Money meets every need." But it can also be rendered, "Money answers everything," in the sense that "money preoccupies everyone."

This collage of texts offers a rich variety of judgments about money that cannot be reduced to a consistent systematic testimony. In the end, the Preacher takes a commonsense, middle-ground approach to avoid extremes. Thus: "Do not be too righteous, and do not act too wise; why should you destroy yourself? Do not be too wicked, and do not be a fool; why should you die before your time?" (7:16–17).

Perhaps as an echo of that middle-ground common sense, Michael Welker warns against both the deification and the demonization of money:

> The fact that the deification and the plain demonization of money might be a distortion can be seen with reference to the broad spectrum of biblical witnesses. . . . At least 300 references in the biblical traditions offer a more subtle criticism than the mere demonization of the function and the potentials of money and monetary communication, or they use the symbolism of money in order to express complex spiritual processes and practices.[14]

Following that cautionary note, Welker offers a helpful distinction in assessing the several dictums about money in the text of Ecclesiastes:

13. Seow, "Social World of Ecclesiastes," 143.
14. Welker, "Kohelet," 97.

> The supposed contradictions between warnings about human restlessness (directed toward comprehensive existential security) and the encouragement energetically to sow and reap and to enjoy life if this is what God has granted, can be resolved if we learn to distinguish between property as wealth (upon which one can capitalize) and property as (a non-marketable) gift. . . . If we follow it through consistently, then Kohelet's message is significantly more innovative. It demands that human property be distinguished in accordance with that which can be converted into wealth and subjected to the channels of trade and that which (as a non-marketable gift) must be kept separate from the market. Thus under "property as gift" we should not only think of "fields, cattle, and all that I own."[15]

As Welker knows, the distinction cannot be clean and simple; his distinction is nonetheless worth pondering. Some property is readily converted into wealth and channeled into trade and some not. In the end, it comes to property as *possession* and property as *gift*. When property is possession, it can be treated as a commodity for use, buying, and selling. But property as gift resists such deployment. The obvious problem and temptation is that the power of commoditization, in our society, is enormously compelling and without restraint. Given intense market ideology, everything becomes regarded as commodity. With commoditization comes restless accumulation and avarice, without the grace to enjoy as gift. It is when all money and possessions have been converted from gift to commodity that the Preacher can declare that it is all vanity.

Finally we may notice the enigmatic saying in 11:1 that seems to encourage generosity and charity:

> Send out your bread upon the waters,
> for after many days you will get it back.
> (11:1)

James Crenshaw suggests the statement encourages making risky maritime investments.[16] But the saying seems to suggest that a generous giver will receive in kind: "By sharing sustenance, one will

15. Ibid., 103.
16. James L. Crenshaw, *Ecclesiastes*, Old Testament Library (Philadelphia: Westminster Press, 1987), 178–79.

invariably receive the same treatment, the same gifts. Hospitality breeds hospitality. . . . 'Good things don't get lost' is precisely Qoheleth's point."[17]

By the time he finishes, the Preacher attests that money has an inscrutable dimension that cannot be readily decoded. It is linked to the God who gives; it is compelling in its power; it is tricky and unpredictable. His teaching is that we should be under no illusion but recognize money for what it is, without being seduced into any ideological explanation of it. It is in a context of "futility" that the reader is invited to enjoyment of the gifts of life while they last. But it is always "while they last," and therefore we are not to esteem the gifts for more than they offer. The gift itself has limited currency and finally we are pushed back to the giver:

> Remember your creator. (12:1)
>
> Fear God, and keep his commandments. (12:13)

"Bottom line" is not clear

IV

The book of Lamentations is linked to the ninth day of Ab, the occasion of the destruction of the Jerusalem temple. In Christian canonical order, it is linked to the prophet Jeremiah. Either way, Lamentations is preoccupied with the loss of Jerusalem and the abiding pain that continues to be emitted from that loss. The book, in five poems, is an artistic articulation of loss and pain. Kathleen O'Connor, Tod Linafelt, and Nancy Lee have probed the way in which this poetic articulation is a great resource for survival and the maintenance of communal identity when all visible props for communal identity have been lost.[18]

The book of Lamentations has no single explanatory assumption about the loss. Early in the poetry, the old connection of deeds

17. William P. Brown, *Ecclesiastes*, Interpretation (Louisville, KY: Westminster John Knox Press, 2000), 102.

18. Kathleen M. O'Connor, *Lamentations and the Tears of the World* (Maryknoll, NY: Orbis Books, 2002); Tod Linafelt, *Surviving Lamentations: Catastrophe, Lament, and Protest in the Afterlife of a Biblical Book* (Chicago: University of Chicago Press, 2000); Nancy C. Lee, *Lyrics of Lament: From Tragedy to Transformation* (Minneapolis: Fortress Press, 2010).

and consequences is assumed, whereby the loss is due punishment for the transgression of Israel. That explanation, however, is found to be inadequate, so that questions are asked both about YHWH's reliability and about Babylonian capricious action in the destruction. The poetry, however, is not primarily explanatory. It seeks rather to give voice to pain concerning elemental loss.

And so it must enumerate losses, among which are money and possessions. Two general points are clear about the loss of money and valuable possessions. On the one hand, the loss of what is precious concerns the splendor of the city but more particularly the splendor of the temple, both its treasure and its brilliant decor. Thus we know that the Babylonian occupiers seized the precious wealth of the temple (2 Kgs. 24:13; 25:13–17; Jer. 52:17–23). On the other hand, it is clear that the loss of such commodity value was not only material but also symbolic, for it signified the honor, beauty, and status of Israel, much as the wealth of Job vouched for his social position. We may notice several allusions in the poetry to the loss of what is of value. In Lamentations 1:7–11, the poetry three times uses the term *ḥmd*, which is rendered "precious things" and "treasure":

> Jerusalem remembers,
> in the days of her affliction and wandering,
> all the *precious things*
> that were hers in the days of old.
> When her people fell into the hand of the foe,
> and there was no one to help her,
> the foe looked on mocking
> over her downfall.
> . . . .
> Enemies have stretched out their hands
> over all her *precious things*;
> she has even seen the nations
> invade her sanctuary,
> those whom you forbade
> to enter your congregation.
>
> All her people groan
> as they search for bread;
> they trade their *treasures* for food
> to revive their strength.

Look, O Lord, and see
how worthless I have become
(1:7, 10–11; italics added)

The usage is of special interest because the term is the same used for the "desire" of the first couple in the garden (Gen. 3:6) and in the tenth commandment, where it is usually rendered as "covet" (Exod. 20:17). The term refers to objects that are especially treasured, that evoke desire and so take on great value. In these verses, the reference seems to be to treasures of the city and the temple. Tod Linafelt notes that the usage is open to some ambiguity:

> The connotation of the Hebrew word used here for "precious things" . . . is debatable. It may mean expensive or treasured possessions, as it does in 1 Kings 20:6 and Joel 4:5, or it may mean children, as it does in Hosea 9:16. One need not decide between these two connotations as the poetry is able to carry both simultaneously. . . . Given the poetic strategy of personification, both connotations are likely on the horizon of the poetry of Lamentations 1 as well.[19]

Elsewhere in Lamentations the loss of children is voiced (2:30; 4:10). Here it seems more likely to refer to valuable commodity. Either way, the point is that Israel now can only remember these treasures and grieve their loss. The same term is used in 2:4, where NRSV renders "all in whom we took pride," but it might better be "all that attracted the eye."

The same ambiguity about valuable commodity and children is voiced in 4:1–2:

How the gold has grown dim,
how the pure gold is changed!
The sacred stones lie scattered
at the head of every street.

The precious children of Zion,
worth their weight in fine gold—
how they are reckoned as earthen pots,
the work of a potter's hands!

19. Linafelt, *Surviving Lamentations*, 40.

Verse 1 is focused on a valuable commodity (gold). The phrase "sacred stones" makes clear this concerns temple ornamentation. But because gold in fact does not tarnish or grow dim, the inconceivable has happened: what could not be tarnished has been tarnished.[20]

But verse 2 opens up the other side of the ambiguity and seems more likely to refer to the children, though the matter is not as clear as the English translation suggests:

> Or the dimmed gold may evoke the children's dimmed future. The lives of the "precious children of Zion, who were weighed as pure gold" (using yet a third synonym for gold) are tarnished and scattered about (4:2). Precious children, once reckoned like pure gold, the community's glittering, shining wealth, its future security, are now as worthless pottery, no more valuable than a cheap jar, easily broken and disposable. How the gold has grown dim.[21]

What follows is a description of cruel mothers who devalue the children as a broken pot may be scorned:

> Zion's children have become worthless, and Zion treats them with even less care than the most despised animals show their offspring. Even jackals nurse their children, but Zion is as cruel as ostriches who are notorious for neglect of their young. . . . Indeed, the terse economical description creates a world of imagination made more horrible by its sparseness.[22]

The poetry is filled with the particulars of loss: "departed majesty" (1:6), "splendor" (2:1), "perfection of beauty" (2:15), "delicacies" (4:5), "inheritance" (5:2), "crown" (5:16). The contrast between a lovely, graceful life and desperate deprivation is caught in this poignant imagery:

> Her princes were purer than snow,
> whiter than milk;
> their bodies were more ruddy than coral,
> their hair like sapphire.

20. O'Connor, *Lamentations*, 61.
21. Ibid.
22. Ibid.

Now their visage is blacker than soot;
they are not recognized in the streets.
Their skin has shriveled on their bones;
it has become as dry as wood.
(4:7–8)

Imagine "hair like sapphire [lapis lazuli]," now gone!

The poem concerns the inexplicable reversal of wealth, power, beauty, luxury, influence, and splendor into a free fall of despair. This loss, vigorously remembered on the ninth of Ab, is a paradigm for all loss, for Christians the crucifixion of Jesus, for our modern barbaric world of Hiroshima, Auschwitz, Chernobyl, all violent disappearances of well-being.[23]

Linafelt has warned us against finding too much hope in the poetry of Lamentations. It is nonetheless the case that Israel, in its loss of money and possessions and all that they signify, must push back behind commodities to the God of fidelity:

But this I call to mind,
and therefore I have hope:

The steadfast love of the LORD never ceases,
his mercies never come to an end;
they are new every morning;
great is your faithfulness.
"The LORD is my *portion*," says my soul,
"therefore I will hope in him."
(3:21–24; italics added)

Because of the covenantal claim of Israel's faith, we may expect relational fidelity to dwell beneath and beyond money and possessions. The remarkable use of the term "portion" with reference to YHWH suggests a treasuring of a relationship that is more valuable than money and possessions that may be acquired . . . or lost.[24] That affirmation, however, is easier to voice than it is to embrace. Only in hints are these voices of Lamentations able to recognize that hope

23. See Alan E. Lewis, *Between Cross and Resurrection: A Theology of Holy Saturday* (Grand Rapids: Eerdmans, 2001).

24. Gerhard von Rad, "'Righteousness' and 'Life' in the Cultic Language of the Psalms," in *The Problem of the Hexateuch and Other Essays* (New York: McGraw-Hill, 1966), 243–66, has exposited the way in which land as "portion" may be displaced by YHWH as "portion."

lies elsewhere beyond what is lost. The final petition hopes for restoration of what has been lost:

> Restore us to yourself, O LORD, that we may be restored;
> renew our days as of old.
>
> (5:21)

The prayer combines relationship and the recovery of what has been lost. Beyond that, 5:22 is an enigmatic ending:

> The appeal in 5:20–22 remains unanswered. The voice of YHWH never sounds in the book of Lamentations. . . . Without such an answer, or perhaps some indication of a salvation oracle, the book of Lamentations remains incomplete. It evidences what Derrida has called a "structural unfinishedness." . . . It is not an incompletion that sits well with readers.[25]

It may well be completed only in God's fidelity that is here left unsaid and unrealized. The relationship between divine fidelity and worldly well-being is not clearly parsed here. Israel may hope in God; but Israel clearly can remember all that has been lost and not received—at least not yet! The idyllic restoration of Job has no counterpart here. This honest articulation of being devalued by the measure of the world is left open and unresolved as the pain persists.

V

The narrative of Esther operates in a complex way as a story of safety of the Jews, but also as a tale of failed patriarchy. Reading it brings to mind the phrase "trophy wife," the capacity of a rich and powerful man to "exhibit" a splendid wife so that she becomes no more than an object in his show of wealth, power, and success. The story begins as the king, Ahasuerus, displays his wealth and power in order to disguise his deep insecurity, indicated by fear of disobedient women (Esth. 1:3–11): "He displayed the great wealth of his kingdom and the splendor and pomp of his majesty for many days, one hundred eighty days in all" (v. 4).

25. Linafelt, *Surviving Lamentations*, 61.

He hopes that the display of his great wealth will make him as strong as he wants to appear:

> Invariably in Esther it ["splendor"] refers to the *public display and consolidation of power over against another's humiliation and/or subordination.* . . . The aim of this party is clearly related to that of the first, namely, to display and thereby secure his honor and greatness over the entire social order.[26]

After the exuberant exhibit of his opulence, the display culminates with his wife, Vashti:

> Furthermore, Queen Vashti gave a banquet for the women in the palace of King Ahasuerus.
>
> On the seventh day, when the king was merry with wine, he commanded . . . the seven eunuchs who attended him, to bring Queen Vashti before the king, wearing the royal crown, in order to show the peoples and the officials her beauty; for she was fair to behold. (vv. 9–10)

The staggering surprise of the narrative is that Queen Vashti refuses to be the king's trophy wife and to be on exhibit. Her refusal evokes enough royal rage that she is promptly and according to careful royal protocol displaced:

> But Queen Vashti refused to come at the king's command conveyed by the eunuchs. At this the king was enraged, and his rage burned within him. . . . "If it pleases the king, let a royal order go out from him, and let it be written among the laws of the Persians and the Medes so that it may not be altered, that Vashti is never again to come before King Ahasuerus; and let the king give her royal position to another who is better than she." (vv. 12, 19)

No reason is given for her refusal. Clearly she refuses his requirement to be an object and is determined to be the agent of her own history. She must have known the risk in her action. It is indeed uncommon for an object to step out of the drama of

26. Timothy K. Beal, "Esther," in Linafelt and Beal, *Ruth and Esther*, 6–7. See Jon D. Levenson, *Esther*, Old Testament Library (Louisville, KY: Westminster John Knox Press, 1997), 44–47.

commoditization for the sake of agency. But wealth has its limits, even if the king could not recognize them.

The narrative intends some mocking humor, for it is acknowledged that the daring action of Vashti (no longer called queen) not only is an embarrassment to the king who could not control his trophy. Her conduct is also a threat to the entire structure of patriarchy wherein wealth requires domination of women. Her refusal, it is feared, will encourage other women to imitate her recalcitrance:

> For this deed of the queen will be made known to all women, causing them to look with contempt on their husbands, since they will say, "King Ahasuerus commanded Queen Vashti to be brought before him, and she did not come." This very day the noble ladies of Persia and Media who have heard of the queen's behavior will rebel against the king's officials, and there will be no end of contempt and wrath! . . . So when the decree made by the king is proclaimed throughout all his kingdom, vast as it is, all women will give honor to their husbands, high and low alike. (vv. 17–18, 20)

Royal rage about the loss of control and domination concludes the Vashti drama. The king will find another trophy wife who will accept a proper role in the drama of wealth and commoditization. The anxiety of the wealthy king propels the story; he soon discovers that his money is no adequate antidote to his anxiety.

The Vashti story is replicated by the account of Esther. Like Vashti, Esther is recruited for the service of the king. When she is "taken" to the king (2:8, 16), she enters his entourage and is made queen. She is content, at the outset, to be the next trophy:

> The king loved Esther more than all the other women; of all the virgins she won his favor and devotion, so that he set the royal crown on her head and made her queen instead of Vashti. Then the king gave a great banquet to all his officials and ministers—"Esther's banquet." He also granted a holiday to the provinces, and gave gifts with royal liberality. (2:17–18)

This is more exhibit of royal wealth, of which Esther is now a part.

Of course the drama of Esther is thicker than the drama of Vashti, even if the plotline is parallel. The thickness of the narrative of Esther concerns the fate of the Jews in Persia and especially of

Mordecai. In 4:1–14 Mordecai recruits Esther to the task of protecting Jews from slaughter. Now the reach of royal opulence is interrupted by the life-or-death risk for Jews. Neither Mordecai nor Esther has an interest in wealth or royal opulence, and the king's great wealth neither attracts nor deters them. Mordecai attests the urgency of the matter to Esther:

> Do not think that in the king's palace you will escape any more than all the other Jews. For if you keep silence at such a time as this, relief and deliverance will rise for the Jews from another quarter, but you and your father's family will perish. Who knows? Perhaps you have come to royal dignity for just such a time as this. (4:13–14)

Back in 1:12 we are given no reason for Vashti's refusal. Now in 4:15–17 we are told nothing about how Esther reached her daring conclusion. What we are told is that she decided to run risks in order to save the Jewish people. She decided to forgo her role as a trophy to help the king deal with his anxiety and to become an active agent in her life and in the history of her people. To do that, she had to renounce her trophy status. Such agency as she chooses clearly falls outside the drama of wealth that reduces to commodity. She renounces commodity and opts for agency; she makes the move from a world of "It" to an arena of "Thou." Esther refuses to be a part of a collection of trophies that the king can exhibit. Instead she takes active responsibility for her future and the future of her people.

As a step along the way to the success of Esther with the king, we may in particular notice the role of Haman in encouraging the king to do honor in the only way he knows, by the insignia of power and wealth. Haman is a full embodiment of the primacy of wealth; he advises the king:

> For the man whom the king wishes to honor, let royal robes be brought, which the king has worn, and a horse that the king has ridden, with a royal crown on its head. Let the robes and the horse be handed over to one of the king's most noble officials; let him robe the man whom the king wishes to honor, and let him conduct the man on horseback through the open square of the city, proclaiming before him: "Thus shall it be done for the man whom the king wishes to honor." (6:7–9)

Haman has unwittingly signed a blank check for his nemesis. But of course the matter backfires completely on Haman and we are reminded, yet again, that the force of male wealth and power is exceedingly limited. The king of course cannot recognize that limit. The king is now allied with Esther, and so the Jews are saved. The narrative has effected a complete role reversal, for now the king is obedient to the will and wish of the Jewish queen. The king has found an engagement that turns out to be more compelling than his usual practice of the display of his enormous wealth.

We may notice one particular at the end of the narrative, when the Jews celebrate relief for deliverance with a day of feasting and gladness. Among the precedents established in the narrative is the gesture of "presents to the poor" (9:22). This gesture stands in ironic contrast to the exhibit of great royal wealth at the beginning of the book, when the poor were not in purview. Thus from 1:4 (wealth exhibited) to 9:22 ("presents to the poor") is a journey from *self-aggrandizing self-congratulatory wealth* to *responsible community* in which wealth is repositioned from ultimacy to a resource for communal well-being. It is a move from *commodity as trophy* to *risky agency* that required refusal of objectification. Timothy Beal notes that the act toward the poor concerns the "more general issues of economic justice."[27] Such a notice parallels the reversal of social status that has taken place through narrative. Historical reality happens outside the reach of commodity where there is no "history."[28] Reliance on commodity, as the king practiced, turns out to be a category mistake, powerful but mistaken.

27. Beal, "Esther," 115.

28. W. Dennis Tucker Jr., *Constructing and Deconstructing Power in Psalms 107–150* (Atlanta: SBL Press, 2014), 26–41, has shown how the imperial ideology of Persia sought to show itself timeless, that is, without history. The commoditization practiced by Ahasuerus is precisely such an effort at timeless nonhistory. In the narrative, first Vashti and then Esther break that timelessness by becoming an agent in her own history.

CHAPTER 10

The Gospels

Performance of an Alternative Economy

It is astonishing that we in the West have been schooled to read the Gospel narratives through a privatized, otherworldly lens that has transposed the story into an individualized, spiritualized account. That schooling reflects the intellectual sophistication, economic affluence, political privilege, and autonomous reasoning of the West that regularly finds a way to tone down the radical material specificity of Jesus. It is clear that Jesus was preoccupied with this-worldly material reality.[1] Jesus was focused on issues related to money and possessions, the ways they are deployed in a world governed by God, and the ways in which they define and skew social relationships.

Two of the initial pronouncements of Jesus indicate his this-worldly accent. One is his initial announcement, according to the Gospel of Mark: "The time is fulfilled, and the kingdom of God has come near; repent, and believe in the good news" (Mark 1:15). This announcement was in Galilee, a cipher for the outlier peasant economy distinct from the urban environment of Jerusalem. In his

1. The various quests for the historical Jesus, including the recent Jesus Seminar, have greatly problematized a critical reading of the Gospel texts. It has not been my task to sort out all of that. Moving into a field of inquiry that is new for me, I have been dependent on the work of other scholars. The wisest book as an introduction I have found to be Luke Timothy Johnson, *Sharing Possessions: What Faith Demands*, 2nd ed. (Grand Rapids: Eerdmans, 2011).

declaration at the synagogue in Nazareth, he reads and comments upon the text from Isaiah 61:1:

> The Spirit of the Lord is upon me,
> because he has anointed me
> to bring good news to the poor.
> He has sent me to proclaim release to the captives
> and recovery of sight to the blind,
> to let the oppressed go free,
> to proclaim the year of the Lord's favor.
> (Luke 4:18–19)

Of Mark's account, we must ask, "Good news for whom?" In the Lukan report an answer is given: the gospel is good news for the poor, the captives, the blind, the oppressed—that is, all those left behind by the dominant economy. His ministry, conducted in subversive act and in disruptive word, concerned the performance of an alternative economy willed by God in defiance of the dominant economy that was legitimated by Rome and practiced by those who accepted imperial hegemony with its exploitative protocols. Thus Richard Lischer, in his reading of the parables of Jesus, can conclude:

> What drives the social, political, ideological, and economic reading of the parables is the conviction that the message of Jesus first took root among the poor. This is a truth so amply attested to in the Gospel that it requires no proof. . . . A sociopolitical reading of the parable [Matthew 20:1–16], then, focuses on economic oppression and makes it the central element of the story. The parable of the Workers in the Vineyard represents a small but vivid slice of first-century social realism. . . . The plots depict codifications of perennial oppression: the characters are not real people but represent the social roles played by the several types of oppressors and the oppressed. The codifications are not merely derived from historical conditions in the time of Jesus; they represent the rules and patterns of many advanced agrarian societies.[2]

In this brief discussion, it is our task to situate the Gospel narrative in a credible economic context that precludes old reading

2. Richard Lischer, *Reading the Parables*, Interpretation (Louisville, KY: Westminster John Knox Press, 2014), 132–35. Note his citation of William Herzog.

habits of privatism and otherworldliness and that considers some representative texts and the way in which they connect with such a context. Obviously the Gospel narratives provide an immense array of materials that might be considered. Here we will focus on a few texts that may illuminate the world of the Gospel testimony with reference to money and possessions. Through this exposition we will have in mind the awareness that Jesus was commending and performing an economy that was sure to collide with established economic patterns and with those who presided over and benefited from such patterns.[3] His term for the alternative economy was "kingdom of God," that is, a social practice and a set of social relationships that are congruent with the God of the covenantal Torah of ancient Israel.[4] His appeal to a political metaphor ("kingdom") assures that his ministry contradicted the dominant kingdom of Rome, wherein a privatized, otherworldly gospel could be acceptable alongside the political economy of Rome; clearly a kingdom that is material and this-worldly has within it an inescapable potential for conflict with established norms and practices.

I

The dominant economy of his day, presided over by Rome and practiced by those who accepted Roman authority, was an economy of extraction. That is why so much attention is given in the Gospels to the tax collectors who were agents who helped transfer money and possessions from those who produced wealth to those who enjoyed wealth. That economy featured an urban center (Jerusalem) that was organized and ordered by the urban elite who enjoyed surplus wealth. It is evident that in Jerusalem many were not among the elite and lived a subsistence existence. The elite who dominated the city depended, of course, on the labor of such subsistence workers. The wealth that sustained the unproductive elite was produced by peasant agriculture, that is, those who lived a subsistence life specified in the Gospel by the cipher "Galilee." Douglas Oakman has

3. Wendell Berry, *Home Economics* (New York: North Point Press, 1987), 57, compellingly distinguishes between "the Great Economy" (kingdom of God) and the "little economy" (a human economy).

4. The phrase "kingdom of God" of course is not exhausted by or contained within the economic sphere.

made a compelling case that the defining reality of this economy was debt, whereby subsistence peasants were kept endlessly and hopelessly in debt to predatory interests.[5]

Peasants who remain always in debt will eventually lose their land.[6] Of course this is an old story in Israel, as old as Pharaoh in Genesis 47:13–25. It is, moreover, as contemporary as today. Thus the *New York Times* reports on how investors make money by offering loans for cars to poor people at interest rates of more than 20 percent, which of course they cannot pay.[7]

The succinct social map of Luke 19:47–48 describes the social relationship of the debtor and creditor classes: "Every day he was teaching in the temple. The *chief priests, the scribes, and the leaders* of the people kept looking for a way to kill him; but they did not find anything they could do, for *all the people* were spellbound by what they heard."

The creditor class wanted to eliminate him, because he contradicted their socioeconomic arrangements. But the "people" were spellbound, and by clustering around him they protected him. They were, we may imagine, spellbound because he enunciated an alternative way in the world that was outside the protocols of persistent debt. The Lord's Prayer of course comes to the subject of debts and their forgiveness. Both Douglas Oakman and Sharon Ringe make clear that the text of the prayer has behind it the provision for the release of debt in the Old Testament (Deut. 15:1–18) and proposes that those who make the petition state their readiness to cancel debts as a basis for forgiveness by God.[8] Such a notion of debt forgiveness would in any case upend any conventional economy and disrupt the privilege of the creditor class; it must have been a welcome offer for the debtors even as it was resisted by the creditors who must have, in the rhetoric of the ancient text, appeared to be

5. Douglas E. Oakman, *Jesus and the Peasants* (Eugene, OR: Wipf & Stock, 2008); Oakman, *Jesus, Debt, and the Lord's Prayer: First-Century Debt and Jesus' Intentions* (Eugene, OR: Wipf & Stock, 2014).

6. See Oakman, *Jesus and the Peasants*, 140, on the dynamics of land loss.

7. Nicholas Kristof, "How Do We Increase Empathy?," *New York Times*, January 27, 2015, A23.

8. Oakman, *Jesus, Debt, and the Lord's Prayer*, 42–91 and passim; Sharon H. Ringe, *Jesus, Liberation, and the Biblical Jubilee: Images for Ethics and Christology*, Overtures to Biblical Theology (Philadelphia: Fortress Press, 1985), 81–90. On the economic dimensions of forgiveness, see Patrick D. Miller, "Luke 4:16–21," *Interpretation* 29:4 (1975): 417–21.

"hard-hearted or tight-fisted" (Deut. 15:7). Such resistance to debt cancellation is evident in current negotiations with the new prime minister of Greece as he seeks redress from the austerity of the European banking interests that respond with the mantra, "There are rules."[9] The rules of conventional economy, of course, are made by the creditor class. It seems clear enough that this teaching about debt cancellation makes a direct connection to the social circumstance of the Galilean peasants whom Jesus addressed. It takes no imagination at all to see how the good news of alternative economics might be welcome news among the debtor class and an abomination to the creditor class that thrives on rules. The Gospel narrative is an interruption of conventional assumptions about money and possessions with enormous practical implications for the ordering of social power.

II

The first texts that I will consider are texts that are common to all three Synoptic Gospels, and so must have been from the common tradition.

1. In Mark 10:17–31 (Matt. 19:16–30; Luke 18:18–30) we have a narrative report that is divided into two characteristic parts, a public encounter and a critical reflection with the disciples. The public encounter concerns a man commonly known as the rich young ruler. He approaches Jesus with an expectation that Jesus knows the answer to the ultimate question of "eternal life." Good rabbinic teacher that he is, Jesus commends to him the commandments of Sinai. But then Jesus moves beyond the commandments to the requirement of his alternative economy. He bids the man, in five imperatives, to disengage from the conventional system of wealth, property, and debt: "You lack one thing; go, sell what you own, and give the money to the poor, and you will have treasure in heaven; then come, follow me" (v. 21).

9. Thus a statement of Wolfgang Schäuble, German finance minister, in commenting on the new Greek government: "The rules accompanying the rescue loans for Greece 'can't just be broken.'" Schäuble also asserted, "We are averse to blackmail." Niki Kitsantonis, "Greece Signals Unwillingness to Cooperate with Auditors," *New York Times*, January 31, 2015.

It is the additional requirement that marks the decisive break with conventional economics that assumes that "treasure in heaven" does not require divestment of treasure on earth. Only so would Jesus then say, "Follow me." Luke Johnson observes that "Jesus demands complete renunciation of possessions for disciples" (see Luke 5:11, 28).[10] The man had "many possessions" and found the break with conventional economy to be too much.

In his reflective exchange with his disciples, Jesus states what they must have concluded: "How hard it will be for those who have wealth to enter the kingdom of God!" (v. 23). The juxtaposition of "wealth" and "kingdom of God" makes clear that Jesus is after an alternative economy that is not preoccupied with wealth. By verse 27 the "how hard" of Jesus has become "impossible." The concluding exchange with Peter makes clear that life with Jesus is about abandoning wealth. Jesus does not say how the "impossible" becomes "possible," an enigma that is at the heart of an evangelical understanding of money and possessions. That lack of clarity allows ample room for interpretive maneuver, but the clarity of his primary requirement is not to be explained away. The "eternal life" about which the man makes inquiry takes on, through this exchange, an altogether different dimension.

2. In Mark 12:13–17 (Matt. 22:15–22; Luke 20:20–26), Jesus is confronted by his adversaries with a trick question, any answer to which is sure to be high risk: "Is it lawful to pay taxes to the emperor, or not?" The question of Caesar and the power of Rome is characteristically a high-risk question that must be answered carefully. But Jesus sees that it is not a serious question: "But knowing their hypocrisy . . ." (v. 15). We may imagine then that his answer to them is a playful one by which he evades the trap they have set for him.

Oakman probes the question "Who controls the land?" and shows how "Caesar's house" stood at the very pinnacle of power and the control of property.[11] Thus in conventional terms the answer is clear; it all belongs to Caesar, so taxes must be paid. The opponents of Jesus know that because of his radicality Jesus cannot very well agree to Caesar's system of taxation. Perhaps they expect him to be

10. Johnson, *Sharing Possessions*, 15.

11. See Oakman, *Jesus and the Peasants*, 141–42, for a summary of the way in which Caesar dominated the economy and all property.

a tax resister. If, on the other hand, he agrees to taxes, he will compromise the radicality of his alternative. He, however, is not stupid. He answers enigmatically.

Alan Culpepper judges that the statement approves taxes because taxes belong properly to Caesar: "In a highly charged political atmosphere, in which he might easily have sided with those who advocated radical and militant efforts to overthrow Roman oppression, Jesus recognized the authority of the state to collect taxes."[12] Culpepper suggests that this line of reasoning is extended by Paul (Rom. 13:7) and by the writer of 1 Peter (1 Pet. 2:13–17). His judgment is seconded by Pheme Perkins:

> Jesus turns from the sociopolitical issue to the theological issue. . . . The coin must belong to Caesar, so it should be returned to him. For Jesus and his disciples, concern over the images on coins was a non-issue. . . . Jesus defuses the political tension inherent in the question. He does not let his opponents escape without reminding them of what really counts: returning to God the things that belong to God . . . in terms of Jesus' instructions about discipleship.[13]

It is no wonder that his listeners were "utterly amazed" by his saying that shrewdly left things open, thereby defying the binary thinking of his opponents (Mark 12:17). He in fact changed the subject upon his opponents. Jesus' performance of alternative is so remote from the world of Caesar that he has no need to answer that trick question concerning Caesar. Like his listeners, we are left to ponder "the things of God" that require greater attention than do coins.[14]

12. R. Alan Culpepper, *Mark*, Smyth & Helwys Bible Commentary (Macon, GA: Smyth & Helwys, 2007), 433.

13. Pheme Perkins, "The Gospel of Mark: Introduction, Commentary, and Reflections," in *The New Interpreter's Bible*, ed. Leander E. Keck (Nashville: Abingdon Press, 1995), 8:673–74.

14. Oakman, *Jesus, Debt, and the Lord's Prayer*, 94, offers an extended chapter with a radical proposal: "This chapter pursues the thesis that Jesus advocated tax resistance as a concrete expression of the 'kingdom of God.' Jesus' historical activity attempted to facilitate the 'eminent domain of God' by brokering the remission of debts and taxes through subversive resistance measures." It is remarkable, however, that Oakman does not take up this text. The other texts cited by Oakman from Luke add up to the judgment by Oakman that taxes should not be paid to Caesar if one is in the Jesus movement; this is not because Jesus opposes taxes but because the taxes paid to Rome fund a mode of power and life that is contradicted by his ministry.

III

Here are two texts shared by several Gospels but not by all of the Synoptic narratives.

1. Luke 12:13–34 is partly paralleled in Matthew 6:19–21, 25–34, but Luke 12:13–21 has no parallel at all, and none of the material is in Mark. Again the text is divided into a public encounter and a reflective instruction to his disciples. The public encounter consists in an exchange of Jesus with a man who is in a dispute with his brother about family real estate. Jesus refuses to engage in his dispute. He makes two responses to the man's request. First, he warns him directly: "Be on your guard against all kinds of greed; for one's life does not consist in the abundance of possessions" (v. 15.) Ched Myers paraphrases: "You are not what you own."[15]

The term rendered "greed" means to grow bigger, to maximize abundance, to yearn for increase.[16] Jesus sees that the man is seduced to want more, even at his brother's expense. He understands that the man is using his energy for accumulation; he reminds him that the accumulation of more wealth cannot be the measure of his life.

His second response to the man is the parable of "a rich man," rich enough to have enough, owning land that produced abundantly. His crops produce so much that he must secure more storage space. It is worth remembering that the Hebrew slaves in Egypt were occupied with building more storage facilities for Pharaoh's massive accumulation (Exod. 1:11)! The man in the parable anticipated that when he had stored more, he would be satisfied in his ample goods. That, however, is nothing more than anticipation that never comes to reality, because his self-congratulatory monologue about accumulation is interrupted by God (anything can happen in a parable!). The man addresses himself as "soul" (*psyche*). But God addresses him as "fool," one who engages in self-destruction by living against

15. Ched Myers, "The Bible and Climate Change" (presentation at Society of Biblical Literature Annual Meeting, San Diego, CA, November 22, 2014). Myers's exposition of this text is quite remarkable!

16. The Greek term *pleonexia* was used recently to describe Vladimir Putin, president of Russia: "She [Masha Gessen] claims that Putin suffers from 'pleonexia,' the insatiable desire to have what rightfully belongs to others" (Tony Wood, "First Person," *London Review of Books*, February 5, 2015, 14). Of course what can be said of Putin can as well be said of the oligarchs who control the U.S. economy.

the grain of God's governance. It turns out that his great accumulation designed to secure *his life* only led to *his death*. Indeed, the question of verse 20 sounds as if he had no family or heirs, so that his accumulation had no future. His is a case not unlike that identified in Ecclesiastes 4:7–8. Finally, at the end of the parable Jesus makes it plain for his listeners by contrasting "treasures stored up" and "rich toward God"; "rich toward self" has no future in the presence of "rich toward God": "So it is with those who store up treasures for themselves but are not rich toward God" (v. 21). Jesus changes the subject on the man by bringing the issue of possessions into the presence of God, where they are completely relativized.

His encounter with the man provides a case study for his instruction to his disciples. The man in the narrative is obviously "worried." He does not have enough. His worry is propelled by his habitation in a culture of extraction that assumes scarcity. The man is propelled by a fear of scarcity. Jesus' disciples, to the contrary, are not to be situated in an economy of extraction, are not to be preoccupied with scarcity, and are not to be propelled by worry. It turns out that the man in the narrative could not add anything to his life by worry about more "things" . . . food or clothing. The man had lost his life (*psyche*) by worry about surplus. Now Jesus invites his disciples to reflect on the actual reality of life (*psyche*) that does not consist in commodities or the accumulation of them. Worry belongs to a practice of accumulation paralleled by a fear of scarcity. Such worry about scarcity is inimical to a world where "our Father," the creator of abundance, governs. It is the Creator upon whom birds and flowers rely. These birds and flowers, practitioners of abundance, are contrasted to Solomon, who, as we have seen, was a practitioner of scarcity, accumulation, and greed. There is a proper "striving" (v. 31), but it is not striving for money and possessions; it is rather for the "kingdom" that defies the commoditization of creation.

In verses 32–34, it is as though the disciples had asked, "How do we do that?" Jesus answers them: Withdraw from the world of fear! The dominant economy is grounded in fear. The national security state, with its surveillance and torture, aims to keep us fearful. The mantra of scarcity tells us that we do not yet have enough. We have not yet done enough. We are not yet enough! Television ads remind us that we do not yet have the product that will make us secure and happy . . . not yet. The antidote to such drivenness is to disengage from such an ideology. "Sell your possessions, and give alms"! The accent is on giving. The contrast is elemental: the man in the parable never gave; he took. A life (*psyche*) of giving is sustainable; it is an alternative treasure, alternative to treasures that erode, wear out, perish: "For where your treasure is, there your heart will be also" (v. 34; see Matt. 6:19–21).

Jesus has masterfully managed the parable to contrast *commodity* with *creation*. Commodity is presided over by fear. Creation is presided over by the God who generously guarantees abundance. It is a stunning either-or!

The version of the same instruction to the disciples in Matthew 6:25–33 is introduced by a very radical either-or that requires his disciples to choose. The choice required is complete and nonnegotiable. In Luke the alternative to worry is to "strive for his kingdom" (12:31). In Matthew it is "to strive first for the kingdom of God and his righteousness" (6:33), that is, his generative neighborliness. The either-or of Matthew 6:24 ("You cannot serve God and wealth") surely merits our attention, especially if "mammon" is translated as "wealth" (as in NRSV) or as "capital." Jacques Ellul insists:

> We absolutely must not minimize the parallel Jesus draws between God and Mammon. He is not using a rhetorical figure but pointing out a reality. God as a person and Mammon as a person find themselves in conflict. Jesus describes the relation between us and one or the other in the same way: it is a relationship between servant and master. Mammon can be a master the same way God is; that is, Mammon can be a personal master . . . He is speaking of a power which tries to be like God, which makes itself our master and which has specific goals. That Mammon is a spiritual power is also shown by the way we attribute sacred characteristics to our money. The issue here is not that idols have been built to symbolize money, but simply that for modern man money is one of his "holy things." Money affairs are, as we well know, serious business for modern man. Everything else—love and justice, wisdom and life—is only words. Therefore we avoid speaking of money. We speak of business, but when, in someone's living room, a person brings up the topic of money, he is committing a social error, and the resulting embarrassment is really expressing the sense of the sacred. This is true for the middle class. Among the working class we find the same sentiment, but in a different form: it is the widespread conviction

> that if the money question is resolved, all problems of the working class and of humankind in general will be solved as well. It is also the conviction that everything that does not tend to solve the money problem is only hot air.[17]

Ellul judges that if the either-or of God/Mammon is taken seriously, the economy must be deprived of its sacred character and its sacred power. That is, it must be "profaned":

> This profanation, then, means uprooting the sacred character, destroying the element of power. We must bring money back to its role as a material instrument. When money is no more than an object, when it has lost it seductiveness, its supreme value, its superhuman splendor, then we can use it like any other of our belongings, like any machine. Of course, even if this relieves our fears, we must always be vigilant and very attentive because the power is never totally eliminated. Now this profound profanation is first of all the result of a spiritual battle, but this must be translated into behavior. There is one act par excellence which profanes money by going directly against the law of money, an act for which money is not made. This act is giving. . . . In the biblical view, this is precisely how giving, which is a consecration to God, is seen. It is, as a matter of fact, the penetration of grace into the world of competition and selling. We have very clear indications that money, in the Christian life, is made in order to be given away. . . . Giving to God is the act of profanation par excellence.[18]

At the end of the Lukan passage, it can be seen that the giving of alms is an act that profanes money, robs it of its sacred quality, and submits it to the rule of God, who is, as Creator, always generously giving.[19] The either-or, in the public encounter and in the

17. Jacques Ellul, *Money and Power* (Downers Grove, IL: Inter-Varsity Press, 1984), 76–77.

18. Ibid., 110–11. Michael Welker concludes concerning a "religious and friendly/family line of thought": "They aim at helping us envisage alternatives to today's morally and politically helpless Manichaeism which uses the rhetorical formulation 'God or Mammon!'" Welker, "Kohelet and the Co-evolution of a Monetary Economy and Religion," in *Money as God? The Monetization of the Market and Its Impact on Religion, Politics, Law, and Ethics*, ed. Jürgen von Hagen and Michael Welker (Cambridge: Cambridge University Press, 2014), 106.

19. On almsgiving, see Gary A. Anderson, *Charity: The Place of the Poor in the Biblical Tradition* (New Haven, CT: Yale University Press, 2013).

instruction in discipleship, is, on the one hand, an exposé of a world governed by money and possessions, and, on the other hand, an invitation to alternative that is free from such anxiety-producing power. Discipleship is the renunciation of that anxiety-producing power; practically that renunciation is performed as generosity that is free of greed and has no fear of scarcity.

2. Mark 14:3–9 is found also in Matthew 26:6–13; John 12:1–8. This narrative episode does not appear in Luke but surprisingly is included in the Fourth Gospel. We will not here be concerned with the drama of the episode itself but only with the much-quoted statement of verse 7:

> For you always have the poor with you, and you can show kindness to them whenever you wish; but you will not always have me.

It is the primacy of Jesus and his death (for which he is anointed) that preoccupies the narrative. Jesus' statement in verse 7 is a response to those who preferred, so they said, that money be spent on the poor rather than on oil for Jesus; this is a proposal to detract from the primacy of Jesus. In the Fourth Gospel the same question is placed in the mouth of Judas the betrayer, and it is said explicitly that the question is a hoax: "He said this not because he cared about the poor, but because he was a thief" (John 12:6).

The intent of the narrative is to focus singularly on Jesus and on the woman's devotion to him:

> The interpretation of the woman's anointing as an act of total and unlimited attention to the person of Christ that for many constitutes the center of the story appears to reflect a meaning that is latent in the text itself. The issue is the woman's relationship to Jesus—a total commitment of herself to him who is going to his death. . . . It is an expression of her relationship to Christ, not simply of recognition of who he is but of devotion to him.[20]

In that context, the statement of verse 7 is curious. It is as if Jesus wanted to assure his detractors that he has not forgotten the poor and that they will have ample opportunity to care for the poor after the crisis of his life and death is completed. His statement

20. Ulrich Luz, *Matthew 21–28* (Hermeneia; Minneapolis: Fortress Press, 2005), 342–43.

concerning the poor is a quote from Deuteronomy 15:11, a text that concerns the cancellation of debt for the poor. It is remarkable indeed that in this dramatic moment Jesus should allude to this most radical text. It is as though his detractors have charity in mind and he summons them to a much more radical action . . . .debt cancellation!

This statement from Deuteronomy 15:11, moreover, is not a statement of resignation, as it is most often taken to be. It is, rather, a summons to vigorous policy and generous practice that refuses "hard-hearted or tight-fisted" attitudes toward the poor. The significance of Deuteronomy 15:11 is indicated by its juxtaposition to verse 4 in the same textual unit, which asserts that "there will be no one in need," that is, no more poor among us. The overcoming of poverty is to be accomplished through debt cancellation. Thus the assurance of verse 4 alongside the summons of verse 11 makes the cancellation of debts of paramount importance to the regulation in Deuteronomy 15. In the Gospel narrative, it is not as though Jesus sets up an antithesis between his anointing and relief for the poor. Relief for the poor via debt cancellation is an ongoing responsibility rooted in the Torah and urged by Jesus, even in this dramatic moment. He insists that his detractors in this episode have much work to do on a continuing basis.

IV

Of course the Gospel of Luke is most directly preoccupied with money and possessions.

1. The Magnificat of Mary (1:46–55) announces primary themes that are to recur in the Gospel of Luke. Her song is an anticipation of the story of Jesus and his ministry that is to follow, and of the story of the early church in the book of Acts. The song is an echo of the Song of Hannah, which anticipates the revolutionary rule of David that is to come in ancient Israel and will effect a social upheaval:

> The bows of the mighty are broken,
> but the feeble gird on strength.
> Those who were full have hired themselves out for bread,
> but those who were hungry are fat with spoil.
> . . . .

The LORD makes poor and makes rich;
he brings low, he also exalts.
He raises up the poor from the dust;
He lifts the needy from the ash heap,
to make them sit with princes
and inherit a seat of honor.
(1 Sam. 2:4–8)

The theme of Hannah, moreover, is reiterated in Psalm 113:7–8:

He raises the poor from the dust,
and lifts the needy from the ash heap,
to make them sit with princes,
with the princes of his people.

That same accent of social upheaval is now on the lips of Mary:

He has brought down the powerful from their thrones,
and lifted up the lowly;
he has filled the hungry with good things,
and sent the rich away empty.
(Luke 1:52–53)

The parallels clearly assume a class analysis of the powerful and the lowly who are, inevitably, the rich and the hungry, respectively. The terms of contrast and reversal clearly pertain to material resources. And while that materiality in what follows in Luke is troped in imaginative ways, the root reality of the material remains. The Gospel of Luke is, from the outset, good news that both challenges present economic arrangements and anticipates alternative arrangements. In addition to the narrative exchange of 12:13–21 considered above, with its warning about "greed," we mention two other texts that are distinctive to Luke.

2. In 14:12–24, the parable of the Great Dinner is told in a distinctive way. In Matthew the second wave of guests, after the first invitees had failed, includes "everyone you find," "good and bad" (22:9, 10). In Luke, however, the initial teaching, without parallel in Matthew, makes a poignant contrast concerning money and possessions: "When you give a luncheon or a dinner, do not invite your friend or your brothers or your relatives or rich neighbors, in case they may invite you in return, and you would be repaid. But when you give a banquet, invite the poor, the crippled, the lame, and the blind" (vv. 12–13).

In the parable itself, moreover, the second wave of invitees includes precisely those who are left behind by a predatory economy: "Go out at once into the streets and lanes of the town and bring in the poor, the crippled, the blind, and the lame" (v. 21).

3. The distinctive accent of Luke is made more explicit in the two parables of Luke 16. In 16:1–13 the enigmatic tale is preoccupied with "dishonest wealth," presumably wealth of the marketplace that is at best transient. The penultimate urging is to be a sharp dealer about such wealth, but to do so in preparation for a time "when it is gone" (v. 9). The follow-up to the parable is the instruction of verses 10–13 that makes a contrast between "dishonest wealth" and "true riches." This in turn morphs into a contrast between "God and mammon" or "God and wealth" (v. 13). Thus the instruction that follows the parable seems to deplore preoccupation with market wealth and also to affirm that there is a very different kind of wealth that is to concern the disciple community.

The second parable in the chapter, also distinctive to Luke, concerns yet again a rich man who in his self-indulgence disregarded the needs of a poor man (16:19–31). The parable evidences Jesus' remarkable capacity to manage and utilize Old Testament traditions that live in deep tension with each other. The poor man is commended to Abraham, the carrier of God's unconditional promise. In the calculation of the alternative economy, the poor man is given unconditional attentiveness and valorization. By contrast, the rich man wants more warning to be given to his brothers who are equally rich. But Father Abraham is unresponsive to the request and does not extend such relief to the rich man or his family. Instead the rich man and his family are left to the tradition of Moses and the Torah, with its summons to a neighborly economy and its harsh sanctions for those who refuse such neighborliness. Thus the map of social relations that is sketched in the tradition of Luke concerns exactly those with ample money and resources and those without such resources. Jesus, according to Luke, exposes the fraudulent wealth as the world entertains it and anticipates a reckoning whereby such imagined wealth is seen to be a hindrance and not an asset. The result of such thinking is the devaluing of what conventional economics values and an insistence on an alternative valuing. Richard Lischer articulates the contemporaneity of the parable:

> It witnesses to the abundance of poverty in our own backyard among people we no longer notice. But in the ultimate fate of

the rich man known to tradition as Dives (Latin for "rich"), it also teaches the poverty of abundance, for wealth establishes its own insulation from the poor and therefore contains the seeds of its own undoing. Dives cannot buy his way out of hell. The parable speaks to the well-off individuals and churches, which, though not exotically rich by Western standards, are insulated from the suffering of others by the many accoutrements of abundance. It is addressed to religious communities that have inherited the biblical language of poverty and lavishly appointed churches in which to talk about it.[21]

V

In Matthew 25:31–46 we have a well-known parable that has no parallel in the other Gospel accounts. The narrative, on the lips of Jesus, imagines a great final judgment before the Son of Man. The contours of the judgment scene are well known and not difficult to decipher. We may linger at the outset over the vision of a world judgment on "all the nations." First of all, it is a parable, an act of imagination, and not a description. This parable, however, insists that there is an "answering" for the management of material resources, an answering that cannot be avoided by more money or more power; and none is immune. The parable is an insistence that material resources (money and possessions) are not an autonomous zone but are situated in a fabric of meaning that will not yield to self-accommodating performances. The image of such judgment is tricky because it may invite hellfire and damnation, which is at best unhelpful and which fails to recognize that this is parable and not report.

I suggest that our thinking about such judgment may consist in two maneuvers. First, I appeal to the words of Václav Havel, the recent president of the Czech Republic. Havel was unwavering in his refusal of Christianity or any other institutional religious claim. But he had a keen sense of the inscrutable mystery of lived reality. For that reason, he resisted the reduction of public life to

21. Lischer, *Reading the Parables*, 108. Nicholas Kristoff, "How Do We Increase Empathy?," *New York Times*, January 29, 2015, observes that because the wealthy are effectively protected from an experience of the poor, they are much less likely to have any empathy for their plight.

its bureaucratic and technical dimensions and insisted that it had a moral dimension that could not be mocked. Thus in the wake of a visit by Pope John Paul II, he said:

> I strongly believe that your visit will remind us all of the genuine sources of real human responsibility, the metaphysical source . . . of the absolute horizon to which we must refer, that mysterious memory of Being in which each of our acts is recorded and in which and through which they finally acquire their true value. . . . Our actions are judged independently of us and of the fact or form of our existence.[22]

Havel did not want to acknowledge God as moral judge; but he recognized the mystery that pervades human life. His biographer comments: "Havel was able to see the mystery of existence in every human action, every human impulse and every human dilemma. And the core of the mystery was moral. He would not discount it as superstition, just as he would not ascribe it to Providence, the Supreme Being, or the superego."[23] This is a way of thinking about the parable that can be compelling for those who resist any simple supernaturalism.

From this may follow a second interpretive maneuver, that is, the recognition that the management of money and possessions is not an autonomous one-dimensional transaction but has deep and thick moral significance that includes accountability. That accountability in the parable is explicit. In less dramatic and explicit ways, however, that accountability among us has do with the fabric of human neighborliness; that fabric is essential to safety and well-being, but it cannot be sustained if and when there is indifference among the moneyed toward those without resources.

It is most probable that the parable in its origin concerned relationships within the Christian community, so that those in the community with resources were in solidarity with "the least" in the community, those without resources. Or alternatively concerning the safety and well-being of Christian missionaries, the parable may have initially concerned the treatment of the Christian "least" by non-Christians who were tested by their treatment of vulnerable Christians.

22. Michael Zantovsky, *Havel: A Life* (New York: Grove Press, 2014), 385–86.
23. Ibid., 387.

But as Ulrich Luz makes clear, a "universal" interpretation of the parable that does not represent Matthew's view is legitimate: "Are we theologically justified in interpreting a text contrary to its original sense when the resulting meaning is central to the gospel and is helpful for modern people who receive it? In this case I would like to answer this question with yes."[24]

When we push beyond that original intent, the parable takes on contemporaneity for us as we consider the least among us. It is not difficult to identify the least in any economic analysis. Once the material requirements for the hungry, thirsty, stranger, naked, sick, and imprisoned, that is, the least, are acknowledged as the ultimate test of money and possessions, it is not difficult to see that unfettered, unregulated predatory economic practices and policies that prey on the vulnerable are indeed "judged" among us.

VI

We do not expect frontal teaching on money and possessions in the Fourth Gospel, because the Gospel of John is characteristically cast in more figurative categories. We may, however, notice the declaration of Jesus in 10:10: "I came that they may have life, and have it abundantly."

Unlike the false shepherds, the good shepherd assures protection and well-being for the sheep. We may, moreover, notice his provision for abundance in two texts concerning the teaching and action of Jesus. In chapter 6, the Fourth Gospel reiterates the feeding miracle whereby Jesus feeds five thousand and has twelve baskets of barley loaves left over: "When they were satisfied, he told his disciples, 'Gather up the fragments left over, so that nothing may be lost.' So they gathered them up, and from the fragments of the five barley loaves, left by those who had eaten, they filled twelve baskets" (6:12–13).

In his teaching at the well, he promises the woman water that will end all thirst: "Those who drink of the water that I will give them will never be thirsty. The water that I will give will become in them a spring of water gushing up to eternal life" (4:14).

The gifts of bread and water attest to the abundance that Jesus gives. The giving of that bread and water are, to be sure, sacramental

24. Luz, *Matthew 21–28*, 283.

acts, so these usages in the Fourth Gospel are always laden with surplus meaning. That, however, does not cause the bread or the water to lose its materiality, so that an economic dimension of abundance is implicit in his words and actions. His promise of abundance is indeed the performance of a new economy that is "from above."

As we have seen, in chapter 12 of John the extravagance of oil for anointing Jesus evoked opposition from Judas, who was mindful, so he said, of the poor. We may see that Judas is portrayed as the antipode of Jesus; he dismisses the abundance of Jesus. Judas thinks in the categories of the old economy, in terms of a zero-sum notion about money. Money used for this will not be available for that. In this case, money used for precious oil will not be available for the poor. Judas has no sense that where Jesus prevails the old economy of parsimony is not in effect, because Jesus' capacity for abundance is generative of all that is needed. In the narratives of Matthew and Luke, Jesus assures the disciples that "your heavenly Father" gives all that is needed. Now his own teaching and performance of abundance confirm the limitless generativity of the new economy. Thus the *parsimony of Judas* and the *abundance of Jesus* provide an epitome of the larger struggle in the Fourth Gospel between darkness and light, between evil and good. The particular conflict between them indicates that the larger struggle has an economic dimension in which his disciples are summoned to participate. Judas assumed that there would be no more gifts given; Jesus, so the gospel attests, is an agent of boundless abundance.

VII

Reading the gospel with reference to economic issues is clear and unmistakable and is required by the Gospel attestations themselves. Such a reading of the gospel, variously attested by all of the evangelists, precludes any privatized, otherworldly, spiritualized reading of the gospel. Such a reading of the gospel claim means, inescapably, a challenge to economics as usual. In our Western capitalist economy, it means a challenge to our most elemental assumptions about money. It is, I judge, the interpretive task of the church to bear witness to the alternative that in the gospel is termed "kingdom." Such an interpretive task is exceedingly difficult and risky because all of us—liberals and conservatives, churched and unchurched—are largely inured to the modern notion of the autonomy of economics and the misreading of the gospel apart from the economy. The testimony of the Gospel texts make clear that an autonomous economy is a deep misconstrual of the gospel, even as a "safe" reading of the gospel is a companion misconstrual. In his pondering of "God and Mammon" in contemporary life, Robert Wuthnow can conclude:

> The basis for assuming that "the poor will always be with you," therefore, is clearly present. Yet the question of why some particular people are poor, rather than others, appears to devolve the issue immediately to the level of individual behavior. In other words, rather than a systemic interpretation of the problem leading to a systemic view of its solution, the systemic diagnosis provides a framework that says, in effect, this is the way it will always be, and then individual attributes are credited with causing people to stay in poverty or to move out of it. The range of relevant attributes itself is considerable. But images of what it has taken the middle class to escape being poor surface most readily, and of these, popular understandings of work, laziness, and financial responsibility are especially apparent. Religious commitment adds authority to these understandings when it translates them from middle-class values into divine absolutes.[25]

The seduction of and equation of middle-class values with divine absolutes is very much with us. In every season, including our own, the teaching and actions of Jesus, as remembered by the church, constitute an urgent wake-up call. Indeed his resolve to restore those "left behind" to full participation in the economy was such a dangerous wake-up call that his adversaries set out to eliminate him right from the outset (Mark 3:6). Economic restoration and full participation of the "left behind"—about which Hannah and Mary sang—requires a reallocation of the material resources of a society. The resisters to his alternative economy sensed that risk immediately! That resistance, of course, did not alter his words or actions; nor did it alter the church's memory of him.

25. Robert Wuthnow, *God and Mammon in America* (New York: Free Press, 1994), 203.

CHAPTER 11

Acts

Community amid Empire

As a sequel to the Gospel of Luke, we expect that the book of Acts will sound some of the radical accents voiced in that Gospel narrative (Luke 1:1–4; Acts 1:1). These radical accents in the Gospel include much that belongs to the common tradition of the Synoptic Gospels but also distinctive Lukan material, including Mary's Magnificat and the parables that we have noted. In our discussion of the Gospel we concluded that Jesus is presented, in his proclamation of the kingdom of God, as announcing and performing an alternative economy of abundance that resists the dominant economy of predatory greed.

While the Acts of the Apostle is surely rooted in historical memory, there is no doubt that historical memory has been shaped in the service of theological testimony. That is, the book is not direct reportage on the early apostles but is an interpretive act that traces the Jesus movement as the carrier of an alternative to imperial modes of reality. Thus the narrative portrays the early apostles under the power of the Holy Spirit—the Spirit of Jesus—who provides energy, courage, and imagination to posit life outside the sphere of imperial assumptions. Because the Spirit-propelled alternative touches every dimension of life, it is no surprise that we have hints and traces of evidence of an alternative economy that is reflective of the radicality of the Gospel of Luke. The point of distinction between "reportage" and "portrayal" is an important one; concerning economic matters we may see that the narrative of Acts is a model for alternative but not a report on a durable practice. Luke Timothy Johnson, in his careful study of the matter, has noticed that the radical account of "shared possessions" occurs only at the outset of the book of Acts and is not later reiterated in the text.[1]

I

The large tension in the book of Acts consists in the interface been *imperial authority* and the *work of the Holy Spirit*. Thus the apostles are regularly propelled by the Spirit to action and proclamation that pivot on the resurrection of Jesus and from that resurrection regularly anticipate a different way of being in the world. As a consequence of such daring and insistent action, it is not surprising that the apostles are regularly summoned into court to appear before imperial officials in order to answer for their gospel claims. The roll call of imperial officials to whom the early church gave answer includes "the tribune" (21:27–22:29), Felix (23:23–24:27), Festus (25:1–12), and Agrippa (25:13–26:32). The empire is continually unsettled because the power of the Spirit, performed by the church, threatens the settled order of the empire.

Given the interface of *Spirit* and *empire*, we may not be surprised that this tension concerns money and possessions as well. Thus the notion of a community that holds money and possessions in common is a radical departure from imperial economics that intends that the privileged and powerful should have an excessive share apart from "the common good." It is in my judgment sufficient to see that the early church is presented as a *community of solidarity* without needing or being able to be precise about economic matters. Johnson notes that the assumptions of the book of Acts allude to Greek models of friendship, for it is in friendship that economic sharing may refuse ordinary predatory practices. Alongside such a Greek model of friendship, no doubt the Jewish tradition of neighbor figures in such practice, for neighborliness of a covenantal

1. Luke Timothy Johnson, *Sharing Possessions: What Faith Demands*, 2nd ed. (Grand Rapids: Eerdmans, 2011), 20–21, 110–27. I am greatly indebted to several of Johnson's discussions.

sort, not unlike friendship, eschews predatory practices.[2] Such a community of friends or neighbors does not require that there be no private property but that money and possessions, as everything else in the purview of the Jesus movement, are distinctive from the ordinary imperial extractive practices. The book of Acts contains a "multiplicity of models and mandates" about economics, and we must recognize that complexity.[3]

II

We may take as our governing reference the narrative of Acts 3:1–10. Peter and John, good Jews that they are, approach the temple to pray. The temple, not surprisingly, was a venue for beggars who sought alms. Alms of course constitute an important act of neighborly charity, but alms have no transformative capacity.[4] They are at best a positive custodial act. The response of the apostles to the beggar's request is direct and dramatic:

> I have no silver or gold, but what I have I give you; in the name of Jesus Christ of Nazareth, stand up and walk. (v. 6)

Peter's statement is a contrast between *"silver and gold"* that the beggar sought and *the transformative name of Jesus* that contains restorative capacity never matched by silver and gold: "Stand up and walk."

This statement need not suggest that the apostles had no coins. They are not, however, in the coin business, because silver and gold of themselves have no transformative capacity and issue no restorative impetus.[5] Thus the apostles break with conventional economics of custodial generosity that maintains the status quo in

2. On the "neighbor" in Lukan narrative, see Luke 10:25–37. It is clear that "neighbor" in this narrative makes more rigorous demands than does "friend."

3. Johnson, *Sharing Possessions*, 23.

4. On responsibility for alms, see ibid., 16–19, and more generally Gary A. Anderson, *Charity: The Place of the Poor in the Biblical Tradition* (New Haven, CT: Yale University Press, 2013).

5. We may connect this exchange with the teaching of Jesus concerning the coins that belong to Caesar. It is not denied that Caesar is entitled to his own coins; but the issue of loyalty of a more serious kind is well beyond the sphere of coins. So here silver and gold are not demonized or dismissed but are recognized as having no transformative power.

their acknowledgment of an alternative power for life that operates outside conventional economics. One may wonder, concerning this particular narrative, whether the absence (refusal) of silver and gold, eschewing conventional resources, is a necessary prerequisite to transformative power. Could it be that a refusal to traffic in conventional custodial economics here attests the basis of transformative power that lies outside conventional status quo economics? That is, conventional practices of money do not constitute the most likely venue for the Spirit's work of restoration.

In this narrative, the transformative imperatives of Peter are effective:

> Immediately his feet and ankles were made strong. Jumping up, he stood and began to walk, and he entered the temple with them, walking and leaping and praising God. (vv. 7–8)

The wonder and amazement evoked by the restoration was no doubt because conventional modes of custodial charity maintenance never issued in such transformative outcomes (v.10).

III

We do not need to take "I have no silver or gold" literally. We may see rather that Peter and John have a different agenda funded in a different way. This disclaimer, nonetheless, pushes us behind Peter and John to the community to which they belong, through which they drew such authority, and to which they were accountable. That community is directly characterized in two important passages. In 2:41–47 the early church community is devoted to "the apostles' teaching and fellowship, to the breaking of bread and the prayers" (2:42). These are the recurring disciplines that sustain and mark the distinctiveness of the Jesus community:

- *Apostles' teaching*. The narrative of Jesus featured in their preaching.
- *Fellowship*. The network of friendship (neighborliness) made alternative economics credible.
- *Breaking bread*. Alan Streett proposes that this act was a counterimperial meal: "The Christian practice of people from all

social strata eating together with everyone getting the same amount and quality of food 'challenged the imperial assumptions of rigid [societal] stratification.' Such a practice would be seen as reactionary at best and subversive at worst. In this sense, Christian meals were counter-imperial. Luke goes on to say, 'All who believed were together and had all things in common. . . .' In breaking bread together they did not perform a mere symbolic act but literally shared their food with each other. The meal had economic ramifications and challenged Rome's economic policy of abundance for the elites and mere subsistence for all others."[6]
- *Prayer*. The community appealed to an authority other than Rome.

Such a mode of community, without accepting it as prescriptive, surely lies behind the declaration of Peter to the beggar. The statement of Peter does not reflect simply a community under discipline, and not simply an alternative economics, but a radically different understanding of the power for life that is operative and effective outside the domain of conventional "silver and gold." The importance of this nexus of community is not an ideological judgment about property. It is rather a reimagining of the nature of worldly reality. In Peter's sermon that follows the transformative restoration of the beggar, he disclaims any power of his own:

> You Israelites, why do you wonder at this, or why do you stare at us, as though by our own power or piety we had made him walk? (3:12)

Peter's disavowal of personal power and private piety suggests a profound contradiction to conventional economics that calls to mind what C. B. Macpherson terms "possessive individualism." Macpherson has written a study of the rise of modern political theory that he traces from Thomas Hobbes through James Harrington and finally to John Locke. The sum of the theory that has become unquestioned concerns the autonomy of the market, the capacity for withdrawal of private property from common use, and

6. R. Alan Streett, *Subversive Meals: An Analysis of the Lord's Supper under Roman Domination during the First Century* (Eugene, OR: Pickwick Publications, 2013), 203–4.

legitimating the claim that an individual person could "possess" all that he could acquire. This was embodied in the several English laws that legitimated "enclosure" to prevent nonowners from having access to property, its grazing grass, and its wood. Thus it was a legal act of private appropriation. In Macpherson's words, Locke asserted that

> the individual right of appropriation overrides any moral claims of the society. The traditional view that property and labour were social functions, and that ownership of property involved social obligations, is thereby undermined. . . . He [Locke] has erased the moral disability with which unlimited appropriation had hitherto been handicapped. Had he done no more than this, his achievement would have to be accounted a considerable one. But he does even more. He also justifies, as natural, a class differential in rights and in rationality, and by doing so provides a positive moral basis for capitalist society.[7]

According to Macpherson, Locke shifted the onus of greed and covetousness away from usurpatious industrial aggression onto the have-nots who by stealth and cunning tried to gain access to the wealth they had been denied. According to Locke,

> It was rational, i.e., industrial, appropriation that required protection against the covetousness of the quarrelsome and contentious who sought to acquire possessions not by industry but by trespass. It was not the industrious appropriator who was covetous, but the man who would invade his appropriation. And rational industrious appropriation required protection only after it had passed beyond the limits of simple small properties and had become unlimited accumulation. Locke's denunciation of covetousness is a consequence, not a contradiction, of his assumption that unlimited accumulation is the essence of rationality.[8]

It would be a gross anachronism to suggest that "possessive individualism" was operative in the ancient world of the book of Acts. I cite Macpherson, however, in order to consider what might

7. C. B. Macpherson, *The Political Theory of Possessive Individualism: Hobbes to Locke* (Oxford: Oxford University Press, 1962), 221.
8. Ibid., 237.

be made, in our reading, about having "all things in common." It did not and does not mean living in a commune, but rather that the property of all is situated in a social-moral context of community. That ancient world of course did not practice possessive individualism; it did, however, legitimate social stratification and distinct social classes and legitimated inequality of social access, social power, and social goods. The common good of the early church spoke deeply against such stratification that was embodied in the imperial pyramid, even as it speaks now against unregulated possessive individualism and accumulation. Macpherson may illumine, without any danger of anachronism, the contrast in the book of Acts between the world of silver and gold and the alternative of the early church in its practice of having "all things in common." I suggest that the reason this radical commonality in the church is stated only at the beginning of the book of Acts is that it is the basis of all that follows in the book. These radical practices, I suggest, are programmatic for the early church in Acts. We may entertain the thought that the bold preaching of Peter and then of Paul continued to be maintained and sustained by a communal practice of shared life. That practice did not need to be reiterated in the text because it is the ground for all that follows. The cunning linkage between *common life* and *the proclamation of the resurrection* is decisive for the apostolic church. The apostolic tradition of Easter proclamation in the face of empire is not a possibility simply because of a good idea but because of grounded, shared bodily practice.

The distinctive passion of the community is reiterated and reinforced in 4:32–37. The narrative weaves together commentary on *communal practice* ("everything they owned was held in common") and *testimony to the resurrection of Jesus*. What was done about money and possessions is linked to the generative force of the testimony and its yield of "great grace." The practice of communal property that eschewed private ownership is, in verse 34, an echo of the old regulation of debt cancellation in Deuteronomy 15:1–18. The assurance that "there was not a needy person among them" refers back to Deuteronomy 15:4, "there will be no one in need among you." The end of poverty concerns the social administration and use of property and goods, a practice here stated generally as a common practice and then specifically with reference to Barnabas: "He sold a field that belonged to him, then brought the money, and laid it at the apostles' feet" (Acts 4:37).

IV

The practice of having "all things in common" (2:44), the exercise of healing power apart from silver and gold (3:6), and the repetition of all things "in common" (4:32) together provide the backdrop for the remarkable narrative of 5:1–11.Whereas Barnabas had brought the money from sold property to the apostles, Ananias and Sapphira did the opposite. They kept back some for themselves. Bradley Chance suggests that the verb "kept back" be rendered "embezzled" and notes that the verb (*enosphisato*) is the same term used in Joshua 7:1 (LXX) concerning the affront of Achan, who also withheld money from the community.[9] Thus the usage intends to suggest a parallel between that ancient narrative concerning Achan that ended in disaster for Israel and the present narrative that will end in an abrupt death of Ananias and Sapphira amid the church. The term is also used in Titus 2:10 concerning slave conduct; slaves are admonished not to "pilfer."

The narrative suggests very close reasoning about the matter:

- When the property was unsold, it was "your own."
- When it was sold, the proceeds were "at your disposal."
- But withholding the money from the sale was an act of deception that the community could not tolerate.

The slippages between (a) the proceeds were "at your disposal" and (b) you "contrived" to withhold is curious. That slippage suggests that submission of the profit to the apostles was not required but was surely expected. Thus it is the dishonesty and the deception that draws the ire of Peter. Indeed Peter escalates the matter and characterizes this simple economic transaction as a great cosmic struggle between Satan and the Spirit; the deception and withholding had violated the work of the Spirit. I wonder if we may see in this narrative a dramatic replay of the initial act of Adam and Eve in Genesis 3:6 where "desire" subverted divine expectation. If the narrative can be seen in the orbit of that ancient memory, it is remarkable the way in which a simple transaction is a venue for the

9. J. Bradley Chance, *Acts*, Smyth & Helwys Commentary (Macon, GA: Smyth & Helwys, 2007), 88.

cosmic struggle in which the church is engaged. In our narrative, as in Genesis 3, deception is the order of the day.

The accusation against Ananias results in his indictment and death (Acts 5:5–6). When the sale and its outcome are portrayed as a testing of the Spirit of the Lord, Sapphira also dies immediately (v. 10). The narrative does not explain the mode of their deaths. We are only struck by the tone, pace, and finality of the account. Withholding from the community is a lie to God and a testing of the Spirit that leads to death. Life consists in telling truth to the community about money. Life consists in conformity to the Spirit. Money, it is recognized, is a great temptation to the contrary and for that reason can be a source of death. It turns out that money has radioactive potential. It is no wonder that the church was seized by "great fear." It is warned that private desire leads to violation of the community and affront against the Spirit. Likely the "great fear" among members of the community is rooted in the awareness that the same dangerous temptation is operative generally. The narrative recognizes that we church members are more likely to follow in the wake of Ananias and Sapphira than in the model of Barnabas.

V

The crisis and contest of gospel vis-à-vis money is front and center in the narrative of 8:9–24 concerning Simon. He is a popular worker of magic who dazzles those who observe his performance. His magic is so effective that he is said to be "the power of God that is called Great" (v. 10). His successful act, however, is interrupted by the gospel proclamation of Philip concerning "the kingdom of God." As a result, Simon's popular following deserts him and is baptized, so that they turn from Simon's magic to the power of the gospel that leads to "signs and great miracles" (v. 13). So great is the impact of Philip's proclamation and the "signs and miracles" that even Simon is baptized, as he joins the community of the church. In this opening scene of the narrative, there is no hint that Simon's baptism is anything other than an act of good faith.

In the next scene, however, the matter is very different. Simon observes that the apostles' laying on of hands causes the reception of the Holy Spirit and the transformative power that comes with the Spirit. Simon wants to receive the Holy Spirit and to have that transformative power; now his true motives are disclosed as he offers the apostles money in order to purchase the laying on of hands that he believes will endow him with power. He is candid to say that he will give them money in order to receive power, that is, so that he may have power to lay on hands in the way that they do. He does not say why he wants this power, what purpose he intends to serve. He might have said that he wanted such power so that he could effectively practice ministry, as do those with the Spirit. But he does not say so. Clearly his desire for such power is an end in itself; he wants to purchase and possess it, as though to regain his former popularity.

Thus it turns out that Simon's conversion and baptism are counterfeit. He still lives in a world of money power in which he assumes that everything is for sale and can be purchased for a price. His offer to the apostles reflects the quid pro quo world of money power; he does not understand that the giving of the Spirit is a gift and cannot be purchased. His bad-faith proposal earns him a severe rebuke and repudiation from Peter:

> May your silver perish with you, because you thought you could obtain God's gift with money! You have no part or share in this, for your heart is not right before God. Repent therefore of this wickedness of yours, and pray to the Lord that, if possible, the intent of your heart may be forgiven you. For I see that you are in the gall of bitterness and the chains of wickedness. (vv. 20–23)

Simon is denied access with the members of the movement who have all things in common. The two phrases "gall of bitterness" (see Deut. 29:18) and "chains of wickedness" (see Isa. 58:6) together link *the worship of false gods* and *the lack of economic justice.*[10] These two accents recur in Israel's faith; *economic injustice* is intimately linked to *idolatry.*

This narrative is yet one more attestation that *the transformative power of the Spirit of God* and *the world of commodity control* are diametrically opposed to each other. The narrative makes clear how gripping is the power of money, even in the face of the gospel. The power of God is not a commodity; the capacity for

10. Ibid., 135.

transformative ministry is not for sale. This is yet one more declaration that "I have no silver or gold, but . . ." (Acts 3:6).

VI

In 16:16–24 the narrative has Paul and Silas in a confrontation with a nefarious moneymaking scheme. The narrative is complex, because in addition to Paul the story features a "slave-girl" who has a "spirit of divination" and "her owners" who use her for moneymaking. The combination of divination and moneymaking draws the narrative into the purview of our topic.

The slave-girl, with her special powers, harasses Paul and his companion with a loud and repeated declaration: "These men are slaves of the Most High God." She is described as having a *puthona* (divining) spirit of divination; the modifier is linked to "python," so that her strange powers suggest, in canonical perspective, an allusion to the serpent in Genesis 3 and perhaps a reference to Satan and the demonic underworld. Her repeated assertion is a nuisance to Paul, who wants her to be silent. Because she is linked to the netherworld of spirits and because Paul exorcises her occupying spirit in the name of Jesus, we can see that she is "demon-possessed" and then freed from the demon in the same way that Jesus, in Luke's account, casts out demons (Luke 4:31–37). Paul manifests his apostolic authority in the act by referring his action to Jesus. It turns out that she, like the demon who recognized Jesus, rightly recognizes Paul's affiliation with the Most High God. She is an authentic witness to Paul and to his God. But Paul finds her an unbearable distraction. As a result, the slave-girl is freed of the demon and so ends her testimony to Paul and Paul's God. At that point she disappears from the narrative.

The narrative, however, turns on the fact that she is a fortune-teller who made a lot of money for her owners, pimps who exploited her. When she was emancipated from such powers, she could no longer perform, resulting in the loss of income for her owners. Not surprisingly Paul becomes the target of her owners, who resent the loss of income; they haul Paul and Silas into court before the magistrates. The accusation made against them of course is not an honest acknowledgment of the loss of money from such an ignoble process; it is rather, "These men are disturbing our city; they are Jews and are advocating customs that are not lawful for us as Romans to adopt or observe" (Acts 16:20–21).

The accusation sounds not unlike the familiar insistence in recent time that "we had no trouble here until outside agitators came and disturbed our way of life." Paul had indeed disrupted the way of life of the moneymakers! The loss of money from such an ignoble enterprise is concealed by appeal to the law. In opposition to Paul and Silas, the moneymakers are joined by the "crowd" that also attacks them. As a result Paul and Silas are stripped, flogged, and imprisoned. The following narrative reports that they were improbably and inexplicably freed from prison by an earthquake that vindicated Paul. By the end of the narrative Paul requires an apology from the magistrates who had wrongly imprisoned him:

> "Are they going to discharge us in secret? Certainly not! Let them come and take us out themselves." The police reported these words to the magistrates, and they were afraid when they heard that they were Roman citizens; so they came and apologized to them. And they took them out and asked them to leave the city. (vv. 37–39)

The story is of interest to us because of the strategic cooperation of *moneymakers* and the voice of the *netherworld* embodied in the slave-girl. It is not clear that the narrative intends to demonize the moneymakers. It is clear, however, that when religious claims are linked to moneymaking, no good will come of it. Thus Paul and Silas have come face to face with a moneymaking enterprise that also has influential access to Roman law court. The moneymakers can mobilize the judiciary against the force of the gospel that eventually, so the story goes, will prevail against the alliance of moneymaking and Roman order. All through the narrative, from Paul's initial act of exorcism (v. 18) to imprisonment (vv. 22–24), emancipation from prison (vv. 25–34), and his ultimate vindication before the magistrates (vv. 38–39), the apostles are unencumbered by neither power, by moneymakers, or by Roman order. Paul's singular testimony twice refers to Jesus: "I order you in the name of Jesus Christ to come out of her" (v. 18). "Believe on the Lord Jesus, and you will be saved, you and your household" (v. 31).

The narrative is a dramatic juxtaposition between *attestation to Jesus* and *the alliance of divination, money, and imperial order*. In the contest between the two, the narrative makes unambiguously clear that the power of Jesus—against the demon who possessed the slave-girl, against the imperial order, and against the money-makers—is decisive and truthful in triumph. The inference may be drawn that in this narrative, Paul could indeed reiterate Peter's earlier declaration, "I have no silver or gold, but . . ." Money and all that is linked to it is here devalued and relativized in society by the power of Jesus on the lips of Paul.

VII

The book of Acts ends with the report that Paul continued preaching in Rome, "proclaiming the kingdom of God and teaching about the Lord Jesus Christ with all boldness and without hindrance" (28:31). The penultimate verse of the book offers a curious, mostly unnoticed report: "He [Paul] lived there two whole years at his own expense and welcomed all who came to him" (v. 30). The phrase that NRSV renders "his own expense" is alternatively "his own hired dwelling." The term *idio* means "belonging only to him," that is, he lived in his own property; he paid for his own housing. The sentence is odd in light of the initial report that the believing community "had all things in common" (2:44; 4:32). I have suggested earlier, however, that this did not mean living in a commune but could allow for the possibility of private property that was held for the common benefit of the community. Here in this final reference Paul does have such property for himself. But of course his ministry required such living arrangements for the common good and prospering of the church community. There is in this statement an element of financial realism. It is likely, however, that the statement intends to assert that Paul was not in ministry for money or personal gain, nor is he dependent upon those to whom he preached. He could, under that circumstance, be "without hindrance" in his ministry of proclamation.

VIII

It is fair to say that the book of Acts is not overly preoccupied with questions of money and possessions. It is equally clear, however, that the singular power of the Holy Spirit that propels the apostolic church in its speech and action was on a collision course with the money interests, assumptions, and practices of the dominant economy. This narrative offers two kinds of evidence for that collision course. First, one can see a systemic encounter in the narrative. The generic practice of "all things in common" was an enactment of Easter faith. This practical, concrete evidence of Easter faith jarred and subverted all old power arrangements, including economic practices of extraction. This evidence was not missed by the authorities who were unsettled by the proclamation that produced such odd practical outcomes. The regular appearances of the apostles before the authorities cannot be separated from the actual practices of the church, a "walk" that corresponded to the "talk." Second, we are offered concrete case studies of the profound tension between gospel and money, or as Luke has it earlier, "God and wealth" (Luke 16:13). It is plausible that this programmatic tension continues to inform the narrative of Acts. Thus:

> "I have no silver or gold, but . . . in the name of Jesus Christ of Nazareth, stand up and walk." (3:6)
>
> "May your silver perish with you, because you thought you could obtain God's gift with money!" (8:20)
>
> "I order you in the name of Jesus Christ to come out of her." (16:18)
>
> "Believe on the Lord Jesus, and you will be saved, you and your household." (16: 31)

The narrative is not indifferent to the need for "possessions and goods" (2:45; see 4:34–35), but such goods are clearly subordinated to the claims, requirements, and possibilities of the gospel. The early church denied the autonomy of money and viewed such autonomy concerning money and possessions as an unacceptable alternative to the gospel.

CHAPTER 12

Paul

Life in the Land of Divine Generosity

As with all things in Paul, his views on money and possessions are scattered through his letters and admit of diversity and complexity. We may order our discussion concerning his views by a recognition of three dimensions of his work: (a) reports on his *personal transformative experience* of Christ, (b) his *theological-Christological reflection* that stands at the origin of Christian tradition, and (c) his work as a *pastoral practical theologian* concerned for the life and witness of the specific congregation that he addresses in his letters.

I

It is impossible to overstate the importance of Paul's personal conversion to Christ that provides for him a new basis of faith and thought. He describes himself as a Torah-keeping Jew, and then immediately and dramatically he is transformed by the overwhelming experience of Christ that places the grace of God at the center of his thinking. He found this radical free gift from God to be subversive of any merit-based religion, whether at the behest of the Roman Empire or in any reductionist form of his own Judaism. As we will see, his rejection of merit-based religion for him spilled over into a rejection of merit-based economics that was displaced by economic generosity that corresponded to the divine generosity of grace. More recent scholarship, notably that of Richard Horsley, Neil Elliott, and Brigitte Kahl, has considered the way in which Paul understands the gospel as a deep and radical alternative to the extractive nature of the Roman Empire with its accent on predatory taxation.[1] It is on this basis that Paul can pose the question to the church in Corinth: "What do you have that you did not receive?" (1 Cor. 4:7). The answer that Paul intends is "Nothing!" Nothing is possessed that is not given. It is all a gift! Paul is dealing with a church community that wants to make socioeconomic distinctions and differentiations among its members; his response is that there is no ground for such differentiations, for all those in Christ share in equal dependence on God's gifts:

> What places all believers, whether in Paul's time or in ours, on common ground is their equal dependence as ones who are the undeserving recipients of God's grace. So who is anybody trying to fool by boasting as if this common ground of grace were not the most important fact about themselves?[2]

This statement, while not directly concerned with economic matters, forcefully pertains to economic matters. All that is possessed is gift. For that reason, money and possessions have no leverage in gospel purview to divide, to make social distinctions, or to stratify according to wealth. As a result, Paul offers his deep and singular conviction concerning the gospel and finds economic differences to be irrelevant and unwelcome, since all depend on divine generosity:

> Not that I am referring to being in need; for I have learned to be content with whatever I have. I know what it is to have little, and I know what it is to have plenty. In any and all circumstances I have learned the secret of being well-fed and of going hungry, of having plenty and of being in need. I can do all things through him who strengthens me. (Phil. 4:11–13)

1. Richard A. Horsley, *Jesus and Empire: The Kingdom of God and the New World Disorder* (Minneapolis: Fortress Press, 2003); Neil Elliott, *The Arrogance of Nations: Reading Romans in the Shadow of Empire* (Minneapolis: Fortress Press, 2008); Brigitte Kahl, *Galatians Re-Imagined: Reading with the Eyes of the Vanquished* (Minneapolis: Fortress Press, 2010).

2. J. Paul Sampley, "The First Letter to the Corinthians," in *The New Interpreter's Bible*, ed. Leander E. Keck (Nashville: Abingdon Press, 2000), 10:837.

The threefold contrast of "little/plenty," "well-fed/hungry," and "plenty/being in need" reflects economic extremes. He denies none of that. All of that, however, is relativized by his confidence in "him who strengthens me." That one in whom he trusts supplies all that is needed; as a result Paul's contentment (sufficiency) is not grounded in self but in the reality of limitless divine generosity. Paul relativizes economic status and circumstance by an awareness that the present order of things is quite provisional and will not last. Thus "the appointed time has grown short":

> From now on, let even those who have wives be as though they had none, and those who mourn as though they were not mourning, and those who rejoice as though they were not rejoicing, and those who buy as though they had no possessions, and those who deal with the world as though they had no dealings with it. For the present form of this world is passing away. (1 Cor. 7:29–31)

The repeated "as though" is framed by two statements concerning the end of the present world arrangement. In verse 29 "the appointed time has grown short." In verse 31 "the present form of this world is passing away." Between the two, Christians can live in defiance of present arrangements and in expectation:

> The evocations invite the Corinthians to imagine the life of faith as one lived in the world but detached or disengaged from the world's values. With these snapshots or vignettes Paul answers the question of how believers can "remain as they are," namely, still living within the world, without being held captive or conformed to the values and structures of the world. The answer: Live in these structures and in these relationships "as if not," as if the world, its structures, and these relationships did not provide life with its value and meaning because one knows that the defining relationship, and therefore value, comes from one's relation to God, in Christ.[3]

It is not a far reach from this statement to the more familiar statement of Romans 12:2 concerning conformity and transformation. Those in Christ are transformed and so do not conform to the present age. In his series of statements of "as though," Paul arrives

3. Ibid., 887.

at economic matters concerning "buying . . . no possessions" and dealing with the world. Paul knows well about buying and having possessions. But they are not definitive for believers who are free to live otherwise. If the present economic world is one of quid pro quo transactions that aim at confiscating the goods and wealth of others, especially from the vulnerable, Christians need not conform to such assumptions and practices. Freedom from these worldly mandates eventuates in a capacity for generosity. As all possessions are gifts, so God "loves a cheerful giver," that is, one who imitates God's own limitless generosity:

> The point is this: the one who sows sparingly will also reap sparingly, and the one who sows bountifully will also reap bountifully. Each of you must give as you have made up your mind, not reluctantly or under compulsion, for God loves a cheerful giver. And God is able to provide you with every blessing in abundance, so that by always having enough of everything, you may share abundantly in every good work. (2 Cor. 9:6–8)

The language of economics is unmistakable. The urging is for bountiful gifts, sowing and reaping bountifully, cheerfully giving, blessing in abundance, enough of everything, sharing abundantly. The attitude that Paul rejects is "extortion" (v. 5), giving reluctantly, under compulsion. Paul weaves together *the generosity of God* and the responding *generosity of the community.* He is quite aware that such a perspective on money and possessions is counter to normal economic practice that traffics in scarcity and ends in parsimony. Paul clearly carries his acute insight into divine grace into an economic practice of generous sharing that evokes abundance. The economic mandates of faith are completely grounded in theological reality that he himself has experienced and embraced. The term "extortion" (v. 5) in NRSV is *pleonexian*, exactly the same term we have seen in Luke 12:15, where it is usually translated "covetousness" or "greed." The rendering "extortion" gives the term a more systemic dimension. Thus Paul urges his addressees to disengage from the economy of extraction and extortion and to embrace an economics of abundance that is grounded in divine generosity. A "cheerful giver" is one who gives in joy and without grudge or reluctance, thus reflective of God's own cheerful generosity.

II

Paul's advocacy of an economy of generosity that defies the parsimony of normal economics is given full play in his appeal for contributions to the Jerusalem church from the Corinthian congregation (2 Cor. 8–9; see Rom. 15:26–27; 1 Cor. 16:1–4).[4] The latter church apparently was reluctant and parsimonious; that is, it acted according to the common worldly norms of what is reasonable. Paul urges this church to think otherwise and to respond to his plea on different grounds. He makes two kinds of arguments. First, he cites the case of the Macedonian church that set a precedent for generosity; even though that church faced a "severe ordeal of affliction," it "overflowed in a wealth of generosity" (2 Cor. 8:2). That church may be a model for Corinth in its full embrace of an economy of generosity.

In his second argument, Paul reminds the church of Corinth of the "big story" of the gospel that is now "retrofitted in economic categories."[5] The true model and embodiment of generosity is the self-giving of our Lord Jesus Christ. He was rich! That is, he possessed all the powers of the Father. But he willingly became poor, that is, entered the risk of human history that led to his suffering and death. And then the punch line: "so that by his poverty you might become rich" (v. 9). This has to be one of the most remarkable and defiant statements in all of gospel rhetoric. It is a defiance of all conventional economic wisdom that it takes money to make money. Paul has recast *salvific categories* into *economic terms*, so that self-giving is a way to generate abundant wealth and well-being for others.

The convergence of the Macedonian model and the christological affirmation together constitute a profound appeal to the church in Corinth. These believers can see in Macedonia that generosity really works and is doable. But behind that concrete ecclesial reality is the christological claim of self-giving. It does not get any better than this! This direct and unqualified linking of theology and economy is at the heart of Paul's conviction about generosity.

4. See Keith Nickle, *The Collection: A Study in Paul's Strategy* (Naperville, IL: Allenson, 1966).

5. J. Paul Sampley, "The Second Letter to the Corinthians," in *The New Interpreter's Bible*, ed. Leander E. Keck (Nashville: Abingdon Press, 2000), 11:123.

Paul writes as a practical theologian. He does not coerce the church, as that would violate the act of self-giving abundance. Nor does he ask for excessive self-giving, even though Christ gave self excessively. He asks only for "a fair balance between your present abundance and their need, so that their abundance may be for your need, in order that there may be a fair balance" (v. 13–14). Paul completes that part of his argument with an appeal to the manna narrative of Exodus 16:18: "The one who had much did not have too much, and the one who had little did not have too little" (v. 15). If ever the biblical tradition provided a case study in divine generosity, the manna story is it. Paul does not go on to remind the church that Israel in the manna story was prohibited from storing up surplus, but the point is readily inferred. Thus we come full circle to his query in 1 Corinthians 4:7: "What do you have that you did not receive?" Manna is all gift; what the church in Corinth has is all gift. It was all given. And now, in a corresponding act of generosity, it may be shared as the church in Macedonia has done.

Macedonia and Achaia have been pleased to share their resources with the poor among the saints at Jerusalem. They were pleased to do this; and indeed they owe it to them, for if the Gentiles have come to share in the *spiritual* blessings of the Jewish Christians in Jerusalem, they ought also to be of service to them in *material* things. Paul agilely translates from spiritual blessing (given by Jewish Christians to Gentile Christians) into material things (to be given by Gentile Christians to Jewish Christians); he does so on the basis of the bodily grace of Jesus Christ.

III

The theme of divine generosity as an impetus for churchly conduct is articulated in the well-known poetry of Philippians 2:5–11. The christological claim of the text, surely normative for the early church, is that Jesus was in "the form of God" and enjoyed "equality with God." Thus the preexistence of Christ came to be normative for the rule of faith, articulated by Irenaeus and then in the normative confessions and symbols of the church. The first rhetorical turn in the poetry is the "but" of verse 7, whereby Christ Jesus relinquished divine status and emptied himself as human and as slave. The term "empty" (*kenosis*) became a tag word for the self-emptying of Jesus from divine status to human vulnerability. We cannot overestimate the radicality of this act of "divine emptying." This self-emptying vulnerability, pushed to its historical extremity, ends in suffering and death. Karl Barth can say of this claim that this servant "has no rights of his own."[6] Paul extends the freighted theme of "emptying" to its ecclesial dimension in a way pertinent to our topic. Hans Urs von Balthasar has written of the radicality of the theme:

> Human thought and human language break down in the presence of this mystery: namely, that the eternal relations of Father and Son are focused, during the "time" of Christ's earthly wanderings, and in a sense which must be taken with full seriousness, in the relations between the man Jesus and his heavenly Father, and that the Holy Spirit lives as their go-between who, inasmuch as he proceeds from the Son, must also be affected by the Son's humanity.[7]

The second rhetorical turn in the poetry is the "therefore" of verse 9, wherein the status of Jesus is reversed as he is exalted as Lord. This double movement of emptying and exaltation receives narrative performance as crucifixion and resurrection.

Paul's citation of this poetry is remarkable for the way in which he turns from the mystery of the self-emptying of Christ to the self-emptying of the church. He takes the self-emptying of Christ, according to what must have been a normative christological tradition by his time, as certain. But his concern, in appeal to that tradition, is to make an argument about the life and conduct of the church. Thus in verses 1–5 he urges that the church, in its concrete practice, must imitate the self-emptying of Jesus Christ. He requires of the church a self-emptying for the sake of others in the community:

> Make my joy complete: be of the same mind, having the same love, being in full accord and of one mind. Do nothing from selfish ambition or conceit, but in humility regard others as better than yourselves. Let each of you look not to your own interests, but to the interests of others. (vv. 2–4)

6. Karl Barth, *Church Dogmatics*, IV/3 (Edinburgh: T. & T. Clark, 1962), 602.

7. Hans Urs von Balthasar, *Mysterium Paschale: The Mystery of Easter* (Grand Rapids: Eerdmans, 1990), 30.

Paul urges that each must look beyond his or her own "interests" (v. 4). The use of that term is not very specific; it can pertain to all sorts of *material* concerns, that is, to money and possessions. The bid is for recognition that the claims of others are to be given precedence over one's own claims. Paul yet again moves agilely from *christological* to *ecclesial* matters; we are then not far removed from economic concerns. One does not need to be Marxist to recognize that much of the disputatious energy in a local congregation concerns matters that are rooted in material reality, even if they are cast in other ways. Self-emptying in economic conduct is done in an assurance that there is more than enough. When one is convinced of the scarcity of goods or for that matter a scarcity of divine grace, one readily becomes parsimonious and exclusionary. Such a stance, however, is inimical to the "mind of Christ."

IV

After his long and complex argument in the Letter to the Romans concerning God's grace that pertains to both Jewish and Gentile Christians, Paul finally arrives at his inventory of appropriate Christian conduct (Rom. 12:1–2). The transitional "therefore" of verse 1 is a clear affirmation that the norms of conduct commended here are rooted in the preceding argument concerning God's overwhelming, self-giving generosity in Jesus of Nazareth. Paul knows very well about the world in which he and his addressees live. It is a world of anxious, fearful calculation. Conformity to such a world situates one amid an economy of anxious scarcity in which others are perceived as threat or as competitor for limited goods.

But of course Paul's urging is for Christians to be transformed (as he had been transformed) and so resistant to such conformity. He himself knows about such transformation, and now he invites his addressees to experience the same. He urges, moreover, that they, like him, are to be a "living sacrifice" offered to God. As his letter makes clear, the God to whom such living sacrifice is offered is not the fearful God of parsimony but is the creator God who assures the flourishing of creation. What follows are the concrete forms such living sacrifice may take in the real world. I will mention only four of these specific mandates.

1. Among the gifts entrusted to the church (it is all gift!) is the gift of giving that is to be done "in generosity" (v. 8).The term rendered "generosity" is elsewhere "liberality" (2 Cor. 8:2; 9:11, 13); it can also be rendered "in sincerity, in simplicity, simply," that is, don't make it complicated. Do it directly and concretely so that the whole body may benefit. Such a mandate clearly assumes an abundance from God.

2. Transformative life includes attentiveness to "the needs of the saints" (v. 13). This mandate concerns sharing resources with others in need in the community of the church. This brief notice may be an allusion to the offering already mentioned in 2 Corinthians 8.

3. The transformed "extend hospitality to strangers" (v. 13). Welcome to strangers indicates an abundance, enough to go around. When we draw tight exclusionary boundaries against strangers, it is because we fear scarcity, for example, not enough grace to include gays, not enough jobs to include immigrants, not enough resources to include Muslims. An economy of scarcity is always propelled to the exclusion of the other. Paul's gospel ethic (that turns out to be a gospel economy) contradicts such fearful parsimony.

4. The transformed need never avenge themselves (v. 19). Vengeance is an act of quid pro quo justice. The reason Paul rejects such action is that he knows that we do not live in a quid pro quo world but in a world of generosity that runs quid beyond every imaginable quo. We have ample evidence of quid pro quo economics among us:

> When powerless labor is kept at an unlivable minimum wage
> When food stamps are denied the poor because they are "unproductive"
> When payday credit arrangements are designed to keep the resourceless deeply in debt

All such economic practices are retaliation by the ownership class against those who do not "deserve" (for whatever reason) an act of generosity. Paul stands in the long covenantal tradition that interrupts such vengeful economics by the practice of Sabbath that lets the working poor have rest alongside the ownership class, by the practice of debt cancellation that allows the vulnerable back into the economy, and by Jubilee that permits a second chance for those who have fallen behind. In recent time we have witnessed the rule of quid pro quo in the stance of the European banking community against the debt in Greece. Quid pro quo economics insists that there is no free lunch, even though the ownership class gorges on free lunches. On all counts, Paul's economics of transformation contradicts the economics of conformity.

V

The Epistles to the Ephesians and the Colossians operate in a different sphere and idiom, but they again show the way in which Paul holds together his theological-christological conviction and his work as a practical, pastoral theologian.[8] In both letters Paul offers a contrast between the old life and the new life of faith. In Ephesians, the old life is characterized in terms of what is to be relinquished:

> So then, putting away falsehood, let all of us speak the truth to our neighbors, for we are members of one another. . . . Thieves must give up stealing; rather let them labor and work honestly with their own hands, so as to have something to share with the needy. Let no evil talk come out of your mouths, but only what is useful for building up. . . . Put away from you all bitterness and wrath and anger and wrangling and slander, together with all malice. (4:25–31)

> But fornication and impurity of any kind, or greed, must not even be mentioned among you, as is proper among saints. Entirely out of place is obscene, silly, and vulgar talk; but instead, let there be thanksgiving. Be sure of this, that no fornicator or impure person, or one who is greedy (that is, an idolater), has any inheritance in the kingdom of Christ and of God. (5:3–5)

This inventory includes all conduct that disrupts a flourishing community. Prominent in the list is attentiveness to economic practices that will skew neighborliness. This includes thievery. In our contemporary context we are increasingly aware of the way in which legal thievery is committed against the vulnerable, as in the

8. I am aware of the critical questions concerning the authorship of Ephesians and Colossians but here treat them according to an assumed Pauline provenance.

practice of wage theft or exploitative interest rates on loans or predatory credit arrangements. While such strategies may not have been on the horizon of Paul, such reference points are a fair extrapolation from his words.

More specifically, the warning on "greed" (again *pleonexia*) is mentioned alongside other damaging conduct. Most important is the linkage of greed (*pleonektēs*) with idolatry, so that exploitative affront against a vulnerable neighbor is equated with false worship. That equivalence, in the horizon of the Sinai commandments, brings together the first commandments on idolatry (Exod. 20:1–6) and the tenth commandment on coveting (Exod. 20:17), which form an envelope for the whole of the Decalogue.[9] That linkage is evident, moreover, in the narrative of the golden calf in Exodus 32, wherein *gold* as commodity value is fashioned into a *god* in a drastic departure from covenant. One cannot, of course, insist that the Letter to the Ephesians is focused on money and possessions; that theme, however, is surely on the horizon of the letter. And since the letter addresses the "dividing wall" that separated the community (Eph. 2:14), economics may be front and center in our interpretation. While the accent in the letter concerns Jewish and Gentile Christians, our own interpretive context suggests that the "dividing wall" that rends the community (church and civic community) is the economic division between haves and have-nots.[10] The letter proposes that the "new self" embraces practices that resist such divisions and distinctions. A context of rivalry and competition may indeed generate "bitterness and wrath and anger and wrangling and slander" (4:31). A self-sufficient indulgence may result in "fornication and impurity" (5:3). Paul urges, against such destructive behavior, a stance of neighborliness that would eschew such competitive hostility.

The matter is not different in the Letter to the Colossians. Again this letter lists the modes of conduct that are to be "put to death" among believers:

9. In *Sabbath as Resistance: Saying NO to the Culture of NOW* (Louisville, KY: Westminster John Knox Press, 2014), I have treated the first and tenth commandments as an envelope for the whole of the Decalogue, at the center of which is the Sabbath command.

10. See Matt Taibbi, *The Divide: American Injustice in the Age of the Wealth Gap* (New York: Spiegel & Grau, 2014). His use of "divide" in his title reflects a "wealth gap" that is as divisive and destructive for society as was the ancient "dividing wall" of which Paul writes.

> Put to death, therefore, whatever in you is earthly: fornication, impurity, passion, evil desire, and greed (which is idolatry). On account of these the wrath of God is coming on those who are disobedient. These are the ways you also once followed, when you were living that life. But now you must get rid of all such things—anger, wrath, malice, slander, and abusive language from your mouth. (3:5–8)

The list is parallel to that in Ephesians and again notes "greed [*pleonexian*] (which is idolatry)."[11] The craving for what belongs to others generates all of these destructive behaviors and is rooted, says the writer, in a mistaken theological commitment. Thus *disordered economics* is grounded in a *mistaken theological loyalty* wherein the pursuit of commodity is taken, in and of itself, as the purpose of life. Such a pursuit will inevitably lead to the disruption of the community:

> Greed refers to the haughty and ruthless belief that everything, including other persons, exists for one's own personal amusement and purposes. Essentially it turns our own desires into idols. It is the overweening desire to possess more and more things and to run roughshod over other persons to get them. It stands opposed to the willingness to give to others regardless of the cost to self. Greed can crave after persons and is never satiated by its conquests but always lusts for more.[12]

The gospel alternative of the "new self" contradicts all of these toxic practices:

> As God's chosen ones, holy and beloved, clothe yourselves with *compassion*, kindness, humility, meekness, and patience. Bear with one another and, if anyone has a complaint against another, forgive each other; just as the Lord has forgiven you, so you also must forgive. Above all, clothe yourselves with love, which binds

11. On this phrase see Brain S. Rosner, *Greed as Idolatry: The Origin and Meaning of a Pauline Metaphor* (Grand Rapids: Eerdmans, 2007). Rosner regards the phrase as a metaphor and concludes: "Thus, at the risk of blunting the affective impact of the metaphor, 'greed as idolatry' may be paraphrased as teaching that *to have a strong desire to acquire and keep for yourself more and more money and material things is an attack on God's exclusive rights to human love and devotion, trust and confidence, and service and obedience*" (173; italics in the original).

12. David Garland, quoted by Nijay K. Gupta, *Colossians*, Smyth & Helwys Bible Commentary (Macon, GA: Smyth & Helwys, 2013), 132–33.

everything together in perfect harmony. And let the peace of Christ rule in your hearts, to which indeed you were called in the one body. And be *thankful*. (3:12–15; italics added)

This list begins in "compassion" and ends in gratitude. Compassion concerns love of neighbor; gratitude concerns love of God. Between these two terms, the repeated accent is on forgiveness:

"*Forgive* each other . . ."
"The Lord has *forgiven* you . . ."
"You must *forgive*."

This usage is no doubt remote from macroeconomics and any policy of forgiveness of debts.[13] The intent here surely concerns a more intimate form of neighborliness. But whether taken in the large sphere of *debt cancellation* or in the more intimate zone of *neighborliness*, forgiveness is the breaking of quid pro quo modes of power whereby those with resources and leverage can prey upon and take advantage of those without resources and leverage. The breaking of the greed cycle is elemental to this gospel ethic; such greed is an act of worship of the gods of self-sufficiency, self-securing, and self-enhancement. Against all such preoccupation with self, the gospel ethic is fixed upon regard for the neighbor as a companion in faith. These two letters imagine and anticipate (a) a drastic disruption of an old mode of life that sets one against another and (b) an entry into a new life "which binds everything together in perfect harmony" (5:14).

Philip Carrington has identified a pattern of rhetoric and content that recurs across these epistles.[14] He proposes, with great persuasiveness, that this pattern is reflective of a primitive Christian catechism that moves from theological affirmation to practical conduct. That pattern consists in these items:

New birth
Putting away evil

13. David Graeber, *Debt: The First 5,000 Years* (Brooklyn: Melville House, 2011), 390–91, ends his book by urging that debts should be canceled: "Nothing would be more important than to wipe the slate clean for everyone, make a break with our accustomed morality, and start again." His judgment is resonant with Paul's urging of forgiveness.

14. Philip Carrington, *The Primitive Christian Catechism* (Cambridge: Cambridge University Press, 1940).

Being subject to one another
Staying alert
Being ready to resist

Carrington suggests, moreover, that the dramatic performance of this new birth is in baptism, whereby the "old self" is put off and a "new self" is embraced.[15] And indeed the long-established tradition of baptism still summons to such *renunciation* and *embrace*:

> Do you renounce Satan and all the spiritual forces of wickedness that rebel against God?
> Do you renounce the evil powers of this world which corrupt and destroy the creatures of God?
> Do you renounce all sinful desires that draw you from the love of God?
> Do you turn to Jesus Christ and accept him as your Savior?
> Do you put your whole trust in his grace and love?
> Do you promise to follow and obey him as your Lord?[16]

The language of renunciation and embrace sounds odd to us even while we utilize it liturgically, because so much baptism has been collapsed into a romantic fog that is remote from the urgency of these epistles written and first read in contexts where the Christian confession mattered enormously.

To the extent that Carrington (himself an Anglican bishop) is correct, we might recover the rhetoric of renunciation and embrace precisely as it pertains to money and possessions; there is no doubt that the predatory economy in which we live and to which we are variously attracted is a form of idolatry, a worship of the self that can leverage other, more vulnerable selves. Andrew Lincoln's verdict on greed sounds like a characterization of our own predatory mainstream culture:

> The fifth vice, "covetousness" . . . , is the insatiable greed whereby people assume that things or other people exist simply for their own gratification. . . . The thought is that all idolatry involves some form of covetousness. When humanity refuses to acknowledge

15. Ibid., 87, 89.
16. *The Book of Common Prayer* (New York: Church Hymnal Corporation and Seabury Press, 1979), 302.

> the various aspects of life as the gift of the Creator, it attempts to seize these things for itself and thereby elevates some desired object to the center of life.[17]

It is impossible to overstate the radicality of this understanding of Christian baptism and Christian life. While the catalogs of vices in Ephesians and Colossians do indeed contain references to sexual perversity and impurity, it is clear that preoccupation with such sexual affronts has greatly hindered the capacity of the church to take seriously the often related economic dimension of the new life to which the church is summoned with reference to this series of acquisitive distortions.

VI

The fact that a like catalog of "desires of the flesh" and "fruit of the Spirit" occurs in Galatians permits us to segue to a final consideration concerning Paul on money and possessions. The "desires of the flesh," against which the church is warned, are "fornication, impurity, licentiousness, idolatry, sorcery, enmities, strife, jealousy, anger, quarrels, dissensions, factions, envy, drunkenness, carousing, and things like these. . . . Those who do such things will not inherit the kingdom of God" (Gal. 5:19–21).

Paul calls them "obvious" (v. 19). It is of note that Paul uses the phrase "kingdom of God," a sharp alternative to the kingdom of Rome. The fruit of the Spirit, by contrast, includes "love, joy, peace, patience, kindness, generosity, faithfulness, gentleness, and self-control" (vv. 22–23).

Brigitte Kahl, in her remarkable study, has shown that the "law" to which Paul is opposed in this epistle is the "law of Caesar":

> The "works of the flesh" . . . are spelled out in a list of vices (5:19–21) that show an exceptionally strong emphasis on community conflicts and tensions. As the conflict-provoking "works of the flesh" according to 5:21 constitute a practice (*prassontes*) that excludes people from the kingdom (or empire) of God, they are tantamount to the "works of the law" as a social practice

17. Andrew T. Lincoln, "The Letter to the Colossians," in *The New Interpreter's Bible*, ed. Leander E. Keck (Nashville: Abingdon Press, 2000), 11:642.

> that in our reading is equivalent to the combat order of Caesar's empire.[18]

Thus the issue concerns actual social practices:

> Paul demands a "crucifixion" of the self-obsessed and self-driven flesh (5:24) and a life entirely shaped by the spirit (5:25). Mutual provocations and envy need to stop, for they are born out of an inflated sense of self-value (*kenodoxoi*) that always competes with the other for honor and recognition (5:26) and is the basic prerequisite for the honor/shame-based power structures of Caesar's empire. The competitiveness among the Galatians imitates, "incarnates," and reproduces the vertical "combat order" of the conquerors, reinscribing it on the "flesh," the carnal existence (*sarx*) of the conquered.[19]

The "fruit of the Spirit" constitute an index of matters that concern "the law of Christ" (6:2), which contradicts the "law of Caesar": "For the whole law is summed up in a single commandment: 'You shall love your neighbor as yourself'" (5:14).

Thus Paul shows how the pivot of the Torah from Leviticus 19:18, accented by Jesus (Mark 12:33), is the order of the new governance of Christ. This *law of neighborliness* is a contrast to the *law of Caesar* that sets one against another: "If, however, you bite and devour one another, take care that you are not consumed by one another" (Gal. 5:15). The imagery of biting and devouring summarizes practices that make community life impossible. It is worth noting that the term "bite" (*nšk*) in the Old Testament has a connotation of economic "bite" (see Exod. 22:24; Lev. 25:37; Deut. 23:20). It is not unlikely that Paul could have made such a connection in his phrase "bite and devour." Conversely, it is of note that the fruit of the Spirit includes "generosity" (Gal. 5:22), so that an economy of abundance is surely in purview.

In his ethical admonition, it is impossible to overstate that Paul's accent on the "law of Christ" concerns positive regard for those who are neighbors: "Bear one another's burdens, and in this way you will fulfill the law of Christ" (Gal. 6:2).

18. Kahl, *Galatians Re-Imagined*, 270.
19. Ibid.

Paul envisions a community of interdependence among sisters and brothers to the benefit of all. Thus we sing:

> We share each other's woes,
> each other's burdens bear,
> And often for each other flows
> a sympathizing tear.[20]

That sense of mutual support and solidarity is the hallmark of the church, a characterization that contradicts, according to Kahl, the combative order of Caesar and that contradicts the usurpatious individualism of our economy that permits the strong to prey upon the weak. It is no accident that in contemporary society the church should be generative of justice ministries that seek to counteract the predatory assumptions of the dominant economy.

Paul's note on bearing each other's burdens is juxtaposed with Galatians 6:5 as a counterstatement: "For all must carry their own loads." Paul surely intends that verses 2 and 5 should be read together. Richard Hays accents the "and" of the two statements: "Paul is saying that we are all personally accountable to God, *and* that we are called to form communities in which we help one another through mutual corrective admonition."[21]

The focus on either of these two statements to the neglect of the other would greatly distort Paul's intent. Verse 2 enjoins aid to one's neighbor; verse 5 summons to personal responsibility. The statement in verse 5 clearly intends that members of the community must each be accountable for their own action and life, but in a community of mutual obligation and responsibility: "The tension between v. 2 and v. 5, then, serves the rhetorical purpose of highlighting Paul's paired "themes of mutual responsibility" and individual accountability.[22] This tension that is intrinsic to the community invites us to reflect on the much-quoted statement of 2 Thessalonians 3:10: "Anyone unwilling to work should not eat."

Chapter 3 of 2 Thessalonians begins with an admonition to pray (3:1). In verse 6, however, the letter turns to practical, material matters and urges that every member of the community has an

20. John Fawcett, "Blessed Be the Tie that Binds," *The New Century Hymnal* (Cleveland: Pilgrim Press, 1995), 393.

21. Richard B. Hays, "The Letter to the Galatians," in *The New Interpreter's Bible*, ed. Leander E. Keck (Nashville: Abingdon Press, 2000), 11:335.

22. Ibid.

obligation to be productive in the service of the common good. This requirement of accountability for the good of the whole sounds like an echo or an anticipation of the juxtaposition we have seen in Galatians 6:2, 5: care for each other and continue on our own. Linda McKinnish Bridges recognizes the economic dimensions of the crisis facing the church in this letter:

> The economic realities are harsh; the rules of the professional group are clear. The economic structure of the artisan community demands that every member work. If one member fails, the entire project deteriorates. If a member of the guild is not properly carrying one's own weight, or handling one's own portion of the load, the entire workshop suffers. The working group depends on the productivity of each member. If, for example, the production is divided among the workers, with some members being responsible for the preparation of the raw goods, such as wood or leather, with another member being responsible for crafting the product, and yet another for cleaning and finishing the product at the final stage of production, then all the members have an important role in the work production of the community. If one member fails to fulfill his role, the entire group suffers.[23]

There is indeed no free lunch! Everyone must bear his or her burden.

It is curious, however, that this dictum of Paul is commonly used to castigate the "unproductive, undeserving poor" who do not, it is said, merit support from the community because they have not worked. Such a reprimanding use of Paul's statement is regularly mouthed by those who do not want to support the "unproductive and undeserving," that is, do not want to bear another's burdens. Such a use of the verse, however, is very often on the lips of those who do not work but who in fact belong to the leisure class and because of great ownership do not need to work. Paul's indictment of idle "busybodies" (v. 11) may pertain exactly to the ownership class that has no need to work in order to contribute to the common good. Abraham Smith suggests that the phrase "idle busybodies" in fact concerns those who cause disorder in the community, so that it

23. Linda McKinnish Bridges, *1 & 2 Thessalonians*, Smyth & Helwys Bible Commentary (Macon, GA: Smyth & Helwys, 2008), 254–55.

is *disorder* and not *laziness* that is the agenda for Paul.[24] "Disorder" in the community may as well be caused by the "idle rich" as by the "undeserving poor," so that what is at stake is contribution to and cooperation with the common good of the community. "Work," that is, work for one's self, can create disorder. The work that is commended here is work that pertains to the well-being of the entire community.

It is clear enough that Paul advocates a very different economy, one that is grounded in Christ's law of neighborliness that is an echo of covenantal Judaism. This alternative economy is expressed in Galatians and Thessalonians with an accent on *the common good*, voiced in the dramatic *contrast of old self and new self* in Ephesians and Colossians, and urged as a *bid for generosity* in Corinthians and Romans. I anticipate that Kahl's focus on the predatory law of Caesar may be a coming pivot point in Pauline interpretation. To the extent that that is true, we can see that Paul on money and possessions invites a radical rethinking of both common practices in a market ideology and common assumptions about Paul's affirmation of "radical grace."

I suggest that there are two interpretive tasks in considering money and possessions in the thought of Paul. The first task is to see that Paul's letters characteristically have a stake in material questions, and any rendering of his theme of grace as spiritual, individualistic, or otherworldly misconstrues Paul. The above discussion makes clear that Paul characteristically urges his readers to an economy that derives from Christ and that contradicts Caesar. The second, more difficult task is to see that Paul's testimony about money and possessions concerns not just the internal life of the Christian community; it is, beyond that, a proposal and an advocacy for the reordering of the public economy. Thus the "law of Christ" contradicts and challenges the law of Caesar and in our time the market ideology (Gal. 6:2). Thus the "kingdom of God" contradicts the kingdom of Caesar (5:21). His appeal to (not imposition on) the church is this: "So then, whenever we have an opportunity, let us work for the good of all, and especially for those of the family of faith" (6:10).

24. Abraham Smith, "The Second Letter to the Thessalonians," in *The New Interpreter's Bible*, ed. Leander E. Keck (Nashville: Abingdon Press, 2000), 11:767–68.

Paul's concern is "especially" for the church, those whom he has addressed in his letters. Beyond that, however, he has in purview the "good of all," that is, the entire world economy. There is nothing parochial or in-house about Paul's vision; it concerns the performance of the new rule of God as the predatory rule of Caesar passes away. Chrysostom can assert: "The way of life that comes from grace takes the whole land and sea as the table of mercy."[25]

The world economy (of land and sea) is reenvisioned as a "table of mercy"! In our contemporary economy, the table of wealth leaves only crumbs for all but the wealthy. For that reason, the image of a table of mercy for all is of immense urgency. It is no wonder that in the black church tradition of my denomination, the Communion table is called the "welcome table." Paul sees that the law of Christ—with each carrying his or her own load and all carrying the burden of each other—works from a welcome table, a table of mercy, that contradicts all exclusions from well-being. This is indeed bread for the world, a reaping of abundance as loaves abound.

25. Quoted by Hays, "Letter to the Galatians," 337.

CHAPTER 13

The Pastoral Epistles

Order in the Household

Three epistles—1 and 2 Timothy and Titus—are dubbed the Pastoral Epistles because they are concerned with the practical pastoral realities of congregational life and are preoccupied with matters of proper leadership in the churches. They reflect a moment in the early Christian movement later than Paul's foundational work and address the quotidian life of a congregation with recurring issues of *sound teaching* (what curriculum to use), *good leadership* (whom can you trust), *good order* (clear procedures), and the *moral life* of its members. The writer of these letters attests that the responsible social conduct of church members constitutes a primary witness to the gospel as the church is present in and observed by its larger cultural context. (Since we cannot identify the writer or writers of these letters, I shall simply refer to "the writer.") One might imagine that this writer long ago knew two of the primary rules of thumb for a faithful pastor:

1. Do not get involved in quarrels that detract from the main work.
2. Do not participate in unfaithful or irresponsible ways in matters of sexuality or money, the two seductions that will most certainly and promptly undo an effective ministry and damage the life of a congregation.

Of these concerns, it is money that concerns us here. The writer urges and assumes that a Christian congregation and its leaders must not be seduced or defined by money, because attraction to money is a powerful impediment to the work of ministry.

I

The positive accent for leadership in these letters is that those who lead must engage in good management of the household. The writer suggests that a church leader, in order to manage a church congregation properly, must first of all be able to manage his (!) household: "He must manage his own household well, keeping his children submissive and respectful in every way—for if someone does not know how to manage his own household, how can he take care of God's church?" (1 Tim. 3:4–5; see 1 Tim. 5:14; Titus 2:5).

The concern is a particular governance of the family, with special attention to the proper discipline and nurture of children and the maintenance of good order in the family:

> Given the sort of authority assumed here, it is noteworthy that the other attributes expected in the supervisor are ameliorative moral qualities that mitigate against any hint of arbitrary or harsh uses of power. To be sober and not a lover of wine means that the supervisor is not corrupted by pleasure, and his judgments are not affected by crass addictions. To be nonviolent and not given to battle means that the leader is not corrupted by envy and vainglory and is able to cultivate cooperation rather than competition, foment peace rather than conflict. Not to be a lover of money means that the leader is not corrupted by avarice and is able to place the community's interests before his own. Likewise, the virtues of prudence and reasonableness point to a leader who applies the best qualities of mind and character to decision making.[1]

To be sure, money is not mentioned in the text of 1 Timothy 3:4–5; but proper household management surely must include administration of money for the family. In 1 Timothy 5:14 and Titus

1. Luke Timothy Johnson, *The First and Second Letters to Timothy*, Anchor Bible 35A (New York: Doubleday, 2001), 224.

2:5, the task of management is assigned to women (in one case a widow), but clearly the role of a woman in this context is under the oversight of the husband to whom she is to be submissive.

It is clear that these mandates pertain precisely to domestic households; in general these epistles do not push outside or beyond the immediate domestic scene. The object of management is the *oikos*, the familial sphere of life. The argument runs from *oikos* to *ekklesia*, from *household* to *church*. When we see that *oikos* is the root of our word "economy," we may judge that this is, in a quite direct way, a summons to "home economics," the proper management of the home, in which money is an unavoidable subject.

If we probe the connection of *oikos*-economics, we may judge that the horizon of these epistles invites us to think of good management of the economy in larger scope, so that the economy is to be marked by generosity, hospitality, and order that make for peaceableness. Douglas Meeks has effectively shown that *oikos* has wider implications when interpreted theologically in a way that invites reflection on a "God-economy" correlation:

> *Oikos* is at the heart of both ecclesiology and political economy. . . . The basic problem is that the church is alienated from both the biblical sense of the economy of God and a critical awareness of its actual situation within our society's prevailing economy. There is insufficient awareness of the way in which the assumptions behind market society have influenced the church and of the way in which the church's worship of God blindly condones prevailing economics. . . . Recent research has shown the pivotal theological, liturgical, and social implications of the concept of *oikos* for the primitive Christian communities.[2]

Of course the extrapolations that Meeks makes concerning *oikos* are not directly articulated in the epistles. There is no doubt, however, that the matters Meeks attests are inchoately present in the epistles. The writer knew very well of the pressure of the larger economy and the way that economy impinged upon the Christian community by way of greedy desire. The writer understood full well that the church was committed to an *alternative economy of generosity* rooted in godliness that contrasted with the power of desire

2. M. Douglas Meeks, *God the Economist: The Doctrine of God and Political Economy* (Minneapolis: Fortress Press, 1989), 33.

that propelled *an economy of greed*. The writer saw, moreover, that the order and conduct of the Christian community was itself a witness to the truth of the gospel. The church community, in its small infrastructure, was indeed acting out an alternative economy.

Such an understanding of *oikos* insists that money matters are understood and practiced within the fabric of the family or the community and cannot be extracted from such a fabric as though it were a zone of autonomy. The precise rhetoric of the Pastoral Epistles requires that money, like all else in the household, is a relational phenomenon and must be kept in the purview of those defining relationships. Thus right money management, like all right management in the family, is testimony about the right ordering of social relationships in the day-to-day life of the people.

II

First Timothy indicates a number of implications from such right management:

1. Church leaders are to be properly paid:

> Let the elders who rule well be considered worthy of double honor, especially those who labor in preaching and teaching; for the scripture says, "You shall not muzzle an ox while it is treading out grain," and, "The laborer deserves to be paid." (1 Tim. 5:17–18)

The writer does not assume that pastoral leaders must take a vow of poverty but asserts that they are entitled to and assured of proper maintenance. In 1 Corinthians 9:9 Paul had already appealed to the same text that is quoted here, Deuteronomy 25:4. This text and its quotation indicate realism about economic necessities.

2. Actual riches are "uncertain" and are not a reliable ground for well-being. Rather than reliance on one's wealth, the writer urges reliance on "God who richly provides":

> As for those who in the present age are rich, command them not to be haughty, or to set their hopes on the uncertainty of riches, but rather on God who richly provides us with everything for our enjoyment. (1 Tim. 6:17)

The term used for "riches" is *ploutos*, the root of our term "plutocracy," governance by the rich. The term suggests quite extensive resources. This statement is of special interest because it uses this term for "rich" three times. First it acknowledges that there are rich people in the church. There is no reprimand for being wealthy. But second, such wealth is seen to be unreliable and no ground for confidence. Most important, however, is the third use of the term that speaks of the God who provides "richly," that is, abundantly. Thus even riches are drawn into the orbit of God's certain abundance that is a proper ground for confidence and reliability.

3. The consequence of such reliance on God's abundance, in the next verse, is that the wealthy are to be "rich in good works," with the same term, *ploutos*: "They are to do good, to be rich in good works, generous, and ready to share, thus storing up for themselves the treasure of a good foundation for the future, so that they may take hold of the life that really is life" (vv. 18–19; see Luke 12:21 for the same usage, "rich toward God" [*ploutos*]).

The fourfold use of the term is an insistence that wealth is not and cannot be autonomous, but is wholly the gift of God and is to be performed by those who receive it in a life of generosity. This is true life; by implication a life lived only out of one's autonomous wealth is no life at all.

III

With such affirmations concerning wealth, we must notice the severe warnings in these letters about money, for the writer sees that ill-managed money is destructive of Christian community and a hindrance to proper witness to the gospel. Each of the letters has a focus on this temptation in the church.

The most extensive passage is 1 Timothy 6:3–10:

> Whoever teaches otherwise and does not agree with the sound words of our Lord Jesus Christ and the teaching that is in accordance with godliness, is conceited, understanding nothing, and has a morbid craving for controversy and for disputes about words. From these come envy, dissension, slander, base suspicions, and wrangling among those who are depraved in mind and bereft of the truth, imagining that godliness is a means of gain. Of

> course, there is great gain in godliness combined with contentment; for we brought nothing into the world, so that we can take nothing out of it; but if we have food and clothing, we will be content with these. But those who want to be rich fall into temptation and are trapped by many senseless and harmful desires that plunge people into ruin and destruction. For the love of money is a root of all kinds of evil, and in their eagerness to be rich some have wandered away from the faith and pierced themselves with many pains.

The text contrasts "godliness" with "gain." While the letter in general urges godly piety, here the focus is on the seduction of wealth that contradicts the practices of godly piety. The writer counsels that godliness brings contentment; as long as there is food and clothing there need be no eager desire for more. But those who engage in godliness for the sake of gain are propelled by ignoble desires ("morbid craving") that disturb and disrupt the community. Human persons themselves neither bring nor take away, that is, possess anything of their own, so that the pursuit of such possessions is in fact an illusion of those who are triggered by "many senseless and harmful desires." The result of such craving is ruin and destruction. It is, moreover, no less destructive when godliness is taken up with an eye on profit.

The conclusion of verse 10 is a well-known statement that recognizes the immensely seductive power of money that leads to forfeiture of faith and a great deal of trouble. While the words are not used here, the contrast of godliness and gain is surely an echo of "God and mammon" we have seen in the Synoptic Gospels (Matt. 6:24; Luke 16:13).

A parallel statement is offered in 2 Timothy 3:2–5:

> For people will be lovers of themselves, lovers of money, boasters, arrogant, abusive, disobedient to their parents, ungrateful, unholy, inhuman, implacable, slanderers, profligates, brutes, haters of good, treacherous, reckless, swollen with conceit, lovers of pleasure rather than lovers of God, holding to the outward form of godliness but denying its power. Avoid them!

The same contrast of godliness and gain is here articulated as "lovers of money" and "lovers of God." The statement is a rigorous either-or that will allow no accommodation of one to the other. The text offers a most extensive catalog of destructive behaviors that are rooted in "love of themselves." Thus "lovers of money" are in fact those who love themselves, who imagine autonomy, who pursue self-sufficiency, and who cause immense destructiveness in the process.

While the either-or seems radical and complete, this statement allows that such lovers of self may and do indeed "hold to the outward form of godliness," so that they are within the church. Such a practice is parallel to the statement in 1 Timothy 6 concerning those who imagine that godliness will produce gain. Such *lovers of self, lovers of money, lovers of pleasure*, that is, those who do not trust their life to God, in fact know nothing of the power of God that comes to those who practice godliness. The concluding imperative, "Avoid them," suggests how dangerous to the community are those given to such distortions of faith in practice. The text does not suggest expulsion or excommunication of such members, but it surely implies a refusal to associate with or to grant power to such persons.

The parallel statement in Titus is brief:

> For a bishop, as God's steward, must be blameless; he must not be arrogant or quick-tempered or addicted to wine or violent or greedy for gain; but he must be hospitable, a lover of godliness, prudent, upright, devout, and self-controlled. (1:7–8)

The statement is a characteristic either-or. In this text, "greedy for gain" is one among many forms of conduct that are contrasted with the habits (virtues) that properly belong to Christian leadership. The love of money or greed for gain is not an isolated matter but belongs to a cluster of seductions, all of which put *the self* over against *the community* and over against *the God of the gospel* worshiped by the community. It is not money but the autonomous self that constitutes the problem, the refusal to submit to and participate in the common good of the community.

IV

The writer of these letters has a clear sense of the church as a vulnerable community whose life, calling, and ministry are pointed upstream in a culture propelled by money. He knows that the pressures, temptations, and seductions of that dominant culture are real and powerful and that the maintenance of the distinctiveness of the Christian community requires great intentionality. Thus in 1 Timothy 3:8–13 the writer brings these several themes together:

> Deacons likewise must be serious, not double-tongued, not indulging in much wine, not greedy for money; they must hold fast to the mystery of the faith with a clear conscience. And let them first be tested; then, if they prove themselves blameless, let them serve as deacons. Women likewise must be serious, not slanderers, but temperate, faithful in all things. Let deacons be married only once, and let them manage their children and their households well; for those who serve well as deacons gain a good standing for themselves and great boldness in the faith that is in Christ Jesus.

"Greedy for money" is among the many destructive habits that are contrasted with "the mystery of the faith." The writer urges and believes that it is possible to maintain a "clear conscience," that is, to live in devotion to the God of the gospel. It is possible to live a life of the gospel in the face of seductive alternatives. Those who so live are qualified for leadership and can exercise management. The outcome of such a life is boldness in faith.

It takes no imagination to see that the same pressures are now upon the church in a market-propelled society. Resistance and alternative to the ideology of money that propels our society is as urgent now in the church as it was then. Resistance and alternative are also possible, now as then.

We may note, in conclusion, that the "sound teaching" that is given in the tradition of Paul is characterized as "the good treasure" (2 Tim. 1:13–14). James Dunn renders it as "fine deposit."[3] Given the foregoing about love of money, it is striking, perhaps daring, that the writer employs an economic term to characterize "the mystery of faith." It is the only reliable currency that requires total investment. Total investment in this "treasure," over against the treasure offered in dominant society, is only possible "with the help of the Holy Spirit." The zone of money, taken autonomously, may

3. James D. G. Dunn, "The First and Second Letters to Timothy and the Letter to Titus," in *The New Interpreter's Bible*, ed. Leander E. Keck (Nashville: Abingdon Press, 2000), 11:837.

be infused with an alien spirit but not with the Holy Spirit of God; therefore, unlike the treasure of the gospel, autonomous money can never yield joy or life. The leadership of the church is to nurture the believing community into an alternative treasure, the one we have in earthen vessels!

CHAPTER 14

The Letter of James

The Deep Either-Or of Practice

Our consideration of the so-called Catholic Epistles will inevitably lead us to focus on the Epistle of James, for it is in this letter that the theme of money and possessions is paramount.[1] It is possible that the seven Catholic Epistles constitute something of a canonical coherence.[2] If that is so, then it is not incidental that James stands first in the canonical sequence. It is unfortunate that the Epistle of James has been so readily caricatured (and thereby dismissed) when it has been situated in a reductionist form of Paul's theme of "grace and works." In fact the Letter of James is an instance of pastoral theology wherein the church must come to terms with the seductions and compromises of faith that characteristically take

1. The theme of money and possessions is not so prominent in other Catholic Epistles, but it is present. See 1 Pet. 1:14–15 on "desires" and holiness and 3:3–5 on adornment that is not packaged as commodity. See 1 John 2:15–17 on "the desire of the eyes, the pride in riches." Not included among the Catholic Epistles, but in purview here as well, is the Letter to the Hebrews; see 10:34 on "better" possessions, 11:26 on "greater wealth," and in 12:16 the contrast with Esau, "who sold his birthright for a single meal."

2. For a possible canonical shape to the Catholic Epistles, see David R. Nienhuis and Robert W. Wall, *Reading the Epistles of James, Peter, John, and Jude as Scripture: The Shaping and Shape of a Canonical Collection* (Grand Rapids: Eerdmans, 2013); David R. Nienhuis, *Not by Paul Alone: The Formation of the Catholic Epistle Collection and the Christian Canon* (Waco, TX: Baylor University Press, 2007); and Peter H. Davids, "The Catholic Epistles as a Canonical Janus: A New Testament Glimpse into Old and New Testament Canon Formation," *Bulletin for Biblical Research* 19:3 (2009): 403–16.

quite concrete form in the church; among the most likely of practical compromises are those concerned with money and possessions. Behind the usual preoccupations of the contemporary church with budgets and stewardship, the epistle sees clearly that a right understanding and practice of money is elementally life or death for the body of the church. We focus on four texts in James that evidence this paramount concern to which the letter returns again and again.

I

In 1:9–11, 12–16, 17–18, and 27, the Letter of James joins together a collage of remarkable themes.[3] The whole is an articulation of a radical either-or of faith vis-à-vis the attitudes and practices of the world.[4] In verses 9–11, the writer imagines economic reversals not unlike those anticipated by Mary (Luke 1:51–53). On the one hand, the lowly brother or sister believer may be "raised up." We would not know that this may refer to economic "elevation" of vulnerable brothers and sisters until we read in context concerning the rich who have been "raised up" by society and are to be "brought low." It is this second element that concerns the writer. The rich will "disappear" because riches are transient and unreliable, with no more staying power than a flower in the hot sun.[5] A social status based on wealth is unreliable, because such a status is evidently reversible. Insofar as the letter is a wisdom tract, it does not surprise us that it picks up an old sapiential theme on the dangerous dynamic linked to money. The statement here constitutes a powerful warning. Its positive affirmation, however, should not be overlooked; it concerns

3. The most immediately helpful study of the Epistle of James for our theme is Elsa Tamez, *The Scandalous Message of James: Faith without Works Is Dead* (New York: Crossroad Publishing, 1985). Tamez understands that the epistle is a scandal to the church whenever the church has signed on to the dominant economy.

4. Luke Timothy Johnson, *The Letter of James*, Anchor Bible 37A (New York: Doubleday, 1995), 175, writes of this either-or: "The establishment of the polar oppositions that James works with throughout the composition is accomplished in these opening verses. . . . First is the contrast between two measures, that which comes from God and that which comes from the world opposed to God. . . . The second set of contrasts is between the attitudes and behaviors consistent with each measure. . . . The third contrast is between the sham religiosity of speech or appearance and a true devotion 'pure and undefiled before God.'"

5. Tamez, *Scandalous Message*, 23–24, enumerates the characteristics of the rich in the epistle.

the valorization of the poor who are being "raised up" to dignity and well-being.[6]

In the next paragraph, one may be tempted, lured, and enticed by one's peculiar "desire." The text does not specify a lust for money, and the notion of desire may be taken more generically as the self-securing desire that propelled the crisis in the garden of Eden (Gen. 3:6). Every and any desire may be included here insofar as it is a desire for life apart from the rule of God. In context, however, the term would seem to refer to desire for wealth that places us yet again in the zone of greed. Here such desire "gives birth to sin," which in turn "gives birth to death"; that is, such greed is a deathly desire.

This extraordinary critique of the desire for self-security is continued in verse 17 by attention to the alternative, "every generous act of giving" that derives from "the Father of lights." Thus the writer contrasts a person of *self-propelled desire* with a person who is situated in *divine generosity* and who therefore in turn is generous. The conclusion drawn at the end of the chapter concerns generosity that is performed toward the resourceless: "Religion that is pure and undefiled before God, the Father, is this: to care for orphans and widows in their distress, and to keep oneself unstained by the world" (v. 27).

"Defilement" is caused by participation in the desires of the world that eventuates in an indifference to orphans and widows. This sequence of themes—riches that perish, desire that leads to death, generosity rooted in God, and actions toward the resourceless—taken together, constitute a teaching that contradicts the easy assumptions of the world: that wealth endures, that desires should be satisfied, that generosity is foolish, and that religion has nothing to do with real socioeconomic need.

> We see the basic contrast between the *measure of the world*, revealed by a foolish religion that fails to control the tongue and indulges or deceives the heart, and the *measure of God*, revealed by a pure and undefiled religion that resists the measure of the world and shows its authenticity by giving gifts to the needy in the

6. Christopher Church, "James," in *Hebrews-James* by Edgar V. McKnight and Christopher Church, Smyth & Helwys Bible Commentary (Macon, GA: Smyth & Helwys, 2004), 341, characterizes the poor as they are presented in the epistle.

> same way God gives them to all creatures. Live as a friend of God and not as a friend of the world. [Italics added.][7]

Christopher Church takes "orphans and widows" as emblematic of all those who are "overlooked, underestimated, passed-by, stepped-on peoples; in the world's eyes such folk are expendable, no names, no accounts, just statistics."[8]

> An HIV-positive patient who lacks insurance coverage
> A preschooler without systemic support
> Abused children
> Undocumented workers
> A minimum-wage father left below the poverty line
> An older woman exposed to lethal summer heat without relief or escape

The writer calls out the church to true religion that refuses privatized spirituality.

II

In 2:1–7 the Letter of James becomes intensely direct in its address to the believing community and observes that practices of social favoritism contradict "our glorious Lord Jesus Christ." The paragraph is basically a reprimand for practicing favoritism and social distinctions without acknowledging them. But of course such a reprimand is inescapably a summons to alternative.

That same social discrimination is continued among us whereby we overestimate and overappreciate well-dressed, well-groomed persons who thereby give evidence of social power and wealth, or conversely, we diminish or dismiss those who are ill-dressed and clearly lack resources. Such social valuing and devaluing is endlessly exhibited in TV ads that bespeak market ideology that contrasts *the worthwhile successful* with *the failed poor*. A dramatic case in point is a TV ad that featured Rob Lowe selling Direct TV.

7. Luke Timothy Johnson, "The Letter of James," in *The New Interpreter's Bible*, ed. Leander E. Keck (Nashville: Abingdon Press, 1998), 12:189.
8. Church, "James," 349–50.

He is handsome, winsome, arrogant, beaming with self-satisfaction. His unattractive counterpart (also played by Rob Lowe, but with a lesser TV service) is poorly dressed, naive to the point of stupidity, and generally unattractive. That such an ad could run over time indicates that our society practices exactly the social differentiations of which the epistle speaks. Rank has its privilege!

But then, that very familiar and "normal" social practice is interrupted by a demanding rhetorical question: "Has not God chosen the poor in the world to be rich in faith and to be heirs of the kingdom that he has promised to those who love him?" (2:5).

This statement is clearly a harbinger of the mantra expressed in our time by liberation theology concerning "God's preferential option for the poor."[9] The writer is succinct. God has chosen the poor! God chose the social rabble of slaves to form Israel (Exod. 12:38). God chose the nobody Jesus as Messiah (see John 1:46). God chose those who are lowly and despised to be the church (1 Cor. 1:26–29). God continues, so insists the writer, to choose the poor to whom to keep promises. There is no need to romanticize the poor. But clearly any practical experience with the poor will evidence a kind of generous, risky openness among some poor that contrasts with the driven control and compulsion among those bent on management success who have bought in to the oppressive requirements of market ideology.

Thus far the paragraph has contrasted "acts of favoritism" against the poor with God's inexplicable but undoubted solidarity with the poor. After the remarkable affirmation of verse 5, the paragraph returns to the "beloved brothers and sisters" who have "dishonored the poor" (v. 6). The verdict against them is sealed with three rhetorical questions that require, in honesty, an affirmative answer:

> "Is it not the rich who oppress you?"
> "Is it not they who drag you into court?"
> "Is it not they who blaspheme" the name of Christ?

9. Tamez, *Scandalous Message*, 35–36, concludes: "The idea that there must be no favoritism within the Christian community does not imply that God is neutral or that God has no favorites. In this context, God's partiality is clear: 'Listen, my dear brothers: it was those who are poor according to the world that God chose . . .'"

Yes, implies the writer. It is the rich who oppress. It is the rich who litigate. It is the rich who mock the God of the gospel. It is the rich who abuse the poor and who receive favorable treatment. The paragraph provides an astonishingly alert social analysis in the midst of which stands the core affirmation of verse 5. It is God's choice that puts the lie to social practice and social valuing that are taken as properly normative among us. Such social favoritism, in its destructiveness, is precisely systemic:

> It is the rich who receive preferential loans.
> It is the rich who benefit from preferential medical care.
> It is the rich who have access to the best education.
> It is the moneyed who ever more earn their money "the old-fashioned way," by sheltered investment, by inheritance, by privileged treatment, none of which requires physical labor.

The writer admonishes the church. But the writer also looks over the shoulder of the church to observe that our socially stratified world is deeply at odds with the most elemental commitments that God has made. It is not surprising that the next verse alludes to "the royal law" of neighborly love (v. 8).

I know of no better articulation of this social differentiation in its patient sketch of two modes of justice than the hair-raising exposition of Matt Taibbi, *The Divide: American Injustice in the Age of the Wealth Gap*.[10] In alternating chapters Taibbi traces out the kind of justice that is meted out to the rich and the poor. Among the rich he observes that the government, that is, the Justice Department, has never taken a first step to indict or convict any of the economic moguls who perpetrated the acts that caused the economic collapse of 2007–2009, a collapse that worked immense hardship on the poor and the near poor. It is as though the wealthy and powerful have been given blanket immunity from prosecution, even though the abuses of public trust are plain for all to see. There can hardly be any doubt that the unrestrained passion for money, influence, and social connection has precluded any serious social accountability.

10. Matt Taibbi, *The Divide: American Injustice in the Age of the Wealth Gap* (New York: Spiegel & Grau, 2014). Concerning "civil forfeiture," see Shaila Dewan, "Unanimous New Mexico Bill on Property Seizure May Die," *New York Times*, April 10, 2015.

By contrast, Taibbi shows the aggressive police action against the poor who are regularly caught up in police sweeps. The ones swooped up are most often acquitted or released without charge after intimidation and harassment, but the process continues to mark the poor as an inconvenience to the social order that insists on and sanctions such ruthless police control. There can be no doubt that social power arrangements serve to invite the rich to "have a seat here, please," while the poor are told to "stand there" or wait outside (v. 3). The evidence is overwhelming. It was so as well in the ancient world. What matters, however, is not finally the social analysis but the gospel interruption: God has chosen the poor. That reality gives the lie to the widespread but ultimately unsustainable practices of neighborly injustice.

III

In James 4:1–4 we have yet another articulation of the deep either-or that is repeatedly traced out in the epistle. That decisive choice is friendship with God or "friendship with the world" (v. 4). There is no middle ground, no both–and, no accommodation. This phrasing sounds, yet again, not unlike "God or mammon." That choice of friendship, in perfectly symmetrical rhetoric, entails enmity for the alternative; thus friendship for the world evokes enmity toward God.

The particulars of this choice are stated in the preceding verses. The problem consists in unrestrained "cravings" that yield a divided self; this is a self that in a faithful way wants what properly belongs to the self created by God but at the same time chooses against that true self. The acknowledgment of the divided self is old and deep in the Old Testament, as old and deep as the double imagination of Genesis. David Wolpe, moreover, can aver of David: "David's division of heart is a leitmotif of his personality."[11]

The narrative of David shows how the man and then the king regularly is double-minded, a person who trusts God and yet who lives otherwise. The traditional attribution of Psalm 51 to David attests to that conflictedness that is evident in the narrative of David.

11. David Wolpe, *David: The Divided Heart* (New Haven, CT: Yale University Press, 2014), 94.

Best known among Christians is the torturous double-mindedness given voice by Paul:

> So I find it to be a law that when I want to do what is good, evil lies close at hand. For I delight in the law of God in my inmost self, but I see in my members another law at war with the law of my mind, making me captive to the law of sin that dwells in my members. Wretched man that I am! Who will rescue me from this body of death? (Rom. 7:21–24)

It is exactly this "war" within the conflicted self that led Sigmund Freud to his stunning insights about the modern self who is conflicted and who uses immense energy in order to conceal from self that conflictedness. The writer of James sees that unrestrained cravings evoke deeply problematic conduct expressed as "conflicts and disputes" (4:1–2). Christopher Church terms it "two-timing God."[12]

As a result of that conflictedness, the self chooses against the self. That counterchoice is expressed here as murder, coveting, and adultery. It takes no imagination to see that this catalog alludes to the Decalogue. The Ten Commandments consist in modes of conduct that commend friendship with God. This is how God's friends act:

> Thou shalt not kill (Jas. 2:11).
> Thou shalt not commit adultery (2:11).
> Thou shalt not covet (4:2).
> Thou shalt not commit adultery (4:4).

This list in our verses is representative and surely includes as well those commands that are not enumerated here. The urge of adultery here likely refers to specific conduct but also functions as a metaphor for broader disloyalty; thus it is a usage that is congruent with the metaphorical usage of Hosea and Jeremiah. It is worth noting that the indictment of David for his predatory seizure of Bathsheba and murder of Uriah is given exactly as violation of the two commandments against killing and coveting (2 Sam. 12:9). Likewise the prophetic indictment of Ahab after the seizure of

12. Church, "James," 385.

Naboth's vineyard turns on the same two commandments (1 Kgs. 21:19). Friendship with the world inevitably and inescapably eventuates in violence.

Cravings that are set against God in friendship with the world are acted out quite specifically, according to this writer. Among the three mentioned, the word for "covet" is *zeloute*, the root of "zeal," that is, "must have," eager passion (4:2). The writer affirms that such actions that contradict friendship with God are undertaken because you do not have, and so want. "You do not have, because you do not ask. You ask and do not receive, because you ask wrongly" (4:2–3).

And the wrong asking is self-centeredness, that is, the seeking of your own pleasure. This brief articulation is a shrewd analysis of the deficient self who is deficient because it does not rely fully on God, who is ready to give generously. The readiness of God to give is well attested in the teaching of Jesus:

> Ask, and it will be given you; search, and you will find; knock, and the door will be opened for you. For everyone who asks receives, and everyone who searches finds, and for everyone who knocks, the door will be opened. Is there anyone among you who, if your child asks for bread, will give a stone? Or if the child asks for a fish, will give a snake? If you then, who are evil, know how to give good gifts to your children, how much more will your Father in heaven give good things to those who ask him! (Matt. 7:7–11)

When one has no friendship with God, however, there can be no proper asking, for proper asking is full, confident, trusting reliance on God.

This analysis might offer a clue to the endless quarrelsomeness in church and in society, because there is wrong asking that is propelled by "your pleasures" that are self-serving and self-seeking (4:3). While this text does not specifically concern money and possessions, as elsewhere in the letter, it is clear that "craving" and "coveting" do pertain to the material stuff that is overly valued in friendship with the world. The letter does not ask for renunciation of pleasure, but it commends pleasure to be shaped and fashioned by the filaments of that friendship with God. The "pleasures" rejected are those rooted in "friendship with the world." One may indeed imagine that such a location of desire would lead to the diminishment of conflicts and disputes. The deep either-or of

asking only for carnal pleasure is always wrong

covenantal faith is voiced in the familiar hymn of Harry Emerson Fosdick that turns from praise to petition in verse 3:

> Cure your children's warring madness;
> Bend our pride to your control.
> Shame our reckless, selfish gladness,
> *Rich in things* and *poor in soul.*[13]

The "warring madness" echoes James's "conflict and disputes." The critique of James knows about "reckless, selfish gladness," and the outcome is predictably "rich in things, poor in soul."[14] Friendship with the world is pursuit of "things" in a way that reduces the God-loved self to poverty. As Christopher Church shows, that seduction and deathly choice is given systemic performance in our society.[15]

IV

In 5:1–6 the Letter of James becomes much more pointed in its accusations, in cadences that echo prophetic rhetoric. Now the addressees are rich people. It may be that the rich are within the church and so are castigated because they disturb and disrupt the practical life of the church. Or it may be that they are outsiders to the church who present a great temptation to church people to imitate the seductions of the world. Either way, verses 1–3 are a critique and warning concerning reliance on wealth. The rhetoric warns of a coming time of misery because the assurances provided by wealth are unsustainable. The value of gold, silver, and clothes is transient, because they rot, rust, and become moth-eaten.[16] The warning is surely reminiscent of the warning of Jesus:

13. Harry Emerson Fosdick, "God of Grace and God of Glory," *The New Century Hymnal* (Cleveland: Pilgrim Press, 1995), 436.

14. Pertinent to the point is the trenchant critique of John Brueggemann, *Rich, Free, and Miserable: The Failure of Success in America* (New York: Rowman & Littlefield, 2010).

15. Church, "James," 390–97.

16. It may be a bit curious to us that clothes are listed along with gold and silver as signs of wealth and targets of accumulation. It was so already with Solomon (1 Kgs. 10:25). See also Luke 20:46 on the seduction of "long robes" for the sake of appearance, and Luke 12:22 on the worry about proper clothes. The accent on clothes in our verses suggests a preoccupation with appearance. But then it is not different among us, with

> Do not store up for yourselves treasures on earth, where moth and rust consume and where thieves break in and steal; but store up for yourselves treasures in heaven, where neither moth nor rust consumes and where thieves do not break in and steal. For where your treasure is, there your heart will be also. (Matt. 6:19–21)

Thus the rich have stored up great wealth in anticipation of a coming time when they will be placed at great risk. The rhetoric calls to mind the bewitched illusion of those who build safe houses and underground shelters stocked with food, who live in gated communities, and who imagine that somehow they will be able to survive and sustain themselves through "the fire next time." Of course such self-securing is the illusion of privatism, because the coming threat will be more severe than that, and because such private resources cannot effectively function apart from social reality. Thus the writer exposes the rich who imagine, by their strategies and plans, that they can outflank the judgment of God.

Peter Brown, in his learned sketch of wealth and poverty in the early church, has shown the way in which the church in the third and fourth centuries devoted great energy and resources to the needs of the poor. He also reports, however, that as wealthy persons entered and dominated the church in the sixth century, attention was turned away from the needy, as the wealthy began to think of their own destiny in this age and in the age to come.[17] As a result, wealth was redeployed from the poor to the construction of great mausoleums to assure the well-being of the wealthy in the age to come, as though such a manifestation of wealth would somehow provide durable protection and privilege. Such a preoccupation with one's own security leads inevitably to the neglect of others. So our writer, in James 5:3, can ponder such surplus amassed for "the last days." In the context of "the last days," one may wonder if the enormous exhibit of wealth in a consumer economy is not evoked by the same assumption that great possessions will assure well-being, no matter what may come.

---

our consciousness of brands of fashion and our preoccupation with appearance. Fashion never stops! See Isa. 3:16, followed by the rich inventory of loss in Isa. 3:18–23.

17. Peter Brown, *Through the Eye of a Needle: Wealth, the Fall of Rome, and the Making of Christianity in the West, 350–550 AD* (Princeton, NJ: Princeton University Press, 2012), 469–77 and passim.

But of course such wealth cannot finally resist the great reversal to come, a reversal that means the end of the world we have worked so hard to perpetuate and control. Great wealth cannot resist the coming new governance, the kingdom of justice and righteousness. The great reversal is mightily anticipated in the Gospel of Luke. It is anticipated first in the Song of Mary:

> He has shown strength with his arm;
> he has scattered the proud in the thoughts of their hearts.
> He has brought down the powerful from their thrones,
> and lifted up the lowly;
> he has filled the hungry with good things,
> and sent the rich away empty.
>
> (Luke 1:51–53)

It is the ground of weeping now and laughing later:

> Blessed are you who are poor,
> for yours is the kingdom of God.
> Blessed are you who are hungry now,
> for you will be filled.
> Blessed are you who weep now, for you will laugh.
> . . . .
> But woe to you who are rich,
> for you have received your consolation.
> Woe to you who are full now,
> for you will be hungry.
> Woe to you who are laughing now,
> for you will mourn and weep.
>
> (Luke 6:20–25)

It is reflected in the parable of the Rich Man and Lazarus:

> In Hades, where he was being tormented, he looked up and saw Abraham far away with Lazarus by his side. He called out, "Father Abraham, have mercy on me, and send Lazarus to dip the tip of his finger in water and cool my tongue; for I am in agony in these flames." But Abraham said, "Child, remember that during your lifetime you received your good things, and Lazarus in like manner evil things; but now he is comforted here, and you are in agony. Besides all this, between you and us a great chasm has been fixed, so that those who might want to pass from here to you cannot do so, and no one can cross from there to us." (Luke 16:23–26)

The theme of the great reversal is not a matter of escapist speculation; it is rather grounded in economic realism that recognizes that such disparity of wealth and poverty is unsustainable. The castigation of the rich (James 5:1–3) is followed by an abrupt summons to reconsider. The reconsideration that follows is an acute social analysis (5:4–6). The passion for great treasure that will secure one's life always requires that something be taken from the table of a vulnerable neighbor. In this case the neighbor is a field hand who is entitled to fair wages. The rich are here condemned for wage theft by fraud. The Bible has long been concerned about wage theft, even as contemporary practices of it become ever more complex and sophisticated:

> You shall not defraud your neighbor; you shall not steal; and you shall not keep for yourself the wages of a laborer until morning. (Lev. 19:13)

> You shall not withhold the wages of poor and needy laborers, whether other Israelites or aliens who reside in your land in one of your towns. You shall pay them their wages daily before sunset, because they are poor and their livelihood depends on them; otherwise they might cry to the LORD against you, and you would incur guilt. (Deut. 24:14–15)

As in the old Torah warnings, such exploitation of laborers by cheap wages or fraudulent practices will evoke a cry of protest, and that cry will be heard by the God who attends to the practice of exploitation. Indeed, at the very outset it was the attentiveness of YHWH to the cry of exploited laborers that set in motion the emancipation of the exodus (Exod. 2:23–25). The Bible knows that *voiced injustice* sets in motion the possibility of emancipation and social transformation whereby the rich are sent away hungry. That cry from below is the engine for new historical possibility, because the cry mobilizes the attentive energy of God's fidelity. Such a cry requires that the "victim becomes conscious."[18] Our writer belongs in that long line from the exodus through the prophets that has no doubt that the victim will become conscious, will cry out, and will mobilize holy power. That holy power will be deployed, it is

18. Enrique Dussel, *Ethics of Liberation in the Age of Globalization and Exclusion*, trans. Eduardo Mendieta et al., translation ed. Alejandro A. Vallega (Durham, NC: Duke University Press, 2013), 242.

anticipated, both as a wrathful force against the exploiter (Exod. 22:21–24) and as great compassion for the victim (Exod. 22:25–27). The victim in the ancient world was the vulnerable laborer. Enrique Dussel indicates their contemporary counterparts:

> The initial question is: Who is the victim to whom the argument is connected? . . . Its subject matter is the suffering of the "concentration camps," which permits the conclusion that "the Enlightenment is totalitarian." . . . This sounds strange to the ears of Erhard's Germany, but is acceptable today to the ears of a Nicaraguan, of the black Africans of South Africa, of the Palestinians in the Israeli-occupied territories, or of the *homeless* in New Delhi . . . or New York.[19]

Dussel updates the critique of the rich from the Letter of James; the contemporary rich are clothed in the rationality of the Enlightenment, but the abuse continues. The paragraph of our text ends with a sweeping judgment against the rich who have "lived on the earth in luxury and in pleasure" (Jas. 5:5). They can live so only for a time, not to perpetuity.

The concluding verse accuses the rich of murder. The phrase "the righteous one" is particularly interesting (5:6). While we might first think that this is an allusion to Jesus as "the righteous one," that is unlikely and would interrupt the argument: "There is no reason to see "the righteous one (*ho dikaios*) as Jesus . . . and even less to identify him with James. . . . The reference is rather more general. Any laborer defrauded in this manner is 'innocent' with respect to the oppressive actions of the rich."[20]

The everyday laborer who earns his wage and does not receive it is the righteous one who is exploited and denied life:

> James continues to develop what we have called "the logic of envy," which seeks to eliminate any competition. In 3:13–4:10 envy was connected to idolatry, that "friendship with the world" that identifies being with having, so that oppression and murder follow as a matter of course (4:1–2). The specific link among idolatry, oppression, and murder is established already by Scripture. . . . but nowhere is it more powerfully stated than in Sir 34:25–27: "The bread of the needy is the life of the poor. Whoever deprives

19. Ibid., 242–44.
20. Johnson, *Letter of James*, 304.

> them of it is a man of blood. To take away a neighbor's living is to murder him. To deprive an employee of his wages is to shed blood."[21]

This indictment of course pertains to immediate practices of wage theft, a practice so well exposed by Interfaith Worker Justice.[22] But the critique of exploitative labor policies not only addresses specific practices but also offers a condemnation of an entire predatory system that is organized against the legitimate rights of laborers. This would include especially credit and mortgage arrangements and union-busting policies that diminish the social power of laborers. Such policies by the greedy rich skew protection and distort dignity for the economically vulnerable.

In the paragraph that follows this text, the writer of James enjoins patience among the faithful. Patience is grounded in the assurance that God brings to social reality a purpose that is marked by compassion and mercy: "You have seen the purpose of the Lord, how the Lord is compassionate and merciful" (v. 11).[23]

V

In these several texts the writer offers a coherent critique of the preoccupation with and pursuit of money and possessions and a material alternative to such preoccupation and pursuit:

> In 1:9–18, 27, wealth will perish; generosity is grounded in a word of truth.

21. Ibid., 304–5.

22. Interfaith Worker Justice is a tireless witness to the legitimacy of workers' rights and to the way those rights are abused and denied by the dominant economy. See the piece that I wrote at the behest of IWJ, "Jubilee," in *Ice Axes for Frozen Seas: A Biblical Theology of Provocation*, ed. Davis Hankins (Waco, TX: Baylor University Press, 2014), 381–82.

23. The patience enjoined in vv. 7–11 may indeed be an appeal for acquiescent acceptance of the status quo. It is, however, the "patience of Job." That patience is urged in confidence of the coming Parousia. It may be that this is an ironic statement, because Job turned out to be profoundly impatient. On our current situation of acceptance of the predatory economy, see Steve Fraser, *The Age of Acquiescence: The Life and Death of American Resistance to Organized Wealth and Power* (New York: Little, Brown, 2014), and Steven Quartz and Anette Asp, "Unequal, Yet Happy," *New York Times*, April 12, 2015.

In 2:1–7, God has chosen the poor, while the addressees of the letter favor the rich in a way that diminishes the poor.
In 4:1–4, friendship with God is to prevail over friendship with the world that leads to contentiousness.
In 5:1–6, wealth is unsustainable when it evokes the cries of the poor.

In these texts we do not have simply economic advice or prudent morality. Rather we have sketched out an ecclesiology for a community that will resist the seductions and temptations of the dominant economy which is propelled by greed and the illusion of self-sufficiency. The letter articulates a deep and unexpected alliance between God and the poor, between the vulnerable and the God of mercy. The summons to the church is to refuse and resist the cravings of the world for self-security and to find in friendship with God a reliable and generative way in the world.

CHAPTER 15

The Book of Revelation

The Ultimate Alternative

The book of Revelation consists in an act of poetic imagination that anticipates a severe ending of the world and the performance of a new world according to the power and purpose of God. The apocalyptic idiom of the poetry permits utilization of well-established Jewish modes of imagination that are here brought to pivot on "the Lamb that was slaughtered" (that is, Jesus) who will be at the center of the new regime (see 5:12).

While the rhetoric of the "end of the world" and the coming "new world" has provided ample ground for much misinformed religious speculation, the world that is to end is not the planet Earth, as dramatic film spectaculars have it, but the ordered cosmos administered by the Roman Empire. Thus the end of the world equals termination of the empire of Rome.

> Since Rome is never named throughout the book, the beast may come to represent "Empire with a capital *E*," power that is seemingly global and beyond effective opposition, as it manifests itself in other places and times. John may be seen as making a distinctive contribution to the prophetic critique of one aspect of imperial power, namely, its inhumane and destructive economic practices. This is a central element of his prophetic eschatology, although it has received relatively little scholarly or popular attention.[1]

1. Ellen F. Davis, *Biblical Prophecy: Perspectives for Christian Theology, Discipleship, and Ministry*, Interpretation (Louisville, KY: Westminster John Knox Press, 2014), 113.

It is that world of Rome that will be displaced by a new world order that is attuned to and credentialed by the creator God whose will is for peace and justice. Thus the apocalyptic imagery and poetic expression are concerned with world change that has to do with socio-economic, political reality embodied in the Roman Empire that is resistant to and adversarial against the God of the gospel. Because the rhetoric addresses this-world realities, it does not surprise that the book of Revelation is preoccupied with the *termination* of the economy of extraction practiced by Rome and the *anticipation* of a coming alternative regime that will perforce practice a different economy. Thus we may organize our discussion of economy in the book of Revelation according to *termination* and *anticipation*.

I

The rhetoric of termination amounts to a vigorous critique and condemnation of the economy of Rome that is committed in wholesale ways to extraction of wealth from its colonies. My discussion of the text is largely indebted to Ellen Davis, who has seen that the massive critique of "Babylon" (read "Rome") in chapters 17–18 (a) appeals to old prophetic poetry in Ezekiel 26–28 against Tyre, the great commercial city-state, and (b) is cast in the particular cadences of Israel's prophetic rhetoric that concerns indictment and sentence.[2]

In Ezekiel 26–28, Tyre receives an extended amount of airtime: "Tyre was the essential agent in the emergence of a new kind of economic system, a mercantile economy based on the circulation of precious metals (silver and gold), which gradually replaced a simpler, more subsistence-oriented system in which goods were bartered."[3] That is, neighborly transactions had been transposed by Tyre into commodity transactions in which the human factor had been completely nullified. The port city of commerce is portrayed as a beehive of traffic in this detailed inventory of commercial goods that passed through the port:

> Tarshish did business with you out of the abundance of your great wealth: silver, iron, tin, and lead they exchanged for your wares.

2. Ibid., 112–15.
3. Ibid., 120.

> Javan, Tubal, and Meshech traded with you; they exchanged *human beings* and vessels of bronze for your merchandise. Beth-togarmah exchanged for your wares horses, war horses, and mules. The Rhodians traded with you; many coastlands were your own special markets; they brought you in payment ivory tusks and ebony. Edom did business with you because of your abundant goods; they exchanged for your wares turquoise, purple, embroidered work, fine linen, coral, and rubies. Judah and the land of Israel traded with you: they exchanged for your merchandise wheat from Minnith, millet, honey, oil, and balm. Damascus traded with you for your abundant goods—because of your great wealth of every kind—wine of Helbon, and white wool. Vedan and Javan from Uzal entered into trade for your wares; wrought iron, cassia, and sweet cane were bartered for your merchandise. Dedan traded with you in saddlecloths for riding. Arabia and all the princes of Kedar were your favored dealers in lambs, rams, and goats; in these they did business with you. The merchants of Sheba and Raamah traded with you; they exchanged for your wares the best of all kinds of spices, and all precious stones, and gold. Haran, Canneh, Eden, the merchants of Sheba, Asshur, and Chilmad traded with you. These traded with you in choice garments, in clothes of blue and embroidered work, and in carpets of colored material, bound with cords and made secure; in these they traded with you. The ships of Tarshish traveled for you in your trade. (27:12–25a; italics added)

It is necessary to recite this long and full inventory of commercial goods in order to glimpse the reach, the wealth, and the power of the city-state that issued in arrogance and lawlessness. Note especially in verse 13 that trade included traffic in "human beings" (*nepeš 'ādām*), that is, slavery. Such a commercial system is opposed to the rule of God and cannot be sustained:

> Because your heart is proud
> and you have said, "I am a god;
> I sit in the seat of the gods,
> in the heart of the seas,"
> yet you are but a mortal, and no god,
> though you compare your mind
> with the mind of a god.
> . . . .
> Will you still say, "I am a god,"
> in the presence of those who kill you,

> though you are but a mortal, and no god,
> in the hands of those who wound you?
> (28:2, 9)

When this critique is transferred to "Babylon" (Rome) in the book of Revelation, the rhetoric is even more intense. Babylon is reckoned to be a whore, so that commerce without morality is regarded as "fornication": "The woman was clothed in purple and scarlet, and adorned with gold and jewels and pearls, holding in her hand a golden cup full of abominations and the impurities of her fornication; and on her forehead was written a name, a mystery: 'Babylon the great, mother of whores and of earth's abominations'" (Rev. 17:4–5).

Such commerce is inimical to God and so will be destroyed. Thus the prophetic indictment is followed by prophetic judgment. God will destroy the power and the arrogance of Babylon:

> For her sins are heaped high as heaven,
> and God has remembered her iniquities.
> Render to her as she herself has rendered,
> and repay her double for her deeds;
> mix a double draught for her in the cup she mixed.
> As she glorified herself and lived luxuriously,
> so give her a like measure of torment and grief.
> Since in her heart she says,
> "I rule as a queen;
> I am no widow,
> and I will never see grief,"
> therefore her plagues will come in a single day—
> pestilence and mourning and famine—
> and she will be burned with fire;
> for mighty is the Lord God who judges her.
> (18:5–8)

The alleged statement of self-congratulation by Babylon is an echo of the self-congratulation by Babylon in Isaiah 47:7–10 in which the mighty empire imagined itself as autonomous, self-sufficient, and of ultimate importance. Such an attitude of course fails to reckon with the ultimacy of YHWH, who has set a severe limit to the autonomy of even the greatest of empires. Because empires must answer to the rule of God, so the text insists, every such effort at autonomy is an exercise in self-destruction.

The combination of critique and threat continues through chapter 18. The chapter is dominated by reference to "merchants" who govern world trade and become rich:

> For all the nations have drunk
> of the wine of the wrath of her fornication,
> and the kings of the earth have committed fornication with her,
> and the *merchants* of the earth have grown rich from the power
> of her luxury.
>
> (18:3; italics added)

But because of pride, arrogance, and indifference to human reality, the merchants will come to a sorry end: "And the *merchants* of the earth weep and mourn for her, since no one buys their cargo anymore. . . . The *merchants* of these wares, who gained wealth from her, will stand far off, in fear of her torment, weeping and mourning aloud" (vv. 11, 15; italics added; see v. 23).

They have been busy with consumer goods that will no longer flourish in the marketplace. The inventory of such goods is not unlike the inventory of Tyre quoted above:

> cargo of gold, silver, jewels and pearls, fine linen, purple, silk and scarlet, all kinds of scented wood, all articles of ivory, all articles of costly wood, bronze, iron, and marble, cinnamon, spice, incense, myrrh, frankincense, wine, olive oil, choice flour and wheat, cattle and sheep, horses and chariots, slaves—and *human lives*. (vv. 12–13; italics added)

It is to be noted that at the end of the list is "human lives," a phrase reminiscent of Ezekiel 27:13. Human persons are listed among consumer goods, as the force of commodity violently sweeps all before it. That final item in the list suggests that human persons, reduced to commodity, can be bought and sold and traded like every other commodity:

> The cargo list of twenty-eight items offers a thumbnail sketch of Roman society, where the superrich might spend the equivalent of five or six million U.S. dollars on one citron-wood wine table. . . . It also highlights political and military power (horses and chariots), as well as the stuff of ordinary life: wine, oil, and grain were the dietary staples for everyone. Probably few Romans would have considered the final item on the list to be a luxury.

> Slave labor was the essential energy supply for the Roman economy; it fueled agriculture, mining, and every other form of industry, as well as every household. Slaves, called *sōmata* ("bodies") in the market, "were treated much like livestock." . . . That status befits their placement here, beside the domestic animals owned by ordinary people, as well as the horses and chariots belonging to the rich.[4]

It does not surprise then, in prophetic discourse, that the poetry ends with an imagined and anticipated negation of Babylon with a repeated "no more" for a power that is unsustainable:

> With such violence Babylon the great city
> will be thrown down,
> and will be found *no more*;
> and the sound of harpists and minstrels and of flutists and
> trumpeters
> will be heard in you *no more*;
> and an artisan of any trade
> will be found in you *no more*;
> and the sound of the millstone
> will be heard in you *no more*;
> and the light of a lamp
> will shine in you *no more*;
> and the voice of the bridegroom and bride
> will be heard in you *no more*;
> for your merchants were the magnates of the earth,
> and all nations were deceived by your sorcery.
> (Rev. 18:21–23; italics added)

The concentration of economic wealth and military power that imagines itself to be beyond challenge will inevitably end in violence toward human persons who have nothing more in their favor than their market value.

If we look for a contemporary analogue to the economic reach of Rome ("Babylon"), Davis is surely right to connect the poetry to current globalization:

> Globalization, the process of worldwide economic integration, both vertical and horizontal, has over the last few decades become

4. Ibid., 129.

the dominant cultural, political, and even biological force; it now leaves untouched no aspect of life on our planet. That new "bio-social" phenomenon—decentralized, transnational, its demands and its reach confined to no discrete territory—may well be the contemporary manifestation of imperial force that some now identify as Empire, with a capital *E*.[5]

While Marshall McLuhan famously imagined and anticipated a "global village" of electronic connection, his anticipation did not include the enormous economic leverage inequality that would follow. That leverage reaches beyond the regulatory capacity of nations, so that the outcome is the concentration of wealth of a transportable kind among the few who have no commitment to any place or to any social infrastructure. Thus Enrique Dussel is surely correct to juxtapose globalization to the reality of exclusion in which persons and societies are simply excluded from economic possibility and so are left behind. Dussel identifies two "absolute limits" to the current economic system:

> a. These limits are in the first place, the ecological destruction of the planet. From the very moment of its inception, Modernity has constituted nature as "exploitable" object, with the increase in the rate of profit of capital as its goal: "For the first time, nature becomes purely an object for humankind, purely a matter of utility; ceases to be recognized as a power for itself." When the earth is seen constituted as an "exploitable object" in favor of quantum, of capital, capital that can defeat all limits, all boundaries, there manifests the "great civilizing influence of capital," and capital now reaches finally its insurmountable limit, where it itself is its own limit, the impassible barrier for ethical-human progress. . . .
> b. The second limit of Modernity is the destruction of humanity itself. "Living labor" is the other essential mediation of capital as such; the human subject is the only one that can "create" new value (surplus value, profit). Capital that defeats all barriers requires incrementally more absolute time of work; when it cannot supersede this limit, it augments productivity through technology—but this increase decreases the importance of human labor. It is thus that there is superfluous humanity (disposable, unemployed, excluded). The unemployed do not earn a salary,

5. Ibid., 115.

> money; but money is the only mediation in the market through which one can acquire commodities in order to satisfy needs.[6]

Saskia Sassen, in her book *Expulsions*, has provided data that show the way in which unmitigated concentrations of capital appropriate and usurp the land, water, and chemical resources of the vulnerable and eventually displace the vulnerable so that they become helpless and disposable.[7] In the United States, moreover, "expulsion" takes the form of incarceration, an effective removal of the devalued and expendable from the gains of economic privatization.

The empire imagines a world that is organized with its own wealth and power at its center. In his remarkable study of fifteenth- and sixteenth-century mapmaking, Walter Mignolo has traced the way in which maps were designed to serve economic interest: "Economic expansion, technology, and power, rather than truth, characterized European cartography early on, and national cartography of the Americas at a later date."[8]

Such mapping was an exercise in imagination aimed at economic control:

> Putting the Americas on the map from the European perspective was not necessarily a task devoted to finding the true shape of the earth; it was also related to controlling territories, diminishing non-European conceptualization of space, and spreading European cartographic literacy, thus colonizing the imagination of people on both sides of the Atlantic: Amerindians and Europeans.[9]

It is not a surprise that the mapping is a product of the Spanish House of Trade. Who else?!

> We are faced with a process of mapping, naming, and silencing that is not strictly related to a reconceptualization of the earth, to which expression New World was commonly associated, but with

6. Enrique Dussel, *Ethics of Liberation in the Age of Globalization and Exclusion*, trans. Eduardo Mendieta et al., translation ed. Alejandro A. Vallega (Durham, NC: Duke University Press, 2013), 39.

7. Saskia Sassen, *Expulsions: Brutality and Complexity in the Global Economy* (Cambridge, MA: Belknap Press of Harvard University Press, 2014).

8. Walter D. Mignolo, *The Darker Side of the Renaissance: Literacy, Territoriality, and Colonization* (Ann Arbor: University of Michigan Press, 1995), 311.

9. Ibid., 309.

> the mapping of the Spanish possessions. . . . The House of Trade was in charge of all maritime affairs, including the regulation of overseas trade and commercial relations. Above all, it was in charge of charting new regions based on geographical records.[10]

It is the work of every economic empire to create a new map of the world in order to place the empire at the center of the world. Thus we may imagine such a map in ancient Tyre and such a map in ancient Rome (Babylon). We may, moreover, attend as well to the way in which U.S. economic interests (allied with military force) imagine the shape of the world designed to assure the flow of money, power, and oil to the benefit of the empire. That breathtaking achievement in every case is contained, eventually, by the poetic force of "no more, no more, no more, no more, no more, no more" (six times!). The reduction of social reality to commodity transactions does not, so the poetry attests, go unanswered. The answer is on the lips of the poet who draws on the old rhetoric of holy disruption. That answer, so the text insists, is from God who will not be mocked. The economics of the empire, that is, the economics of commoditization, has no long-term future.

II

The absolutist claims of the imperial economy are answered by counterdiscourse that refuses the destructive concentration of wealth and imagines otherwise. Enrique Dussel, in his critique of "globalization and exclusion," identifies counterdiscourse as constitutive of a different kind of modernity, in which those on the periphery of power have an important role to play. He is wont to say that such counterdiscourse is a part of Enlightenment rationality when modernity is properly understood. He cites, as a case in point, Bartolomé de Las Casas as a voice of counterdiscourse who was himself part of Enlightenment Europe. But Dussel also recognizes that

> Bartolomé de Las Casas would not have been able to formulate and articulate his critique of the Spanish conquest of the Americas if he had not himself lived in the periphery and heard the

10. Ibid., 286.

> cries and witnessed the tortures to which indigenous people were being submitted. It is that Other who is the actual origin of this counterdiscourse that took root in Europe.[11]

That countervoice that sounded in the midst of European hegemony came from outside Europe:

> This is why the study of thought (traditions and philosophy) in Latin America, Asia, and Africa is not a task that is anecdotal or parallel to the study of philosophy *as such* (which would be that which is European in character) but instead involves the *recovery* of a history that incorporates that counterdiscourse that is nonhegemonic and that has been dominated, silenced, forgotten, and virtually excluded—that which constitutes the alterity of Modernity.[12]

Dussel mentions both Kant ("a key hegemonic philosopher") and Marx (a countervoice within Europe). What is most telling for our study, however, is that Dussel, in speaking of "that Other" who is the "actual origin of this counterdiscourse," capitalizes "Other." It is a strange usage. But the capital *O* in "Other" may indicate that even this rigorously secular liberationist must recognize that in the counterdiscourse against "globalization and exclusion" something of holy insistence beyond human explanation is at work. In any case, Dussel allows that current social analysis must include "peripheral alterity."[13] Following Emmanuel Levinas on "the other," Dussel judges that there is a "metaphysical desire" that is the "drive of alterity."[14] Dussel goes to considerable length to try to articulate all of this without reference to "God."

In the context of our study, however, we need not employ such rhetoric of circumlocution but can readily say about the context and the text that it is God who is the "metaphysical desire" who is the "drive of alterity." The economics of empire that reduces the Other to commodity allows for no such alterity. What is not allowed in the imperial economy, however, shows up in the poetic utterance of the book of Revelation.

11. Dussel, *Ethics of Liberation*, 45.
12. Ibid., 46.
13. Ibid.
14. Ibid., 269. See Emmanuel Levinas, *Totality and Infinity: An Essay on Exteriority* (Pittsburgh: Duquesne University Press, 1969).

Thus the book of Revelation that claims to be utterance from the Other is indeed antihegemonic counterdiscourse. That counterclaim about an alternative is voiced in Revelation 19–22; after the anticipated fall of "Babylon" in chapter 18, it sketches out in lyrical fashion the alternative governance that issues in alternative economics.

a. The celebrative doxology of 19:1–3 declares the defeat of and judgment against the "great whore" who practiced the fornication of commoditization:

> He has judged the great whore
> who corrupted the earth with her fornication,
> and he has avenged on her the blood of his servants.
> (v. 2)

b. The celebrative doxology acknowledges new governance: "On his robe and on his thigh he has a name inscribed, 'King of Kings and Lord of Lords'" (19:16). The language is reminiscent of the ancient psalms of enthronement that speak of the displacement of false gods, the exaltation of YHWH, and the consequent rejoicing of all of creation (Pss. 96–99).

c. The counterdiscourse celebrates the faithful who "had not worshiped the beast or its image and had not received its mark" (20:4). The declaration is designed to authorize and evoke resistance to the hegemonic power of Rome. These lines suggest that such resistance was possible and that some did genuinely resist. It remains an open question now among the faithful whether resistance to the economy of globalization and exclusion is possible. It is all too easy to be branded (with the mark of the empire) by the preferred commodities that purport to make life safe and happy, but the counterdiscourse invites resistance to such branding.

d. The "book of life" is beyond the reach or editing of Rome. That book, concerning those who have resisted and chosen otherwise, records the names of those who have remained steadfastly outside the defining power of the hegemon (20:12).

e. Ellen Davis offers an innovative riff on the declaration that there is "no more" sea (21:1).[15] Rather than appeal to the usual equation of sea with chaos, Davis suggests, with compelling force, that the disappearance of the sea means the termination of commercial

15. Davis, *Biblical Prophecy*, 133–36.

domination by Rome that regarded the Mediterranean Sea as "our sea." Global domination depends on control of transport by land and by sea, and now by air as well (so space exploration!). The termination of such transport of commerce may suggest an option for local commerce that does not require such great transport. And indeed resistance to and refusal of globalization and exclusion places accent on the local. It asks a village to remain human and humane in economics.

f. The new heaven, new earth, and new Jerusalem anticipated here (21:1–4) allude back to Isaiah 65:17–25, with its vision of social newness. That poetic vision is striking for its accent on economic matters:

The poetic anticipation of Isaiah concerns a coming time when there will be no more infant mortality, a time that will require an infrastructure of good health care that will only come about when human persons are taken seriously and not reduced to commodities (v. 20).

That vision anticipates a retention of one's own property without economic displacement that arises from debt and foreclosure or, alternatively, from war and predatory confiscation (vv. 21–22). Either way, the new economy will be one without usurpatious expulsion of the kind practiced in globalization.

That vision anticipates a healed, reconciled creation in which none of the disruptions of the environmental crisis are any longer operative (v. 25). The termination of "hurt or destroy" specifies that the distorting, destructive force of empire no longer pertains. The poet can envision a peaceably ordered economy in which the vulnerable are no longer subject to abuse and exploitation.

That new Jerusalem will be occupied by those written in the book of life, that is, the ones who have not worshiped the beast. The counterdiscourse imagines a social scene without threat and danger.

g. We have noted the sixfold "no more" in Rev. 18:21–23. Davis judges that the "no more" of 21:4 is a completed seventh usage of the phrase. The parallelism of 21:4 indicates the end of death and by implication asserts that the force of Rome was indeed an agent of death. It takes no imagination, in our current economy where those left behind are bereft of life resources, to see that the current system of globalization and exclusion is in fact an agent of death that systematically produces wealth and power that provide no succor or relief to the resourceless.

h. It is no wonder that the counterdiscourse can conclude: "And the one who was seated on the throne said, 'See, I am making all things new.' Also he said, 'Write this, for these words are trustworthy and true'" (21:5). "All things new" means that all of the old power of death has lost its force. With reference to the economy, the new regime will no longer operate to displace and expel. The newness is surely more than economic; but it is economic in part.

One of the spin-offs of "all things new" is free water. Davis has a rich suggestive statement, following Maude Barlow, on "water conservation, water justice, and water democracy."[16] Peter Brabeck-Letmathe, then the chief executive officer of Nestlé, which markets bottled water, declared that the notion of "a right to free water" was "an extreme solution," and that placing a price on water for sale was essential to appreciating its value.[17] That is, treating water as commodity would permit assigning it only to those who could purchase it (expulsion). But here the counterdiscourse refuses to think that the gift of creation can be controlled and administered as commodity, because it is all free. Water as free rather than a commodity is indeed "all things new." The concluding invitation of Revelation 22:17 (with an allusion to Isa. 55:1–2) accents the point. Not only is water free. Life is free, given by the generous Creator, not needing to be earned or purchased or deserved. Free water and all that follows from it would contradict the imperial claim that the gift of creation is to be bottled for purchase. Indeed, the reduction of the gifts of creation to purchasable commodity may be the ultimate pornography of the market.[18]

16. Ibid., 137–39.

17. Quoted by Sassen, *Expulsions*, 192: "The one option, which I think is extreme, is represented by the NGOs, who bang on about declaring water a public right. This means that as a human being you should have a right to water. That's an extreme solution. The other view says that water is a foodstuff like any other, and like any other foodstuff it should have a market value. Personally I believe it's better to give a foodstuff a value so that we're all aware that it has a price, and then that one should take specific measures for the part of the population that has no access to this water and there are many different possibilities there."

18. The Greek root of "pornography" is utilized in Rev. 17:1, 5, 15–16; 19:2; 21:8; 22:15; we may judge that extreme commoditization of human economy is indeed a gross act of pornography.

i. The full performance of the new creation, with its fruit trees, is for “the healing of the nations” (22:2). As long as the economy is monopolized by an imperial superpower, the nations cannot enjoy a healthy existence. The text speaks at a time when Rome is the single superpower. Such a single superpower, whether Rome then or the United States now, greatly distorts international possibility. Of course the single superpower readily, perhaps inevitably, imagines that it is the indispensable nation. Such an imposed status, however, cannot deliver on its promise of healing for the nations that can come about only through discourse and policy that are dialogic and not imposed. The prophetic exposé of Babylon (Rome) (chaps. 17–18) and the lyrical alternative (chaps. 19–22) are worthy of our attention, because we live now, as many did then, accepting the hegemony of the single superpower as a normative given. Such an acceptance, however, requires closing one's eyes to the human costs of such power. The counterdiscourse, now as then, refuses to close eyes and insists upon both seeing and saying otherwise.

Finally the church prays for the coming of Lord Jesus and his kingdom (22:20). Such a prayer is a bid that the kingdom of God should displace the kingdom of Rome and its economy of extraction. The hope that propels faith is not escapism from socioeconomic, political reality. It is rather a resolve that all such social reality should be ordered by the rule of Christ according to the neighbor law of love.

III

It would be a misreading of the book of Revelation to conclude that the witness of the book is against wealth. Its polemic, rather, is against wealth that is situated in the autonomy, self-sufficiency, and arrogance of Rome. That wealth is no advantage and may indeed be a cause for judgment: “Then the kings of the earth and the magnates and the generals and the rich and the powerful, and everyone, slave and free, hid in the caves and among the rocks of the mountains” (6:15; see Isa. 2:19–21).

But wealth situated in obedience to God is acceptable and approved. Thus in 3:17, the church in Laodicea is chided for imagining it is wealthy when in fact it is “wretched, pitiable, poor, blind, and naked.” That same church, however, in the next verse, is invited to real wealth: "Therefore I counsel you to buy from me gold refined by fire so that you may be rich; and white robes to clothe you and to keep the shame of your nakedness from being seen; and salve to anoint your eyes so that you may see" (v. 18). Real wealth is richness that has endured suffering for the sake of the gospel, that is, has actively opposed the hegemony of Rome. The outcome of such obedience is that blindness will be turned to sight, so that one may see faithfully and truly. The measure of wealth then is adherence to the God of the gospel rather than to the norms and passions of Rome.

The book of Revelation, moreover, is not at all embarrassed with the wealth of gold, so long as it is gold devoted to the glory of God (see 1:12; 4:4; 5:8; 8:3; 9:13; 14:14; 15:6–7; 21:15, 18). The address to the church in Smyrna allows for wealth, but it is wealth filtered through affliction and poverty in readiness for obedience (2:9–10).

The jarring rhetoric of the book resituates all economic questions in terms of imperial hegemony and life in obedience outside of that hegemony. For us in our social circumstance, I suggest that the testimony of the book functions to make strange what we have come to regard as normal life in the empire. It turns out that life in accordance with empire that reduces everything to commodity is a deep perversion of the coming kingdom that is the true norm for the book of Revelation and for our life in the world.

BIBLIOGRAPHY

Ackroyd, Peter. *Studies in the Religious Tradition of the Old Testament*. London: SCM Press, 1987.

Adams, Samuel L. *Social and Economic Life in Second Temple Judea*. Louisville, KY: Westminster John Knox Press, 2014.

Anderson, Gary A. *Charity: The Place of the Poor in the Biblical Tradition*. New Haven, CT: Yale University Press, 2013.

Balentine, Samuel E. *The Torah's Vision of Worship*. Overtures to Biblical Theology. Minneapolis: Fortress Press, 1999.

Balthasar, Hans Urs von. *Mysterium Paschale: The Mystery of Easter*. Grand Rapids: Eerdmans, 1990.

Baptist, Edward E. *The Half Has Never Been Told: Slavery and the Making of American Capitalism*. New York: Basic Books, 2014.

Barth, Karl. *Church Dogmatics*. III/2, *The Doctrine of Creation*. Edited by G. W. Bromiley and T. F. Torrance. Edinburgh: T. & T. Clark, 1960.

———. *Church Dogmatics*. IV/3, *The Doctrine of Reconciliation*. Edited by G. W. Bromiley and T. F. Torrance. Edinburgh: T. & T. Clark, 1962.

Beal, Timothy K. "Esther." In *Ruth and Esther*, by Tod Linafelt and Timothy K. Beal. Berit Olam. Collegeville, MN: Liturgical Press, 1999.

Beckert, Sven. *Empire of Cotton: A Global History*. New York: Knopf, 2014.

Berger, Peter. *Pyramids of Sacrifice: Political Ethics and Social Change*. Garden City, NY: Doubleday, 1976.

———. *The Sacred Canopy: Elements of a Sociological Theory of Religion*. Garden City, NY: Doubleday, 1969.

Berry, Wendell. *Home Economics*. New York: North Point Press, 1987.

Berthoud, Gerald. "Market." In *The Development Dictionary*, edited by Wolfgang Sachs, 74–94. 2nd ed. New York: Zed Books, 2010.

Biddle, Mark. "The Biblical Prohibition against Usury." *Interpretation* 65 (2011): 115–37.

Bittman, Mark. "Don't Ask How to Feed the 9 Million," *New York Times*, November 11, 2014, A23.

Blenkinsopp, Joseph. *Ezra–Nehemiah: A Commentary*. Old Testament Library. Philadelphia: Westminster Press, 1988.

Blomberg, Craig. *Christians in an Age of Wealth*. Grand Rapids: Zondervan, 2013.

Boer, Roland. *The Sacred Economy of Ancient Israel*. Louisville, KY: Westminster John Knox Press, 2015.

Boer, Roland, and Christina Pettersen. *Idols and the Nations: Biblical Myth and the Origins of Capitalism*. Minneapolis: Fortress Press, 2014.

The Book of Common Prayer. New York: Church Hymnal Corporation and Seabury Press, 1979.

Botha, Phil J. "'Wealth and Riches Are in His House' (Psalm 112:3): Acrostic Wisdom Psalms and the Development of Antimaterialism." In *The Shape and Shaping of the Book of Psalms: The Current State of Scholarship*, edited by Nancy L. deClaissé-Walford, 105–28. Atlanta: SBL Press, 2014.

Braulik, Georg. "The Sequence of the Laws in Deuteronomy 12–26 and in the Decalogue." In *A Song of Power and the Power of Song: Essays on the Book of Deuteronomy*, edited by Duane L. Christensen, 313–35. Winona Lake, IN: Eisenbrauns, 1993.

Bridges, Linda McKinnish. *1 & 2 Thessalonians*. Smyth & Helwys Bible Commentary. Macon, GA: Smyth & Helwys, 2008.

Brink, Andre. *Rumors of Rain*. New York: Penguin Books, 1984.

Briones, David E. *Paul's Financial Policy: A Socio-theological Approach*. Library of New Testament Studies 494. London: Bloomsbury, 2013.

Brown, Peter. *Through the Eye of a Needle: Wealth, the Fall of Rome, and the Making of Christianity in the West, 350–550 AD*. Princeton, NJ: Princeton University Press, 2012.

Brown, William P. *Ecclesiastes*. Interpretation. Louisville, KY: Westminster John Knox Press, 2000.

Brueggemann, John. *Rich, Free, and Miserable: The Failure of Success in America*. New York: Rowman & Littlefield, 2010.

Brueggemann, Walter. "The Countercommands of Sinai." In *Disruptive Grace: Reflections on God, Scripture, and the Church*, edited by Carolyn J. Sharp, 75–92. Minneapolis: Fortress Press, 2011.

———."The God Who Gives Rest." *The Book of Exodus: Composition, Reception, and Interpretation*, ed. by Thomas B. Dozeman et al. Leiden: Brill, 2014, 565–90.

———. "Heir and Land: The Royal 'Envelope' of the Books of Kings." In *The Fate of King David: The Past and Present of a Biblical Icon*, edited by Tod Linafelt, Claudia V. Camp, and Timothy Beal, 85–100. New York: T. & T. Clark, 2010.

———. *Ice Axes for Frozen Seas: A Biblical Theology of Provocation.* Edited by Davis Hankins. Waco, TX: Baylor University Press, 2014.

———. "Psalms 9–10: A Counter to Conventional Social Reality." In *The Bible and the Politics of Exegesis*, edited by David Jobling, Peggy L. Day, and Gerald T. Sheppard, 3–15. Cleveland: Pilgrim Press, 1991.

———. *Reality, Grief, Hope: Three Urgent Prophetic Tasks*. Grand Rapids: Eerdmans, 2014.

———. *Sabbath as Resistance: Saying No to the Culture of Now.* Louisville, KY: Westminster John Knox Press, 2014.

———. *Solomon: Israel's Ironic Icon of Human Achievement*. Columbia: University of South Carolina Press, 2005.

———. *Testimony to Otherwise: The Witness of Elijah and Elisha*. St. Louis: Chalice Press, 2001.

Brueggemann, Walter, and Davis Hankins. "The Affirmation of Prophetic Power and Deconstruction of Royal Authority in the Elisha Narratives." *Catholic Biblical Quarterly* 76:1 (2014): 58–76.

Cahn, Edgar S. *No More Throw-Away People: The Co-Production Imperative*. Washington, DC: Essential Books, 2000.

Carrington, Philip. *The Primitive Christian Catechism*. Cambridge: Cambridge University Press, 1940.

Cavanaugh, William T. *Migrations of the Holy: God, State, and the Political Meaning of the Church*. Grand Rapids: Eerdmans, 2011.

Chance, J. Bradley. *Acts*. Smyth & Helwys Bible Commentary. Macon, GA: Smyth & Helwys, 2007.

Chaney, Marvin L. "'Coveting Your Neighbor's House' in Social Context." In *The Ten Commandments: The Reciprocity of*

Faithfulness, edited by William P. Brown, 302–17. Louisville, KY: Westminster John Knox Press, 2004.

Childs, Brevard S. *The Book of Exodus: A Critical, Theological Commentary*. Old Testament Library. Philadelphia: Westminster Press, 1974.

———. *Introduction to the Old Testament as Scripture*. Philadelphia: Fortress Press, 1979.

Chirichigno, Gregory C. *Debt-Slavery in Israel and the Ancient Near East*. Sheffield: JSOT Press, 1993.

Church, Christopher. "James." In *Hebrews–James*, by Edgar V. McKnight and Christopher Church. Smyth & Helwys Bible Commentary. Macon, GA: Smyth & Helwys, 2004.

Clements, Roland E. "Patterns in the Prophetic Canon." In *Canon and Authority: Essays in Old Testament Religion and Theology*, edited by George W. Coats and Burke O. Long, 42–55. Philadelphia: Fortress Press, 1977.

Crenshaw, James C. *Ecclesiastes*. Old Testament Library. Philadelphia: Westminster Press, 1987.

Cruesemann, Frank. *The Torah: Theology and Social History of Old Testament Law*. Edinburgh: T. & T. Clark, 1996.

Culpepper, R. Alan. *Mark*. Smyth & Helwys Bible Commentary. Macon, GA: Smyth & Helwys, 2007.

Daley, Suzanne, "After Harvest, Spanish Town Fights over Leftovers," *New York Times*, April 3, 2015, A5.

Davids, Peter H. "The Catholic Epistles as a Canonical Janus: A New Testament Glimpse into Old and New Testament Canon Formation." *Bulletin for Biblical Research* 19:3 (2009): 403–16.

Davis, Ellen F. *Biblical Prophecy: Perspectives for Christian Theology, Discipleship, and Ministry*. Interpretation. Louisville, KY: Westminster John Knox Press, 2014.

———. *Scripture, Culture, and Agriculture: An Agrarian Reading of the Bible*. Cambridge: Cambridge University Press, 2009.

Dewan, Shaila, "Police Department Wish List when Deciding which Assets to Seize," *New York Times*, November 10, 2014, A12.

Dewan, Shaila, "Unanimous New Mexico Bill on Property Seizure May Die," *New York Times*, April 10, 2015, A14.

Diest, Ferdinand E. *The Material Culture of the Bible: An Introduction*. Edited by Robert P. Carroll. Sheffield: Sheffield Academic Press, 2000.

Dixon, Sandra Lee. *Augustine: The Scattered and Gathered Self.* St. Louis: Chalice Press, 1999.

Dodd, Nigel. *The Social Life of Money*. Princeton, NJ: Princeton University Press, 2014.

Duchrow, Ulrich, and Franz J. Hinkelammert. *Transcending Greedy Money: Interreligious Solidarity for Just Relations*. New York: Palgrave Macmillan, 2012.

Dunn, James D. G. "The First and Second Letters to Timothy and the Letter to Titus." In *The New Interpreter's Bible*, edited by Leander E. Keck. Vol. 11. Nashville: Abingdon Press, 2000.

Dussel, Enrique. *Ethics of Liberation in the Age of Globalization and Exclusion*. Translated by Eduardo Mendieta et al. Translation edited by Alejandro A. Vallega. Durham, NC: Duke University Press, 2013.

Elliott, Neil. *The Arrogance of the Nations: Reading Romans in the Shadow of Empire*. Minneapolis: Fortress Press, 2008.

Ellul, Jacques. *Money and Power*. Downers Grove, IL: Inter-Varsity Press, 1984.

———. *On Being Rich and Being Poor: Christianity in a Time of Economic Globalization*. Edited by William H. Vandenberg. Toronto: University of Toronto Press, 2014.

Eubank, Nathan. *Wages of Cross-Bearing and Debt of Sin: The Economy of Heaven in Matthew's Gospel*. Beihefte zur Zeitschrift für die neutestamentliche Wissenschaft 196. Berlin: Walter de Gruyter, 2013.

Exum, J. Cheryl. *Song of Songs*. Old Testament Library. Louisville, KY: Westminster John Knox Press, 2005.

Fackenheim, Emil L. "New Hearts and the Old Covenant: On Some Possibilities of a Fraternal Jewish-Christian Reading of the Jewish Bible Today." In *The Divine Helmsman: Studies on God's Control of Human Events*, edited by James L. Crenshaw and Samuel Sandmel, 191–205. New York: KTAV Publishing House, 1980.

Fishbane, Michael. *Sacred Attunement: A Jewish Theology*. Chicago: University of Chicago Press, 2008.

———. *Text and Texture: Close Readings of Selected Biblical Texts*. New York: Schocken Books, 1979.

Fraser, Steve. *The Age of Acquiescence: The Life and Death of American Resistance to Organized Wealth and Power*. New York: Little, Brown, 2014.

Glory to God. Louisville, KY: Westminster John Knox Press, 2013.

Goodman, Lenn Evan. *Love Thy Neighbor as Thyself*. Oxford: Oxford University Press, 2008.

Gordis, Robert. *Poets, Prophets, and Sages: Essays in Biblical Interpretation*. Bloomington: Indiana University Press, 1971.

Gowan, Donald E. *When Man Becomes God: Humanism and* Hybris *in the Old Testament*. Pittsburgh: Pickwick Press, 1975.

Graeber, David. *Debt: The First 5,000 Years*. Brooklyn: Melville House, 2011.

Gupta, Nijay K. *Colossians*. Smyth & Helwys Bible Commentary. Macon, GA: Smyth & Helwys, 2013.

Gutiérrez, Gustavo. *On Job: God-Talk and the Suffering of the Innocent*. Maryknoll, NY: Orbis Books, 1987.

Haidt, Jonathan. *The Righteous Mind: Why Good People Are Divided by Politics and Religion*. New York: Pantheon Books, 2012.

Hamilton, Jeffries M. *Social Justice and Deuteronomy: The Case of Deuteronomy 15*. Society of Biblical Literature Dissertation Series 136. Atlanta: Scholars Press, 1992.

Hankins, Davis. *The Book of Job and the Immanent Genesis of Transcendence*. Evanston, IL: Northwestern University Press, 2015.

Hardt, Michael, and Antonio Negri. *Empire*. Cambridge, MA: Harvard University Press, 2001.

Hays, Richard B. "The Letter to the Galatians." In *The New Interpreter's Bible*, edited by Leander E. Keck. Vol. 11. Nashville: Abingdon Press, 2000.

Horsley, Richard A. *Covenant Economics: A Biblical Vision of Justice for All*. Louisville, KY: Westminster John Knox Press, 2009.

———. *Jesus and Empire: The Kingdom of God and the New World Disorder*. Minneapolis: Fortress Press, 2003.

———, ed. *Paul and Empire: Religion and Power in Roman Imperial Society*. Harrisburg, PA: Trinity Press International, 1997.

Hudson, Michael. *The Lost Tradition of Biblical Debt Cancellations*. New York: Henry George School of Social Science, 1993.

Japhet, Sara. *I & 2 Chronicles: A Commentary*. Old Testament Library. Louisville, KY: Westminster/John Knox Press, 1993.

Johnson, Luke Timothy. *The First and Second Letters to Timothy*. Anchor Bible 35A. New York: Doubleday, 2001.

———. *The Letter of James*. Anchor Bible 37A. New York: Doubleday, 1995.

———. "The Letter of James." In *The New Interpreter's Bible*, edited by Leander E. Keck. Vol. 12. Nashville: Abingdon Press, 1998.

———. *Sharing Possessions: What Faith Demands*. 2nd ed. Grand Rapids: Eerdmans, 2011.

Joyce, Paul. *Divine Initiative and Human Response in Ezekiel*. Journal for the Study of the Old Testament Supplement Series 51. Sheffield: JSOT Press, 1989.

Kahl, Brigitte. *Galatians Re-Imagined: Reading with the Eyes of the Vanquished*. Minneapolis: Fortress Press, 2010.

Kaufman, S. A. "The Structure of the Deuteronomic Law." *Maarav* 1:2 (1978–1979): 105–58.

Kessler, Rainer. *Debt and the Decalogue: The Tenth Commandment*. Leiden: Brill, 2015.

Kierkegaard, Søren. *Stages on Life's Way*. New York: Schocken Books, 1967.

Klein, Ralph W. *I Chronicles: A Commentary*. Hermeneia. Minneapolis: Fortress Press, 2006.

Knight, Douglas. *Law, Power and Justice in Ancient Israel*. Louisville, KY: Westminster John Knox Press, 2011.

Koch, Klaus. "Is There a Doctrine of Retribution in the Old Testament?" In *Theodicy in the Old Testament*, edited by James L. Crenshaw, 57–87. Philadelphia: Fortress Press, 1983.

Kraus, Hans-Joachim. *Psalms 60–150: A Commentary*. Minneapolis: Augsburg, 1989.

Kristoff, Nicholas, "How Do We Increase Empathy?" *New York Times*, January 29, 2015, A23.

Krugman, Paul, "Money Makes Crazy," *New York Times*, February 13, 2015, A25.

Krugman, Paul, "Nobody Understands Debt," *New York Times*, February 9, 2015, A15.

Lancaster, John. *How to Speak Money: What the Money People Say—and What It Really Means*. New York: W. W. Norton & Co., 2014.

Lee, Nancy C. *Lyrics of Lament: From Tragedy to Transformation*. Minneapolis: Fortress Press, 2010.

Levenson, Jon D. *Creation and the Persistence of Evil: The Jewish Drama of Divine Omnipotence*. San Francisco: Harper & Row, 1988.

———. *Esther*. Old Testament Library. Louisville, KY: Westminster John Knox Press, 1997.

Levinas, Emmanuel. *Totality and Infinity: An Essay on Exteriority*. Pittsburgh: Duquesne University Press, 1969.

Lewis, Alan E. *Between Cross and Resurrection: A Theology of Holy Saturday*. Grand Rapids: Eerdmans, 2001.

Linafelt, Tod. "Ruth." In *Ruth and Esther*, by Tod Linafelt and Timothy K. Beal. Berit Olam. Collegeville, MN: Liturgical Press, 1999.

———. *Surviving Lamentations: Catastrophe, Lament, and Protest in the Afterlife of a Biblical Book*. Chicago: University of Chicago Press, 2000.

Linafelt, Tod, Claudia V. Camp, and Timothy Beal, eds. *The Fate of King David: The Past and Present of a Biblical Icon*. New York: T. & T. Clark, 2010.

Lincoln, Andrew T. "The Letter to the Colossians." In *The New Interpreter's Bible*, edited by Leander E. Keck. Vol. 11. Nashville: Abingdon Press, 2000.

Lischer, Richard. *Reading the Parables*. Interpretation. Louisville, KY: Westminster John Knox Press, 2014.

Longmann, Tremper, III. *Song of Songs*. New International Commentary on the Old Testament. Grand Rapids: Eerdmans, 2001.

Luz, Ulrich. *Matthew 21–28*. Hermeneia. Minneapolis: Fortress Press, 2005.

Macpherson, C. B. *The Political Theory of Possessive Individualism: Hobbes to Locke*. Oxford: Oxford University Press, 1962.

Marshall, Christopher D. *Compassionate Justice: Gospel Parables on Law, Crime, and Restorative Justice*. Eugene, OR: Cascade Books, 2012.

Meeks, M. Douglas. *God the Economist: The Doctrine of God and Political Economy*. Minneapolis: Fortress Press, 1989.

McLellan, David. *The Thought of Karl Marx: An Introduction*. New York: Macmillan, 1971.

Mignolo, Walter D. *The Darker Side of the Renaissance: Literacy, Territoriality, and Colonization*. Ann Arbor: University of Michigan Press, 1995.

Milgrom, Jacob. *Leviticus 23–27*. New York: Doubleday, 2001.

Miller, Patrick D. "The Human Sabbath: A Study in Deuteronomic Theology." *Princeton Seminary Bulletin* 6:2 (1985): 81–97.

———. *Israelite Religion and Biblical Theology: Collected Essays*. Journal for the Study of the Old Testament Supplement Series 267. Sheffield: Sheffield Academic Press, 2000.

———. "Luke 4:16–21." *Interpretation* 29:4 (1975): 417–21.

———. *Sin and Judgment in the Prophets*. Chico, CA: Scholars Press, 1982.

Miranda, José Porfirio. *Marx and the Bible: A Critique of the Philosophy of Oppression*. Maryknoll, NY: Orbis Books, 1974.

Morgan, Donn F. *Between Text and Community: The "Writings" in Canonical Interpretation*. Minneapolis: Fortress Press, 1990.

Murphy, Kelly J. "Wisdom over Gold: Scribal Power, Politics, and the Poor." (SBL 2014 Economics Program Unit).

Myers, Ched. "The Bible and Climate Change." Presentation at the Annual Meeting of the Society of Biblical Literature, San Diego, CA, November 22, 2014.

———. "'Pay Attention to the Great Economy!' Reflections on Luke 12:13–34, Earth Cosmology and Sabbath Economics." Paper delivered to the Forum on Faith, Economy, and Ecology, Washington, DC, 2009.

Neusner, Jacob. *From Politics to Piety: The Emergence of Pharisaic Judaism*. Eugene, OR: Wipf & Stock, 2003.

The New Century Hymnal. Cleveland: Pilgrim Press, 1995.

Newsom, Carol A. *The Book of Job: A Contest of Moral Imaginations*. Oxford: Oxford University Press, 2003.

Nickle, Keith. *The Collection: A Study in Paul's Strategy*. Naperville, IL: Allenson, 1966.

Nienhuis, David R. *Not by Paul Alone: The Formation of the Catholic Epistle Collection and the Christian Canon*. Waco, TX: Baylor University Press, 2007.

Nienhuis, David R., and Robert Wall. *Reading the Epistles of James, Peter, John, and Jude as Scripture: The Shaping and Shape of a Canonical Collection*. Grand Rapids: Eerdmans, 2013.

Nisula, Timo. *Augustine and the Functions of Concupiscence*. Leiden: Brill, 2012.

Noth, Martin. "The 'Re-presentation' of the Old Testament in Proclamation." In *Essays on Old Testament Hermeneutics*, edited by Claus Westermann, translated by James Luther Mays, 76–88. Richmond: John Knox Press, 1963.

Oakman, Douglas E. *Jesus and the Peasants*. Eugene, OR: Wipf & Stock, 2008.

———. *Jesus, Debt, and the Lord's Prayer: First-Century Debt and Jesus' Intentions*. Eugene, OR: Wipf & Stock, 2014.

O'Connor, Kathleen. *Lamentations and the Tears of the World*. Maryknoll, NY: Orbis Books, 2002.

Oreskes, Naomi, and Erik M. Conway. *The Collapse of Western Civilization: A View from the Future*. New York: Columbia University Press, 2014.

Patrick, Dale. *Old Testament Law*. Atlanta: John Knox Press, 1985.

Perkins, Pheme. "The Gospel of Mark: Introduction, Commentary, and Reflections." In *The New Interpreter's Bible*, edited by Leander E. Keck. Vol. 8. Nashville: Abingdon Press, 1995.

Premnath, D. N. *Eighth Century Prophets: A Social Analysis*. St. Louis: Chalice Press, 2003.

The Presbyterian Hymnal. Louisville, KY: Westminster John Knox Press, 2001.

Rad, Gerhard von. "'Righteousness' and 'Life' in the Cultic Language of the Psalms." In *The Problem of the Hexateuch and Other Essays*, 243–66. New York: McGraw-Hill, 1966.

———. *Studies in Deuteronomy*. Studies in Biblical Theology 9. Chicago: Henry Regnery Co., 1953.

———. *Wisdom in Israel*. Nashville: Abingdon Press, 1972.

Ringe, Sharon H. *Jesus, Liberation, and the Biblical Jubilee: Images for Ethics and Christology*. Overtures to Biblical Theology. Philadelphia: Fortress Press, 1985.

Risen, James. *Pay Any Price: Greed, Power, and Endless War*. New York: Houghton Mifflin Harcourt, 2014.

Roberts, J. J. M. *Nahum, Habakkuk, and Zephaniah*. Old Testament Library. Louisville, KY: Westminster/John Knox Press, 1991.

Rosner, Brian S. *Greed as Idolatry: The Origin and Meaning of a Pauline Metaphor*. Grand Rapids: Eerdmans, 2007.

Sampley, J. Paul. "The First Letter to the Corinthians." In *The New Interpreter's Bible*, edited by Leander E. Keck. Vol. 10. Nashville: Abingdon Press, 2000.

———. "The Second Letter to the Corinthians." In *The New Interpreter's Bible*, edited by Leander E. Keck. Vol. 11. Nashville: Abingdon Press, 2000.

Sanders, James A. *Torah and Canon*. Philadelphia: Fortress Press, 1972.

Sandoval, Timothy J. *Money and the Way of Wisdom: Insights from the Book of Proverbs*. Woodstock, VT: Skylight Paths, 2008.

Sassen, Saskia. *Expulsions: Brutality and Complexity in the Global Economy*. Cambridge, MA: Belknap Press of Harvard University Press, 2014.

Schmid, H. H. "Creation, Righteousness, and Salvation: 'Creation Theology' as the Broad Horizon of Biblical Theology." In *Creation in the Old Testament*, edited by Bernhard W. Anderson, 102–17. Philadelphia: Fortress Press, 1984.

Schauble, Wolfgang, "We Are Averse to Blackmail," *New York Times*, January 31, 2015, A3.

———. *Gerechtigkeit als Weltordnung*. Tübingen: J. C. B. Mohr, 1968.

Seitz, Christopher R. *Word without End: The Old Testament as Abiding Theological Witness*. Grand Rapids: Eerdmans, 1998.

Seow, Choon-Leong. "The Social World of Ecclesiastes." In *Money as God? The Monetization of the Market and Its Impact on Religion, Politics, Law, and Ethics*, edited by Jürgen von Hagen and Michael Welker, 137–58. Cambridge: Cambridge University Press, 2014.

Smith, Abraham. "The Second Letter to the Thessalonians." In *The New Interpreter's Bible*, edited by Leander E. Keck. Vol. 11. Nashville: Abingdon Press, 2000.

Smith, Adam. *The Theory of Moral Sentiments*. Oxford: Clarendon Press, 1976.

Sommers, Benjamin D. *The Bodies of God and the World of Ancient Israel*. Cambridge: Cambridge University Press, 2009.

Steinbeck, John. *The Grapes of Wrath*. New York: Penguin Books, 1939.

Streett, R. Alan. *Subversive Meals: An Analysis of the Lord's Supper under Roman Domination during the First Century*. Eugene, OR: Pickwick Publications, 2013.

Sullivan, Paul, "Having Enough, but Hungry for More," *New York Times*, January 18, 2014, B5.

Taibbi, Matt. *The Divide: American Injustice in the Age of the Wealth Gap*. New York: Spiegel & Grau, 2014.

Tamez, Elsa. *The Scandalous Message of James: Faith without Works Is Dead*. New York: Crossroad Publishing, 1985.

———. *When the Horizons Close: Rereading Ecclesiastes*. Maryknoll, NY: Orbis Books, 2000.

Trible, Phyllis. *God and the Rhetoric of Sexuality*. Overtures to Biblical Theology. Philadelphia: Fortress Press, 1978.

Tucker, W. Dennis, Jr. *Constructing and Deconstructing Power in Psalms 107–150*. Atlanta: SBL Press, 2014.

Tuell, Steven S. *First and Second Chronicles*. Interpretation. Louisville, KY: Westminster John Knox Press, 2001.

Wafawanaka, Robert. *Am I Still My Brother's Keeper? Biblical Perspectives on Poverty*. Lanham, MD: University Press of America, 2012.

Welker, Michael. "Kohelet and the Co-evolution of a Monetary Economy and Religion." In *Money as God? The Monetization of the Market and Its Impact on Religion, Politics, Law, and Ethics*, edited by Jürgen von Hagen and Michael Welker, 96–108. Cambridge: Cambridge University Press, 2014.

Westermann, Claus. *Basic Forms of Prophetic Speech*. Philadelphia: Westminster Press, 1967.

———. *Genesis 1–11: A Commentary*. Minneapolis: Augsburg Publishing House, 1984.

———. *Prophetic Oracles of Salvation in the Old Testament*. Louisville, KY: Westminster/John Knox Press, 1991.

———. *What Does the Old Testament Say about God?* Atlanta: John Knox Press, 1979.

Wheeler, Sondra Ely. *Wealth as Pearl and Obligation: The New Testament on Possessions*. Grand Rapids: Eerdmans, 1995.

Wilson, Robert R. *Prophecy and Society in Ancient Israel*. Philadelphia: Fortress Press, 1980.

Wood, Tony. "First Person." *London Review of Books*, February 5, 2015, 13–16.

Wuthnow, Robert. *God and Mammon in America*. New York: Free Press, 1994.

Whybray, R. Norman. "Qoheleth, Preacher of Joy." *Journal for the Study of the Old Testament* 23 (1982): 87–98.

———. *Wealth and Poverty in the Book of Proverbs*. Journal for the Study of the Old Testament Supplement Series 99. Sheffield: Sheffield Academic Press, 1990.

Wolpe, David. *David: The Divided Heart*. New Haven, CT: Yale University Press, 2014.

Yoder, Christine Roy. "The Shaping of Erotic Desire in Proverbs 1–9." In *Saving Desire: The Seduction of Christian Theology*, edited by F. LeRon Shults and Jan-Olav Henriksen, 148–63. Grand Rapids: Eerdmans, 2011.

———. *Wisdom as a Woman of Substance: A Socioeconomic Reading of Proverbs 1–9 and 31:10–31*. Beihefte zur Zeitschrift für alttestamentliche Wissenschaft 304. Berlin: Walter de Gruyter, 2001.

Zantovsky, Michael. *Havel: A Life*. New York: Grove Press, 2014.

Zenger, Erich. "Geld als Lebensmittel? Über die Wertung des Reichtums im Psalter (Psalmen 15.49.112)." *Jahrbuch für Biblische Theologie* 21 (2006): 73–96.

INDEX OF SCRIPTURE

INDEX OF SUBJECTS

of human beings, 25, 267, 269–70
as pornography, 277, 277n18
vs. power of Holy Spirit, 214–15
Sabbath countering, 51–52
of sexuality, 168, 169, 180–81
temptation to, 151, 169, 173
of water, 277, 277n17
common good, 6–7, 10
and resurrection, 211, 218
wealth disturbing, 5–6, 64, 115, 129, 150–51, 212–13
wealth used for, 6–7, 136, 183, 206–7, 211, 235–37
Communion, 238
community
coveting inimical to, 17–18
self *vs.*, 41–42, 127, 129, 143–44, 149–50, 183, 225–26, 229–30, 234, 237, 244–45
wealth destroying, 112–13
conformity *vs.* transformation, 221–22, 226–28
conscription, 62, 68, 69
consumerism, 143–44
social implications of, 144, 146
contemporary issues, xi
Conway, Erik M., 9n3
Corinthians, 223–24
corporate ideology, 69
corruption, 50–51, 120
counterdiscourse, 273–78
definition of, 273
peripheral figures and, 273–74
in Revelation, 275–78
covenant. *See* Torah
Covenant Code, 50–51
coveting, 15–33, 176, 232–33, 256–58
commandment against, xii–xiii, 16–18, 25–26, 38–39, 58, 147, 229, 229n9
emancipation from, 20–21, 23
as inimical to community, 17–18
land, 18–19
misunderstanding of, 16–17
taking as part of, 17–18, 38
creation
abundance of, 107–8, 110–11
vs. commodity, 194
and deeds-consequences, 121
in Job, 134
and justice, 106
materiality of, xxi, 11, 12
narrative, 18
Sabbath and, 15
wisdom and, 112, 117–18, 126
credit, 6, 27, 45, 101–2, 227
creditor class
economic rules made by, 189, 189n9
Jesus and, 188–89
Crenshaw, James, 173
crucifixion
of the flesh, 234
of Jesus, 178, 225
Cruesemann, Frank, 49
Culpepper, Alan, 191
Cyrus, 77, 87

Daley, Suzanne, 49n8
Daniel, 8–9, 162n19
David, 4–5
and Bathsheba, 65, 256
blessing God, 83–85
census of, 65
double-mindedness of, 255
promise to, 56, 109–10
as Robin Hood character, 64
as taker, 65, 70, 81–83
and the temple, 81–83
Davidic dynasty, 64–70
God and, 106–7
reduced focus on, 111–12
rejection of, 110, 111
Davis, Ellen, 265, 266, 269–71, 275–76
Day of the Lord, 145–46
deacons, 246
death, 113–15
accumulation leading to, 193, 213
end of, 276–77
globalization as agent of, 277
wealth limited by, 113–14
debt
and class divisions, 39–40, 93
in the European Union, 189, 189n9, 228
land loss resulting from, xiv, 53, 188
and popular insurrections, 45, 93n21
slavery, xx, 46–47, 48, 52, 93
threat of, to farmers, xiii, 188

and weights and measures, 50, 127–28
merit
vs. gift, 135–36, 137, 138, 219–20, 227–28
and work, 235–36
messiah, Cyrus as, 77
methodology, xix–xx, 1–13, 186–87, 202
mənûḥâ (security), 164, 164n2
Micah, 147–48
middle class
perspective of, 169–70
values, 204
Mignolo, Walter, 272–73
Milgrom, Jacob, 53
Miller, Patrick, 44, 51, 97
minimum wage, 151, 227
ministry, money as impediment to, 239–40
Miranda, José, 74–75
mišneh (double portion), 160n17
mišpaṭ (justice), 63
money and possessions
addictive quality of, 8
attraction to, damaging ministry, 239–40
avoiding extremes in, 172–73
belonging to God, 4–5, 10, 61
contextualization of, 117–18, 127, 129, 136, 195–96, 200, 210, 211
gained through conquest, 82, 83
as gifts from God, 1–3, 9, 66, 83–85, 171, 173, 174
held in common, 211–12, 217
as holy things, 194–95
idolatry stemming from, 8–9, 10, 25, 31, 60, 61–62, 194–95
indifference to, 119–20
injustice stemming from, 5–6, 10
international power of, 85–86
lacking transformative power, 207, 207n5, 208
mismanagement of, 5, 6
obedience rewarded by, 3–4, 9–10
Pastoral Epistles warning about, 243–45
profaning, 195
renouncing, 190
restoration of, through Jubilee, 52–53
sharing, 6–7, 10
as source of death, 213
theses concerning, 1–9
money crops, 49
morality, 123, 201, 210, 239
Mordecai, 182
Moses, 8, 31
interpreting Torah, 38
negotiating with God, 30
Myers, Chad, 192

Naaman, healing of, 72
Naboth's vineyard, 5, 71, 124, 256–57
Naomi, 164
Nathan, 65, 70
national security, 86n9
nations, healing of, 278
Nebuchadnezzar, 87, 162n19
Nehemiah
on debt and interest, 94
foreign wives expelled by, 90–92
not exploiting people, 95
restoration under, 87
temple tax used by, 85
neighborliness, xii–xiii, xxi, 5, 6–7, 35
in Acts, 206–7
children socialized into, 40–41
in Luke, 207n2
vs. market ideology, 10
in Paul, 228–29, 231, 234–35, 237–38
social order founded upon, 17
neighbors
definition of, 6–7, 45
ethics oriented to, 17
vs. foreigners, 45
poor as, 27
solidarity between, 7
in tenth commandment, 17–18, 24, 25–26, 38
vs. workers, 20
nepeš, 11–12
nepeš 'ādām (human beings), 267
Nestlé, 277
newness, 276–77
Newsom, Carol, 137–38

CPSIA information can be obtained
at www.ICGtesting.com
Printed in the USA
BVHW070808070119
537203BV00003B/224/P

9 780664 262808